inventing late night

inventing late night

Steve Allen
and the original
***tonight* show**
ben alba

foreword by jay leno

 Prometheus Books

59 John Glenn Drive
Amherst, New York 14228-2197

Published 2005 by Prometheus Books

Inquiries should be addressed to
Prometheus Books
59 John Glenn Drive
Amherst, New York 14228–2197
VOICE: 716–691–0133, ext. 207
FAX: 716–564–2711
WWW.PROMETHEUSBOOKS.COM

09 08 07 06 05   5 4 3 2 1

Library of Congress Cataloging-in-Publication Data

Alba, Ben, 1957–
    Inventing late night : Steve Allen and the original Tonight show / by Ben Alba.
        p. cm.
    Includes bibliographical references and index.
    ISBN 1-59102-342-4 (hardcover : alk. paper)
    1. Allen, Steve, 1921–2000. 2. Entertainers—United States—Biography.
3. Tonight show (Television program) I. Title.

PN1992.4.A4A65 2005
791.4502'8'092—dc22

                                                                    2005017191

Printed in the United States of America on acid-free paper

To my mother, with love and gratitude.

In memory of Steve Allen, whose early encouragement and support made this project possible.

ACKNOWLEDGMENTS

*T*hanks to Mitch Morinec for assisting with research, tape transcriptions, and the bibliography and index. To Chris Elder, for additional research assistance. To Andrea Cartolano, for her last-minute typing and collating assistance. To Richard Erickson, Steve Farwick, Joan Hackett, Gioia Heiser, Dave Nightingale, Lester Northe, Tim O'Shea, Judith Rutherford, and Winnie Taylor, who contributed valuable ideas and materials that I incorporated into the text. To Tamara Dawson, Marie Allen, and Bobby Allen for tediously researching and compiling the appendix of over a thousand Allen-era *Tonight* show guests from the original, antiquated, user-unfriendly network logs. To Bill O'Neill, a lifelong Steve Allen fan who read many of my early drafts and kept telling me to write more.

Thanks to Bill Harbach, the *Tonight* show's first producer, for his untailing cheer and patience amid my many follow-up calls over the past several years. To Rick Ludwin at NBC for his warm and enthusiastic support. To Rick Kogan at the *Chicago Tribune* for telling me, more than anyone else, "Don't give up!" To American pop icon Andy Williams, through whom my interest in Steve's career grew and eventually blossomed into this book. To Glen Weissenberger, dean of DePaul University College of Law, because it helps to have a loyal Allen admirer for a boss. To my students, who have probably learned more about Steve Allen than any other group of law students in America.

Thanks to Kathryn Leigh Scott, Gail Polevoi at *Emmy* magazine, Bill Bike, and Karen Nazor for their professional advice. Thanks to Chicago's Museum of Broadcast Communications and its president, Bruce DuMont, for facilitating my initial contact with Steve Allen. Thanks to the wonderful folks at Prometheus Books: to Steven L. Mitchell for believing in this project; to Chris Kramer and Heather Ammermuller for poring over every word, letter, comma, and colon; and to Jackie Cooke and Jon Kurtz for their savvy art direction.

Special thanks to Jay Leno for graciously contributing the foreword. Finally, my humble thanks to Jayne Meadows Allen and Bill Allen, who patiently helped me unravel and appreciate the seemingly endless layers of an extraordinary and decent human being and who generously contributed many of the rare archival photos that bring this story to life.

CONTENTS

How Steve Allen emerged as a radio talent and developed the elements that would eventually light up late-night television. The events that positioned him to reign as television's first late-night king. How Allen's role as creator of the groundbreaking format remained a well-kept secret for decades.

The September 27, 1954, premiere and the nightly innovations that followed: the single-guest show, the single-theme show, the road show and live segments from across the country, Broadway shows visit *Tonight*, episodes on McCarthyism and other political themes,

Steve Allen's brush with the mob, a wealth of jazz artistry, a ground-breaking showcase for artists of color, musical tributes, and the establishment of the studio audience as a comedy goldmine.

How "Carnac the Magnificent," "Jay Walking," "Stupid Human Tricks," zany stunts, exotic animal antics, and other popular features of late-night television comedy originated with Steve Allen. With comments by Jay Leno, David Letterman, and Bob Costas.

Tonight writers Stan Burns (*The Carol Burnett Show*), Herb Sargent (*Saturday Night Live*), and Bill Dana ("Jose Jimenez") explain how they successfully combined their fresh, hip writing with Allen's ad-lib wit and audience-bonding ability. They, along with NBC senior vice president Rick Ludwin, also discuss how the censorship pendulum has swung in different and sometimes unexpected directions over the past five decades.

Before there was Kevin Eubanks, Paul Shaffer, or even Doc Severinsen, there was Skitch Henderson. TV's first late-night banana recalls how conducting the *Tonight* show band went from being a dreaded sentence to the career achievement for which he wants to be remembered most. In addition, Severinsen recalls how he began his late-night career under Henderson and how the role of the late-night house band grew under Allen's influence.

Contents

FOREWORD

BY JAY LENO

*S*teve Allen had a tremendous influence on me. He was the inspiration for everything we do here. He started the very first *Tonight Show* in 1954.

When I was a kid, I remember the first time I had stayed up to midnight and saw twelve o'clock on a clock at night. And when you're six or seven, and you see a clock hit twelve for the first time at night, it's like, "Oooh, this is magical!" I looked over, and Steve Allen was on TV. That's always been in my mind. His face is a part of my childhood.

Steve Allen was the first modern comedian that I saw on TV. Most comedians up to that point came from vaudeville, and they were song-and-dance men and clowns. He was the first wise guy— always had a quip, always had a line. The first wise guy that my mom liked. He wasn't a wise guy in the sense that he was ever mean or nasty to people. He was just so quick on his feet and so smart. He always used his intellect. He always had smart jokes. He always brought the audience to a higher level. He rose above the lowest common denominator when he went for his jokes. That was the thing I most admired about him.

Steve Allen was an innovator. When he started this program, there was nothing to fashion it after. Nobody had ever done this before! He made it what it is. He was the first guy to put audience members on TV, read angry letters to the editor, do characters on the show, and take the cameras into the street in search of "found comedy."

All this stuff you see on all these late-night shows, network or syndicated—it started with Steve. There's nothing new. It all started with him.

INTRODUCTION

"*I*f you have ever turned on the TV after the 11 o'clock news and laughed, you owe Steve Allen a debt of gratitude."

That's what *Entertainment Weekly* wrote when Allen died on October 30, 2000. Numerous other tributes celebrated the enduring legacy of one of television's most creative and innovative minds.

Newsweek crowned him "The Father of Late Night, the man who created the TV-talk-show format we go to sleep with and led the way for Johnny, Dave and Jay. . . . He created an insomniac's paradise and changed television forever."

"All of us who have hosted *The Tonight Show* owe a debt of gratitude to Steve Allen," acknowledged Johnny Carson in a statement issued upon Allen's death. "He was a most creative innovator and a brilliant entertainer."

"His early work is really the foundation for what late-night shows have become," said David Letterman on the day Allen died. When he had Allen as a guest on his NBC daytime show twenty years earlier, he told his hero, "You started the whole thing. You're the reason we have a desk here. You're the reason talk shows are what they are today."

The *Tonight* show—America's longest-running nighttime entertainment program and most successful late-night show—marked its fiftieth anniversary on September 27, 2004. It all seems so simple: the home base desk, the opening monologue, the announcer/sidekick, the horsing around with the bandleader, the breezy celebrity chats, the wacky stunts, the comedy sketches, the cameras roaming backstage and outside the studio, the irreverent observations of passersby, the offbeat and eccentric guests, and the ad-lib banter with the studio audience.

Five nights a week.

But this formula did not exist before Steve Allen. If America stayed up late at all, it was only to doze in front of tired movie reruns. Drawing from his unique combination of gifts—wit, freewheeling silliness, musical talent, and an amiable manner—Allen invented the format that made late-night television fashionable and *Tonight* a national institution. He also drew from another gift that dwarfed all of his others: a rare ability to ad-lib his way out of anything. "He was one of the sharpest guys off the cuff," said current *Tonight* host, Jay Leno. "Allen was more improvisational than anyone in high-stakes television is today," *Newsweek* noted. The *Chicago Tribune* assessed Allen as one of the first entertainers "to find ways of being funny on television peculiar to the medium."

Allen created the *Tonight* show and served as its original host from 1954 to 1957. Much of what has succeeded on late-night talk shows over the following fifty years was introduced, in some form, during Allen's early years in television. Even conventions identified with later hosts—like "Jay Walking," "Stump the Band," "Stupid Human Tricks," "The Tea-Time Movie with Art Fern," and even "Carnac the Magnificent"—owe their origins directly to the early Allen shows. Before Dave was giving away canned hams, Steve was giving away salamis. And before Johnny found fun with exotic animals brought by Jim Fowler and Joan Embery, Steve was getting up close and personal with tigers, elephants, and tarantulas.

Through Allen's direct descendants—Jack Paar, Johnny Carson, and Jay Leno—NBC continued to build the grand *Tonight* tradition. Buoyed by the enormous profit potential of *Tonight*, the network cloned the show for David Letterman and Conan O'Brien. NBC's senior vice president of specials, variety programs, and late night, Rick Ludwin, acknowledged that the Letterman and O'Brien shows probably would not exist today had there not been Steve Allen "because Steve proved that not only would people stay up late to watch television, but that the premium would be on funny—and that the more unpredictable and wilder, the better."

Other networks replicated the Allen template with variety talk shows of their own hosted by Merv Griffin, Joey Bishop, Dick Cavett, Pat Sajak, Joan Rivers, Arsenio Hall, Magic Johnson, Chevy Chase, Craig Kilbourn, Dennis Miller, Jimmy Kimmel, Jon Stewart, Craig Ferguson, and a host of others—all with the same basic look, but not always with the same level of success.

Under Allen's guidance, *Tonight* not only defined late-night television but also influenced modern television entertainment. It blazed the trail for classic '60s and '70s comedy variety shows like *The Carol Burnett Show, Rowan and Martin's Laugh-In, The Smothers Brothers Comedy Hour,* and *SCTV,* as well as contemporary programs like *Saturday Night Live.* The original *Tonight,* explained Allen, was "very experimental, a canvas on which we could paint anything we wanted," including dramas, segments from Broadway shows, musical tributes, wild stunts, political debates, and remote segments from around the country—all groundbreaking and mostly never before attempted on live network TV. *Tonight* was the vehicle by which Allen pioneered the road show, the single-theme show (a format popularized by Phil Donahue and Oprah Winfrey), and the single-guest show (later adopted by hosts like Dick Cavett, Charlie Rose, and Bob Costas).

Allen's *Tonight* was the spawning ground for comedians like

Jonathan Winters, Don Knotts, Shelley Berman, Buddy Hackett, Louis Nye, Don Adams, Jackie Mason, and Mort Sahl. It launched the singing careers of Andy Williams, Steve Lawrence, and Eydie Gorme and showcased cultural icons like Carl Sandburg, James Michener, Billie Holiday, Leonard Bernstein, Willie Mays, Abbott and Costello, Martin and Lewis, and Grace Kelly. It presented the network debut of Hal Holbrook's classic characterization of Mark Twain and the whimsical comedy of Jim Henson's Muppets. Allen founded a living museum of American jazz by regularly featuring Count Basie, Duke Ellington, Dave Brubeck, Lionel Hampton, Gene Krupa, Dizzy Gillespie, Ella Fitzgerald, and dozens of other jazz legends on the show. In its posthumous tribute to Allen, *Variety* noted that he provided TV exposure to renegade talents like Jack Kerouac and Lenny Bruce at a time when other broadcasters still considered them taboo.

In addition, Allen's social conscience permeated the show's fabric. He frequently booked African American musicians, singers, and athletes to appear prominently on *Tonight* in an era when they were rarely visible on television. He devoted entire shows to race relations, organized crime, McCarthyism, drug addiction, and other serious topics. A nondrinker himself, he once downed six vodkas throughout the course of a live broadcast to demonstrate what happens to drivers who drink. He promoted charitable causes, including support for the disabled, needy families across America, and orphans overseas. And even when he moved from late night into prime time, he was not afraid to risk his career by publicly opposing the death penalty in a controversial case involving convicted serial rapist Caryl Chessman in 1960.

The unprecedented success of *Tonight* led NBC in 1956 to gamble on slating Allen in a prime-time comedy series opposite the Sunday night king of the era, Ed Sullivan. Not only did Allen's Sunday night show win critical acclaim and rescue NBC from a longtime ratings drought, but also it launched one of the fiercest ratings wars between NBC and CBS in television history. In 1980, NBC aggressively tried to woo Allen back to late night with a program to air after Johnny Carson—a move that backfired embarrassingly on the network but ultimately paved the way for David Letterman to enter the late-night arena.

The stellar achievements of Allen and his colleagues should long ago have dictated the compilation of a *Best of Steve* or *The Tonight Show: Season One* archival video series. Tragically, nearly all of NBC's Allen-era *Tonight* kinescopes, along with thousands of films and tapes of other early shows, were destroyed. Only about two dozen shows survive because, Allen once lamented, "Some idiot in charge of the network storage facility in New Jersey needed to clear some shelf space."

The creative spirit and camaraderie behind the birth of the *Tonight* show are recalled by the people who were there—fifty years ago. Conductor Skitch Henderson remembered the band members leaping onto their chairs and the audience fleeing the Hudson Theatre when a bunch of trained circus snakes was suddenly spooked by the harsh studio lights. Doc Severinsen, a young horn player in the Allen *Tonight* band, remembered when there was no budget for arrangements, which meant that each musician had to write out his own part. Director Dwight Hemion recalled coaxing Eydie Gorme to sing a number perched perilously on a tree branch above the thundering waters of Niagara Falls—on live TV. Singer Steve Lawrence recalled how Allen had successfully fought the NBC brass' attempt to dump him and Gorme, the show's resident singing duo, because they were Jewish. Producer Bill Harbach admired Allen's on-air condemnation of a bigoted viewer who had written to chastise Allen for giving Lena Horne a friendly kiss on the cheek on a previous night's show. And Allen himself recalled how he and his wife, Jayne Meadows, had to live under round-the-clock police protection after he spoke out on the show against organized crime and was subjected to death threats, a tire slashing, and a stink bomb erupting in the Hudson Theatre.

Especially remarkable is how the versatile Allen and his talented team pulled off their clever feats using primitive technology. All of the Allen-era *Tonight* broadcasts were live, back when stagehands hadn't yet learned how to hold cue cards, clunky TV cameras plodded across the stage like elephants, and the harsh lighting needed to transmit an acceptable picture made some performers look like ghouls. There was no tape delay because, as Bill Harbach noted, "There was no tape!" (with a "Don't you get it?" tone in his voice). In contrast to the army of writers employed by late-night shows today, Allen's *Tonight* show began with a writing staff of one: himself. Vulgar humor, virtually a staple in today's programs, was scrupulously policed by network censors.

According to *Variety*, Allen's "inventive, wry, cerebral style of comedy influenced . . . most prominently Steve Martin and David Letterman." They, along with contemporary figures like Billy Crystal, Bill Maher, and Jay Leno, pay tribute to Allen as a major influence on their work. In addition, Allen's legendary peers—including Sid Caesar, Carl Reiner, Jonathan Winters, and Larry Gelbart—offer revealing insights about their dear friend.

The reflections collected here offer an entertaining, behind-the-scenes look at the birth of a television institution and the brilliance of the Inventor of Late Night, whose influence continues to make America stay awake and laugh—night after night after night.

Chapter 1

THE NIGHT BEFORE *TONIGHT*

Although millions of Americans alive today grew up with the Tonight *show as hosted by one of Steve Allen's successors, few realize that it was Allen who actually created it. But to say that he deliberately set out to "create" the* Tonight *show is not quite accurate. Rather, the elements that came to define* Tonight *emerged out of Allen's early life experiences and a series of creative experiments in which he discovered and developed his personal strengths in radio and television.*

*B*orn on the day after Christmas in 1921 in New York City to a vaudeville couple, Stephen Valentine Patrick William Allen grew up immersed in showbiz culture. His father, Billy Allen, was a vaudeville straight man and singer. His mother, Isabelle Donohue— better known by her stage name, Belle Montrose—was one of seventeen children in a poor family and began her entertainment career at age nine by joining the circus. It was her mother's decision to apprentice her out to their neighbors, the Watson Sisters, a pair of aerialists who traveled the world with the Barnum and Bailey Circus. "One less mouth to feed," justified Belle's weary mother, Bridget

Donohue, who years earlier had been abandoned by her illiterate husband. Belle tried her hand as an aerial acrobat and over the next few years graduated to chorus girl and later comedienne, working on the road with a series of acts and partners, and meeting her future husband in the process.

Steve, too, was a child of the road. When he was only a few months old, he became ill while his parents were performing in San Francisco, and he had to be hospitalized—and ended up being left there for several months while they continued to tour the country. Not long after his first birthday, one of Belle's sisters, Rose, traveled to San Francisco to take him from the hospital back home to Chicago. Steve marked the reunion by slapping his mother's face with all his might. She angrily responded by striking him back, alarming his aunt Rose, who seized the boy from her and considered keeping him herself.

When Steve was eighteen months old, Billy Allen died. Belle became the family breadwinner and typically had to work late at night. Baby-sitters were not always easy to find, especially in strange towns across the country. "I can dimly remember waking up alone in the middle of the night in various hotel rooms," recalled Allen, "wondering where I was and where my mother was. Sometimes I would get up, get dressed, and go out into the night looking for her." One sitter turned out to be a young vaudevillian named Milton Berle, who worked with Belle and cared for two-year-old Steve.

"I was just a teenager," remembered Berle, "and one of the acts on the bill with me was a very, very funny lady, Belle Montrose. And one evening, after she came off stage, she looked at me and she said, 'Hey, sonny, you see that stroller over there? Could you keep an eye on my little Stevie?' So I did."

Allen regarded his mother as a wonderful companion and comedienne who exerted a tremendous comedic influence on him. As a young boy, he sat through countless movies and live acts in any number of theaters, waiting for his mother to come on. Belle was known for her airheaded, addle-brained onstage persona that became the trademark of another vaudeville wife, Gracie Allen (no relation). Belle's was a casual style of comedy—"low-volume, not big like Jackie Gleason's humor," as Allen put it. Allen absorbed "her mannerisms, her way of throwing off hand gestures, her attitudes, and the way she looked and talked."

Decades later, on one of Allen's television shows, the two re-created a vaudeville routine that she frequently had performed with her husband—she as the dimwit amateur actress and he as the suffering emcee who had to interview her before a live audience. The routine exemplified her masterful comic timing and also made clear the source of Allen's own timing:

BELLE (confused): Everybody thunk? Thought? *Thinks* that I have all
     the earmuffs—
STEVE: No, no. Earmarks.
BELLE: All the earmarks . . . of an *earmuff.*
STEVE (impatiently): No!
BELLE: An earache.
STEVE: No, no.
BELLE: Of a birthmark?
STEVE: No, not a birthmark. Earmarks of an *actress.*
BELLE: Oh, that old thing.
STEVE: An actress, yes.
BELLE: Of course, I'm not a regular mattress—
STEVE (exasperated): ACTRESS!
BELLE (startled): Of course, I'm not a regular actress, and if I make
     any mistakes, look them over—over*look* them (nodding her
     head in satisfaction).

Although Belle influenced her son's comedy talents, she also subjected him to her drinking problem. "If she didn't have a drink, then there was a problem," chuckled Allen warmly, with no visible trace of bitterness. But one of the wiser decisions Belle did make was to enroll her son in piano lessons for three years. "I made up little songs at first," he recalled, "but afterward lost interest in music." Actually, it was the ability to *read* music that Allen never seemed to pick up, whereas his ability to play melodies and harmonies by ear emerged and later blossomed.

Belle's success in show business, like that of many other performers, fluctuated perilously. She earned as much as $700 a week, and when she had that kind of money, she placed Steve in a boarding school, such as Bishop Quarter School at East Avenue and Lake Street in Oak Park, Illinois, or St. Joseph's Institute in LaGrange, Illinois, a quiet Chicago suburb. An order of strict nuns ran the latter school, where Steve spent the third through fifth grades. The rest of the time, when it was not feasible to take the boy on the road, Belle sent him to Chicago to live with a succession of aunts, uncles, and grandparents on her side (the Donohues) and even strangers for months at a time. Consequently, he bounced around between eighteen schools (including high schools in Chicago, Los Angeles, and Phoenix) and two colleges.

The other Donohues, like Allen's mother, were high spirited, independent, argumentative, popular, wild, unruly, unstable, and irrational—in other words, he explained, "flighty Irish." They lived in neighborhoods scattered throughout Chicago's South Side, including Hyde Park and the Back of the Yards, and subjected those neighborhoods to their endless bickering and quirks. "Instead of answering the door calmly, in a civilized way," Allen wrote, "the members of the family would start up like a flock of startled quail, some running into bedrooms, others hiding behind curtains and peeking out of windows to see what enemy was invading their privacy."

During his formative years, Steve was surrounded mainly by

women ("I have no recollection of my father," he would later write in *Mark It and Strike It* [1960]). In the absence of a father, he found a father figure in his uncle Steve Donohue, who devoted countless hours to his young nephew, taking him to the Lincoln Park Zoo, to the circus, or just for long walks in the park. Allen remembered how at every intersection his uncle would lecture him on looking both ways before crossing the street. There was more advice: "Take deep breaths and keep your back straight like a soldier. Drink lots of milk. Get plenty of exercise." Uncle Steve admired Clarence Darrow, Luther Burbank, Thomas Edison, and Abraham Lincoln.

But Uncle Steve couldn't hold down a job. He drank hard and got into bar fights, coming home late, drunk, bloodied, and wild; breaking dishes; and stumbling in the dark. Late one stormy night, little Steve and his terrorized aunt Mag surreptitiously watched Uncle Steve standing on the porch outside their apartment on 60th Street just off Halsted, where torrents of rain drenched his long underwear. "My God," said Aunt Mag, "if anybody sees him out there like that, we'll all be arrested." Uncle Steve began yelling to someone on the street, affecting a southern accent: "Pahdon me, podnuh, but ah was wonderin' if pe'haps you maght have a cigarette."

"I got a fit of giggles and laughed so hard my aunt had to press her hand over my mouth," Allen later recalled. "I don't remember what happened after that, but I fell asleep happy."

At Uncle Steve's funeral in 1958, Allen curiously noticed how his uncle, dressed for the first time in an elegant suit, looked handsomer, healthier, younger, and more at peace in death than he ever was in life. Despite his uncle's overwhelming failure in life, Allen found himself indebted to him: "His advice was excellent, his example deplorable. And yet by listening to him I learned what to do, and by watching him I learned what *not* to do."

John O'Rourke met Allen in the sixth grade at St. Thomas the Apostle School in Hyde Park. He lived just a few blocks away from

Allen and his mother, who at the time were living in a second-floor apartment above a grocery store at 55th Street and Kenwood. He and Allen and their friends used to hang out together after school in another friend's basement, which had a Ping-Pong table and a piano.

In a 2005 interview, O'Rourke remembered Allen as a popular kid: "He knew more than everybody. He read more, and he had a lot of charisma. And he could stay out later than most kids." On Halloween, Allen would get into some of his mother's stage outfits, walk down the street, and scare people. He and O'Rourke snuck into the 1933 World's Fair held at Chicago's Northerly Island. Unlike his peers, who had never been anywhere outside the city, Allen, at age eleven, had been everywhere.

The worldly Allen had an imaginative mind. He started a game where he and his friends would refer to each other by pronouncing their names backwards. In class, where most other students were afraid to open their mouths, he was not afraid to voice his opinions about many topics and sometimes would even correct his teachers. "He wouldn't be snippy with the nuns because they were tough ladies, but he'd just voice his opinions," remembered O'Rourke. "He'd been more places and read a lot more than probably any other student the nuns had encountered." Allen's precociousness, however, didn't always sit well with the good sisters. During the course of one school year, a nun wound up breaking three different wooden pointers across Allen's back.

Allen looked back on his topsy-turvy childhood with affection because he felt genuine love and concern from his quirky, if not tragic, elders. One stabilizing factor was his family's love of humor and ability to find it in almost any situation. One such situation occurred in 1938, when sixteen-year-old Steve, his mother, and Aunt Mag were living in the rundown Hotel Raleigh on Chicago's Near North Side. Suddenly in the mood for background music, Allen turned on the radio, fiddled with the tuner, and settled on a station playing ballroom dance music. The 1930s was the decade when nearly every home in America had a radio, and big-scale dramas, quiz shows, and comedies were broadcast for the mass market. Television, however, was still in its infancy. It would be another year before NBC would inaugurate regular TV service by broadcasting the opening ceremonies of the 1939 World's Fair in New York.

Allen lay on the floor near the radio with a book, while his mother and aunt played cards in the next room. They had no idea that he had tuned into Orson Welles's legendary radio play, *War of the Worlds*, and, like millions of other listeners across the country, had missed the opening disclaimer that the entire broadcast was make believe.

The innocuous dance music was interrupted by a series of bulletins from CBS News—first reporting a series of mysterious explosions on Mars, and later reporting meteor showers over Princeton, New Jersey. Soon afterwards, a spaceship landed with grotesque leathery creatures emerging from within. National Guard troops dispatched to the scene were immediately massacred. "The contents of the news broadcast were inherently unbelievable," recounted Allen, "and yet we had it on the authority of the Columbia Broadcasting System that such things were actually happening." Then the announcer reported more spaceships observed over Cleveland, Detroit, and—gulp—*Chicago*.

"Jesus, Mary, and Joseph!" exclaimed Aunt Mag. "We'll be killed right here in this hotel!"

"There's only one thing to do," Allen's mother bravely declared. They would all flee to nearby Holy Name Cathedral. After fluttering around the room and bickering about whether Aunt Mag would need to take her glasses or hat, the three departed their eighth-floor suite, missing the reassuring finale to the program.

As they stood in the dim hallway, waiting for the elevator, Allen's mother admonished a dignified-looking young woman holding a little girl in her arms, "Run for your life!" She then turned to her son and ordered, "Button your overcoat, Stevie. You'll catch cold when we go out."

The young woman looked blankly at Belle. A wild-eyed Aunt Mag began shouting at her. The woman started laughing.

"Go ahead and laugh," snapped Aunt Mag. "But for the sake of that dear baby in your arms, don't you laugh!" The woman eyed the relatively even-keeled Allen quizzically, prompting him to explain to her, "We just heard on the radio that there's something up in the sky."

Apparently, Allen's explanation didn't help. The woman and her child began retreating a few steps down the hall—"walking backward," noted Allen, "so as to keep an eye on us." This inflamed Aunt Mag, who by now was on a roll: "'You ought to get down on your knees, instead of laughing at people! We're going to church to pray, and that's what you ought to be doing right this minute, *praying!*'"

At that moment, the elevator doors opened, revealing the customarily cheerful, smiling elevator operator. "Never had I seen a smile fade so fast," mused Allen. The three charged into the elevator, and Belle and Aunt Mag practically pounced on the poor boy with their hysterical warnings about an interplanetary invasion. The boy was petrified—not at the thought of invaders from Mars, but by the fact that he was trapped in a tiny elevator with three lunatics from Earth.

The elevator boy slid the throttle all the way forward for a full-speed ride down to the first floor. He slid the folding doors of the cage open, and the three thundered past him into the lobby. To their surprise, the atmosphere was, well, normal. "It was a scene of lobbylike calm," recalled Allen. People were sitting or dozing in overstuffed chairs. Some were smoking cigars. Others were reading newspapers. The conversations were subdued.

Such tranquility was disarming. The three had planned to warn everyone in the lobby about the crisis and then sprint across Dearborn Street, pausing only in the event that a sudden spaceship attack should cause them to take cover. A frustrated Aunt Mag tried to apprise the blasé desk clerk that the world was about to end.

Meanwhile, Allen overheard a radio at the other end of the lobby. Instead of an urgent crisis update, what he heard was an announcer calmly reading a commercial for tomato soup. A light-bulb suddenly went on in Allen's mind. He told his mother and Aunt Mag, and the three embarrassed souls tip-toed, eyes downcast, toward the elevator, "excruciatingly aware that all heads were turned toward us, and that the clerk was smiling at us in a frightfully patronizing way," remembered Allen.

"We'll have to move out of this place," shuddered Allen's mother. But before they ever made it to the elevator, they broke into shrieks of laughter, forcing them to sit down and create even more of a scene in the hotel lobby than the panic they had displayed only moments earlier.

The young Allen's ability to extract humor so quickly out of a situation foreshadowed his aptitude for spontaneous, off-the-cuff comedy. "Funny things used to pop into my head all of the time when I was a little boy in school—and I'd start laughing," Allen told *Redbook* magazine in 1954. "Other kids and their mothers told me I could make my living with my jokes. But my humor met with a very mixed reception from my teachers, some of whom thought I was a young show-off."

EARLY EXPERIENCES IN BROADCASTING

In 1939, television attempted nightly experimental broadcasts solely in New York, where most of the few television sets that existed were located. Viewership was so minuscule, in fact, that NBC mailed weekly postcards containing its program schedule to a list it kept of known TV set owners.

29

That same year, Allen was attending Hyde Park High School in Chicago. There were days when he would alight the streetcar at Stony Island and 62nd Street, and, instead of heading toward the campus, he would stroll toward the windy lakefront, wander the hallowed halls of the Museum of Science and Industry, or sit in Jackson Park and write poetry. He might take in a movie at the Tivoli Theater on Cottage Grove, walk under the "L" tracks at 63rd Street, or invite a girl to the Walgreens at 63rd and Stony Island, where they would sit in a booth and indulge in hot cocoa and cookies wrapped in transparent paper.

A kindly teacher recognized the bright, inquisitive student lurking beneath Allen's disinterested exterior and took him under her wing. She had Allen attending classes regularly, and she made him an editor of a school magazine. This teacher, Mrs. Marguerite Byrne, encouraged him to enter essay contests, and he won a $100 prize in a Civitan club contest. She also encouraged him to submit material to Chicago newspapers, and the *Chicago Tribune* published his jokes and light verse in its famous "Line-o'-type" column.

Allen dreamed of becoming a newspaper reporter, but his asthma got so bad that he and his mother left Chicago and moved to Phoenix, where the hot desert climate cleared his symptoms immediately. He enrolled in Phoenix Union High School, where he completed his senior year and developed his interest in journalism by writing humorous features and sports stories for the school paper. This led in 1941 to his acceptance of a journalism scholarship to Drake University in Des Moines, Iowa, where he joined the university newspaper and became the sole writer of humorous material (as well as the first freshman in the school's history to be assigned a regular feature).

While in college, Allen played piano in the dance band and discovered that his musical abilities could attract more attention and popularity than his painfully shy personality ever did. He also took a course in radio production, which awakened his interest in the medium. Although his first year at Drake was idyllic, his $1,000 scholarship expired at the end of that year, and he could not afford the next year's tuition. In addition, his asthma began to catch up with him. In the fall of 1942, Allen transferred to Arizona State Teachers College (now Arizona State University) in Tempe.

A career in radio, however, continued to beckon. Ultimately, Allen chose radio over journalism when he discovered that "while there seemed to be many brilliant men on newspapers, the radio field impressed me as one swarming with idiots." He dropped out of Arizona State a few months later to take a fifty-dollar-a-week part-time job at Phoenix radio station KOY, announcing, piano playing, record spinning, and acting. He also wrote advertising and news copy and soap opera scripts and took on "as many additional duties as I desired, as long as it was understood that I would demand no additional salary."

By this time, NBC and CBS had recently been granted commercial licenses for their New York stations, thus marking the birth of commercial television. Throughout the 1940s, most television programs would continue to be seen only in New York, which held the honor of being America's TV capital.

One of Allen's regular assignments at KOY was to drop an Alka-Seltzer tablet into a cup of hot water for an on-air commercial and exclaim, "Listen to it fizz!" One night, just two minutes before the commercial, Allen discovered that the Alka-Seltzer bottle was empty. He dashed to the men's room and found a small can of Bi-so-dol, another antidote of the day, "that belonged," he recalled, "to a staff newscaster who evidently hadn't been listening to my Alka-Seltzer commercials." Confident and relieved, Allen raced back to the studio, just in time to start the commercial, only to discover—in that instant—that Bi-so-dol doesn't fizz. After two seconds of dead air, Allen recovered by doing "as nice a vocal impersonation of a stomach tablet's fizz as you've ever heard."

In a weekly man-on-the-street interview program, Allen and fellow KOY announcer Bill Lester asked passersby for whom they intended to vote in the 1944 presidential election—Roosevelt or Dewey—and why. The show, which was originating that week from a Phoenix supermarket, was progressing smoothly until Allen and Lester discovered, without warning, that the store had run out of customers. With ten minutes of airtime left to fill, Allen and Lester desperately took turns posing as imaginary customers and interviewing each other. Allen became "Walter Kline," an elderly tobacco-chewing geezer who preferred Dewey because "it's time for a change." Lester posed as "A. K. Johnson" from Tucson and chit-chatted with Allen. They went on that way, carefully splitting the votes down the middle and saying nothing unkind about either candidate.

Allen didn't recover quite as nicely from pitfalls that awaited him in other assignments. While doing live commentary on a parade from the rooftop of the KOY studios, he watched in horror as his carefully prepared notes about each of the floats blew away. His predicament was compounded when the parade came to a grinding halt, leaving him straining to find different ways to describe the Boy Scout drum-and-bugle corps that was marching in front of him—in place. That afternoon, his coverage of a rodeo show was similarly abysmal. Fresh from Chicago, Allen's knowledge of western speak, "gleaned entirely from cowboy movies, seemed to consist solely of words like hombre, ornery sidewinder, no-good varmint, chuck wagon, and six-gun, none of which appeared appropriate to the task at hand," he recalled. Allen proceeded to describe a "'steer-milking contest'—a phenomenon," he would later acknowledge, "theretofore unknown to biological science, not to mention the cattle business."

Despite these mishaps, Allen had begun to develop his glibness speaking into a mike, even if he felt the need to practice by talking to himself as he drove through the streets of Phoenix, describing things and people he observed along the road.

SMILE TIME

While at KOY, Allen collaborated with singer and fellow announcer Wendell Noble to form Noble and Allen, an upstart comedy team that played clubs in the Phoenix area. Their act was a hodge-podge of goofiness consisting of Allen playing piano, Noble singing, and the two clowning in jokes and sketches. In 1946, Noble moved to Los Angeles to work at KHJ, an affiliate of the Don Lee/Mutual network. Once Allen saved up $1,000, he, too, followed, and the two teamed up again—this time, on a daily morning show being carried by Don Lee/Mutual along the entire West Coast. The program, *Smile Time*, was based on their Phoenix act and packed a punch into its fifteen-minute timeslot. It was a fast-paced cavalcade of songs, patter, goofy characters, jokes, zany time checks and weather reports, soap-opera parodies, and nonsense (Allen: "Hey, Wendell, how are the letters coming in?" Noble: "By mail, mostly") squeezed into a twelve-page script. There were even mock band remotes: *"From the beautiful Aragon Ballroom, high atop the fabulous Hotel Fabulous, in the heart of downtown Gallup, New Mexico, just a short forty-five-minute drive from the ball-bearing center of the world, Leavenworth, Kansas. . . ."*

The *Smile Time* theme song was cheerfully silly: *"It's* Smile Time *// Chase your blues away because it's* Smile Time *// The way to start the day is just to sing this minute // Put rhythm in it // And smile, 'cuz it's* Smile Time *now!"*

The show was an instant hit, but its wild success alarmed the two partners. "Somehow we had talked our way into a big break," explained Allen. "But now it suddenly occurred to us that we really weren't ready for such a giant step. Within the short space of two

33

weeks, we had used up all our tested material and were staring with horror at the bottom of the comedy barrel." In desperation, there was only one thing to do: Go to secondhand bookstores and buy every joke book they could find and adapt or lift as much material as they could. But even this wouldn't cut it for a daily twelve-to-fifteen-page script. Allen dredged and recycled the humorous verse he had written for his high school magazine and the Drake University paper.

Just as the boys were reaching the point of collapse, the Mutual brass called them in. "Boys," declared a beaming executive, "we like what you're doing. In fact, we like it so much that we're going to put you on the air coast-to-coast starting next month!"

At twenty-four, Allen was starting to attract national attention. The network permitted him to hire another player, June Foray, a petite, young actress with a growing reputation for character voices. (She would later be revered as the voice of Rocky the Squirrel and Natasha Fatale on the *Rocky and Bullwinkle* animated series, as well as Grandma on Warner Brothers' *Looney Toons*.) She was capable of doing any dialect, any age, comedy or drama, which was just what Allen wanted for his sketches. On *Smile Time*, recalled Foray in 2003, she played everything: "Irish, Brooklyns, Mexicans, and loudmouths," thereby relieving Noble of having to play old ladies and society matrons.

In addition, the show's budget increased to allow for the hiring of a young organist, Skitch Henderson, who had just been discharged from the Air Corps (and who in 1954 would lead the band on Allen's *Tonight* show). Henderson remembered the show: "Their 'orchestra' was me on piano. And we gave away groceries to get an audience. That's the way that the salami thing [Allen giving away salamis] started on the *Tonight* show."

The music and silliness and lightning pace were unusual for the era and soon became a national wake-up call. "Here it was, seven-fifteen in the morning," said Foray, "and people would show up in the auditorium before they went to work and watch us."

Foray found Allen a fascinating and complex personality: "Steve had no inhibitions about comedy. He could be outrageous in his comedy. But in person he was very quiet. And here he was, a songwriter, played piano beautifully, and he told me that he could never read music. That's what was so wonderful about Steve. His talent just opposed his nature."

For Allen, *Smile Time* became the GED equivalent of a high school course in radio comedy: "I knew almost every old joke ever written, had learned how to write new jokes on every conceivable subject; and the simple business of performing five times a week had given a certain professional polish to my work."

During *Smile Time*'s run, television's first mass audience—an "East Coast network" comprising New York, Philadelphia, Schenectady, and Washington, DC—tuned in to the 1947 World Series. A total of 3.9 million people watched the games—3.5 million of them in bars, the primary recipients at the time of television broadcasts, where most people encountered their first television set. This eventually triggered a revolution of home TV set purchases.

ATTRACTING A FOLLOWING

By 1948, network television was just getting off the ground. CBS and ABC opened for business that year, and landmark shows hosted by Milton Berle, Ed Sullivan, Arthur Godfrey, and Ted Mack premiered. Still, less than 2 percent of all US homes owned a television set.

In early 1948, after a two-year run, Mutual dropped *Smile Time*, and Allen accepted an offer to host a nightly thirty-minute records-and-talk program, *Breaking All Records*, at KNX, the CBS Los Angeles affiliate. At first, he considered the move from network star back to a local disc jockey a sort of demotion—"a big step in the wrong direction." But then he began to attract an avid local following that encouraged him to play records less, talk more, and keep playing piano. Allen saw that this would be in his own best interest: "Perceiving at once that by playing a great many records I would be performing an estimable service for Bing Crosby, Frank Sinatra, Dinah Shore, et al., but doing very little for myself, I determined immediately to make the music on the new program secondary in importance to its humor. Therefore, I wrote out a seven- or eight-page script each evening, read it in an offhand conversational manner to create the impression that I was speaking more or less extemporaneously and played a little less music than instructed."

After two months, frowning station bosses ordered him to go back to doing what they had hired him to do: play records. Like a spoiled boy, Allen went on the air and reported the entire exchange to his listening audience, who came to the rescue, flooding the KNX mailroom in the next two days with over four hundred letters of support. Fans declared that they were more interested in Allen's banter than in the records. KNX relented and let Allen gab. It was a smart move. The popularity of the show (now *The Steve Allen Show*) continued to grow, and Allen started receiving letters from a few listeners wanting to visit the studio. Allen obliged, still wondering why a dozen or so drop-in visitors a night would want to watch a guy "in his shirt-sleeves sitting at a table reading from a script and introducing recordings." Observing that "twelve people laughing in a small room sounds like a larger number," Allen saw the number swell to over a hundred, and the show moved to a larger studio, all for an 11 p.m. *radio* broadcast. In another eighteen months, Allen would not be playing any records on the show at all.

Buoyed by the show's growing success, KNX expanded the show to an hour. Up to this point, Allen had been adhering to radio's tightly scripted format, slavishly writing his own comedy scripts to perform on the air. Disappointed that his $175-a-week salary failed to keep pace with his expanding duties and timeslot, not to mention the show's growing popularity, he decided to take the lazy way out. Rather than spend even more time writing scripts, he began interviewing more and more guest entertainers—something he discovered he could do well and with far less preparation.

Allen's new approach worked until one night, when the scheduled guest, actress/singer Doris Day, failed to show up. Her agent had forgotten to tell her about the booking. Allen was suddenly forced to fill twenty-five minutes of air. He had already used up all of his minimal, prepared script, and he had played both sides of Day's new record.

Suddenly, without quite knowing why, Allen found himself hauling the clunky studio floor microphone into the audience, where he chatted with visitors. The audience response stunned him and gave rise to another revelation. "Whatever was said was greeted with almost hysterical laughter," recalled Allen. "I was astounded to learn that audiences would laugh more readily at an ad-libbed quip, even though it might not be as funny as a prepared and polished joke."

"Others in radio had wandered into audiences before Allen— gabby guys like Art Linkletter and Bert Parks," wrote entertainment columnist Gerald Nachman in his 2003 book, *Seriously Funny*. "But they lacked Allen's ingenuity and verbal dexterity," opting for more contrived conversation starters ("Who's the oldest lady in the audience?" "Who can describe a spiral staircase without using his hands?"). "His background as a jokesmith allowed him to go beyond mere audience chitchat," continued Nachman, and create jokes on the spot.

Although Allen sensed an epiphany, he wasn't sure he could pull it off night after night: "Believe me, that wasn't easy at first. I used to think of my ad-lib while my guest was talking. Then I found the secret: base your ad-lib on what is said or done."

From that night on, Allen incorporated audience interviews into every program, and he eventually stopped writing comedy material altogether, just showing up at the studio within fifteen minutes of airtime. He would select a few letters and newspaper articles for the opening ten-minute monologue, which would be followed by the celebrity guest interview, a musical number he would play or sing, and the all-important ad-lib banter with the audience.

The show graduated to an even larger studio and became a late-night cult hit not only in southern California but also in other parts of the United States, for a local show beamed from a fifteen thousand-watt station such as KNX could on certain nights (depending on the atmospheric conditions) be picked up several states away. Allen received upwards of two thousand fan letters a week, and he reported receiving mail from as far away as Florida and New England. Katherine Hepburn and Fanny Brice headed a club that staged listening parties around the show. The show became the darling of the comedy elite, including Jack Benny, Bob Hope, Fred Allen, Groucho Marx, Milton Berle, Red Skelton, and Phil Silvers, many of whom were occasional guests. But the more Allenesque type of guest might be a burlesque dancer, a lobster, a waiter from a posh Hollywood restaurant (who brought a seven-course dinner that Allen consumed on the air), or a tiger.

By now, hundreds of fans—men in business suits and ties, women in sensible skirts and blazers—were lined up around the block on Sunset Boulevard in front of the theater at CBS. Ushers would be on duty, along with a cop and a CBS night watchman. The audiences would average three hundred or four hundred on a week-night. "After a while," recalled Allen, "we'd have a thousand persons there on Saturday night, and I'd have to do two shows. My twenty-five-minute show was lengthened to forty-five minutes a night, five nights a week, but I was still getting only $100 a week."

PIC magazine captured the flavor of the midnight show and its amiable twenty-nine-year-old host this way: "No script, no format, no stars, and one lone phonograph record. What does Allen do that can fill the Columbia Broadcasting System's largest radio studio at midnight? Almost no one on the Pacific Coast can tell you—least of all Allen." Groucho Marx, one of Allen's biggest boosters, said, "Allen, the trouble with you is you're too damn good" and later called him "the funniest Allen since Fred."

Smile Time alum June Foray helped Allen out on Saturday nights, when there was one broadcast of the show to the East at five o'clock and a second performance for the West Coast at eight. Foray remembered that some of the actors would imbibe at a bar next door to the studio, often shortly before airtime. One actor got so sloshed that, in the middle of the show, "he just walked off the stage." It was the calm and quick-thinking Allen who saved the day, Foray recalled: "Everybody recovered because Steve did. He could talk his way out of anything. So everybody felt very comfortable."

One night, Allen conned his audience into participating in a national, fraternity-style prank. He convinced listeners, at the count of ten, to sound their automobile horns, so that engineers at CBS stations all over the country could "measure" his show's automobile listenership with "audiometers." Thousands all over the country bought into the practical joke, which today might be dubbed "Horns across America."

The Steve Allen Show enjoyed a nearly three-year run through 1950. Pleased with Allen's phenomenal rise on its Los Angeles affiliate, CBS brought him to New York to find him a network program. The announcement of his first network assignment also attracted the attention—and approval—of a growing segment of Allen's audience: college students, who dug Allen's irreverent yet good-natured jabs at guests, audience members, sponsors, CBS officials, and even himself. The *Daily Trojan*, the student newspaper of the University of Southern California, wrote: "When CBS decided to make *The Steve Allen Show* the summer replacement for *Our Miss Brooks* last month, the only ones who were not surprised were local college students. As far back as two years ago, when Steve Allen was first starting out as a comic, students formed the nucleus of his group of admirers. Now, still composed mostly of students, the number of Allen fans has reached the point where anyone who shows up outside CBS studios after 11:15 p.m. in hopes of getting in is considered, by them, a rank optimist." (Allen remained popular with college audiences throughout his career; his last concert, a one-man music and comedy show, took place the night before his death before a sold-out crowd at Victor Valley Community College in Victorville, California).

The Transition into Television

Allen's local radio successes caught radio and television programmers by surprise, as the shows were low budget and largely unpromoted. His radio background proved invaluable, for it facilitated his successful transition into entertaining on TV. The great comedians of vaudeville and nightclubs simply adapted their stage acts to television. In contrast, Allen's television comedy sprung from his ability on radio to ad-lib, interview, and connect with audiences in loose, extemporaneous fashion. His very first television experience came in 1949 as the unlikely announcer/commentator for wrestling matches, which required him to ad-lib and get laughs—two talents he would have to summon to compensate for his virtual ignorance of the sport.

But Allen didn't dare admit his ignorance to the ABC exec who recruited him for the assignment. At the time, wrestling was a very popular television attraction. The ABC exec thought Allen could do a funny but reasonably knowledgeable commentary on what was happening in the ring. Allen decided to prepare for his assignment by watching three nights of televised wrestling matches on KTLA that were announced by the jovial, fast-talking former actor Dick Lane. Once Allen was settled into the announcer's booth at Ocean Park Arena in Santa Monica, his meager preparation got him through the first five minutes of the match. The rest would be up to him and whatever he could conjure.

"Leone gives Smith a full nelson now," ventured Allen on the spot, "slipping it up from either a half-nelson or an Ozzie Nelson. Now the boys go into a double pretzel bend with variations on a theme by Velox and Yolanda. Whoops, Leone takes his man down to the mat! He has him pinned; now they roll. It's sort of a rolling pin." Allen's confused, unorthodox descriptions of the various holds had audiences laughing from outside the arena. He would even comment about the more bizarre people attending the match, as well as the haze permeating the arena: "There's lots of cigar smoke in the air here. I don't like to say that this joint is too smoky, but this is the only wrestling arena in town where they cure hams from the ceiling." Allen's career as a wrestling announcer lasted several months before ABC decided to replace the matches with old movies.

After CBS radio gave Allen a weekly prime-time show, CBS television believed it could groom him for national small-screen stardom and gave Allen his first network television show. *The Steve Allen Show* premiered at 11 a.m. on Christmas Day, 1950, and was later moved into a thirty-minute, early evening slot. Allen's new television show required him to uproot himself and his family (consisting of his wife, Dorothy Goodman, and their three sons) from their home base in Los Angeles and move to New York. The reasons were technological. In 1950, it was not possible to originate a live network broadcast from L.A., since the West Coast was not yet hooked up to the television coaxial cable that carried the TV signals linking the East and Midwest. The link to the West Coast would not be completed until September 1951, when America would finally enjoy coast-to-coast television.

The Steve Allen Show, which ran through 1952, was a daily television version of Allen's old Hollywood radio show—part music, part comedy, and part talk. It featured Peggy Lee as the regular vocalist and Llemuel, a huge, lovable, and affectionate South American llama. The show introduced audiences to routines that would later become Allen trademarks, including wild physical stunts, reading funny items in the newspaper, and prank phone calls. One day, he read an ad, "Leiberman Brothers' third floor is now open to the public," and commented to the studio audience, "I wonder what's been going on on the third floor that we couldn't get in on until today?" Allen picked up the phone, called the company on the air, and asked that question to the man who answered. "The first time he hung up on me," recalled Allen. "I called back four times, and it all got screams from the audience."

On another day, an annoying clatter outside the stage doors of the studio began to disrupt the proceedings. Unable to ignore the disturbance, Allen had the ushers open the back door, and he took a hand mike in search of the source of the noise. He found an elderly Italian gentleman running a cement mixer. A bemused but quick-thinking Allen decided to interview the laborer for several minutes, to the screaming laughter of the studio audience. The workman, who even apologized for the disturbance, was probably unaware that he could be heard in the studio, not to mention throughout the entire country. "It didn't matter much what either of us said," concluded Allen. "It was the situation itself that was funny." And it was that particular situation that prompted him to interview fewer celebrities and more "just plain folks."

The show was only a modest ratings success. When CBS canceled it in 1952, Allen came up with an innovative way to mark the final broadcast. Ten minutes before the show's end, the stagehands proceeded—on the air—to dismantle the set and cart off the scenery, Allen's breakfast table/desk, and his piano. Allen bid good-bye to

Miss Lee, Llemuel, and the other cast members, and he thanked the studio audience and television viewers for their support. With three minutes of air left and the orchestra softly playing the show's theme song, Allen donned his coat and hat. The camera followed him as he walked across the now bare and deserted set, through the large stage door, and out into the street. An outside camera picked up the shot as Allen walked down the street, fading into the crowd under the pale New York sunlight. In the days that followed, Allen received a flood of letters from women reporting that their children had "cried uncontrollably as my tiny figure vanished in the distance and that they, too, were reduced to tears by the sight and by the realization that the program would be seen no more. Here was another surprising example of the power of television to arouse the emotions of an audience."

CBS kept trying to carve out opportunities for Allen. In 1953, it assigned him to host a ninety-minute Saturday night program, *Songs for Sale*, in which songwriter wannabes had their tunes performed by professional singers and evaluated by a panel of experts. The show ran for a year and a half under Allen, who parted company with CBS when the network wanted to move the show into weekday afternoons, in order to open up the Saturday evening slot for a then-unknown comedian who had been working on New York's DuMont station: Jackie Gleason.

Although Allen's radio experience factored into his successful transition into television, there were daunting adjustments to television that even the most skilled radio entertainers struggled to make. The atmosphere of the typical radio studio was "controlled, respectful, tomb-like silence," explained Allen, void of even the slightest distraction. "Supporting performers are sometimes even dismissed for crossing their legs or for distracting in other ways the attention of the studio audience at a crucial moment during a broadcast—and with considerable justification. If the audience is distracted, it does not laugh."

Allen found the mayhem of the early television studio to be the opposite extreme.

> I shall never forget my shock at the first few months in TV. I was horrified to learn that instead of being separated from the spectators by one thin microphone and a few feet of conditioned air, I was now required to reach them through a squirming jungle of cameras, lights, props, microphone dollies, scenery, stagehands, cameramen, audio-men, and lighting men, all creeping around in the darkness in full view of the audience; assorted production assistants who strode about with headphones, muttering audibly while receiving communications from the control booth; and a sprinkling of actors, musicians, announcers, and dancers.
>
> Trying to make an audience laugh under these circumstances is a little like working on the stage of a theater while between you and the footlights the Harlem Globe Trotters run through a few fast-moving plays. Television audiences in some studios are usually so intrigued at being behind the scenes that they can scarcely take their eyes off the technical equipment to look at the actors.
>
> Many times I have sat at home with friends watching one or another comedian reap three or four seconds of silence for what was obviously an excellent joke. The reason may easily have been that just as the comic was delivering the line, a stagehand walked in front of the studio audience with a ladder, or that a line of chorus girls moved into position off camera. Of course, the home viewers are not aware of these distractions; all they see is the clown with egg on his face.

Since the new medium was visual, holding a script in one's hand suddenly became a no-no. Cue-card reading became the norm, but since there were yet no experienced cue-card holders, many an on-camera performer had to endure awkward instances of cue cards being dropped or flashed in the wrong sequence. In addition, unlike in radio, early television studios were extremely uncomfortable, given the massive amount of light necessary to transmit an acceptable picture—which, in turn, called for anyone on camera to be pasted with heavy makeup.

Allen found that such unending chaos made it more difficult to be funny on television than in radio, where "the only thing that moves is the comedian's mouth." He told *Redbook*, "On second thought, when everything goes right on my show, I'm sunk. I depend for laughs on what pops into my head. And if everything moves smoothly, nothing may pop. But television being what it is, I think I have little cause to worry."

A whole school of early television hosts came out of radio and into TV in the early '50s, including Arthur Godfrey, Dave Garroway, Jack Paar, Garry Moore, and Johnny Carson. Although they were heralded as television pioneers, Allen said that neither he nor his contemporaries felt that way at the time. Rather, he believed that their entry into TV was more likely accomplished by stumbling rather than strategy:

> As a freshman at Drake University in 1941, I had quite casually taken a snap-course in radio production and immediately perceived that, while the newspaper business was likely to be a demanding profession, almost anyone not cursed with an annoying speaking voice could find work in radio. And several years' experience in that medium accidentally placed me in that enormous job-pool from which the first wave of television personalities were drawn. Thus, far from having to make any willed attempt to get into TV, I was pulled into it, along with hundreds of others, as if we all were in the grip of an enormous vortex. It was simply a matter of being in the right place at the right time.

THE FAILURE OF *BROADWAY OPEN HOUSE*

In 1950, the year CBS was signing Steve Allen to a television contract, Sylvester "Pat" Weaver, NBC's vice president in charge of programming (and later president), was exploring new programming avenues. In addition to the network's lineup of daytime soaps and prime-time comedies and variety shows, Weaver saw the potential for a network to fill the early-morning and late-night hours with original programming and commercial time sold by the network. He was developing a late-night show to be called *Broadway Open House.* It would be vaudeville in style, featuring comedy skits, music, and dance. Network execs were skeptical, wondering who would be staying up to watch. Given the absence of any real competition other than reruns of old movies, Weaver was convinced that an original late-night network show would be profitable.

The first choice for host was not Steve Allen but the "other" hot young Hollywood comic, Don "Creesh" Hornsby. Like Allen, Hornsby was in his late twenties, played piano and composed novelty songs, and got laughs the then-new way, by ad-libbing. Unlike Allen, Hornsby was bombastic, manic, and more physical in style, with high energy and lots of props—a cross between modern-day comedians Leo "Gallagher" Anthony and Scott "Carrot Top" Thompson. At one point in his nightclub act, Hornsby would swing from a trapeze bar while engaging in nonstop patter, or he would run around the stage yelling, "Creesh! Creesh!" He would point a high-beam railroad yard flashlight at startled audience members and engage them in comical banter. Other not-so-subtle gimmicks included walking through the audience with a rubber gila monster, wearing a cheerleader's megaphone dunce cap–style over his head, magically pulling brassieres out of women's blouses, and spraying sections of the audience with pressurized dry ice from a fire extinguisher.

With his high energy, ad-lib wit, and physical style, Hornsby convinced NBC that he was a natural for television. But in the tradition of the twisted movie plot, Hornsby was stricken with polio just days before the premiere of his new late-night show. He had just flown into New York to meet with the NBC brass. Two days later, on May 22, 1950, he was dead.

In show-must-go-on fashion, NBC replaced Hornsby with two veteran comics. One was Morey Amsterdam, who hosted the show on Mondays and Wednesdays. (He would ascend to greater heights as the wise-cracking Buddy Sorrell on *The Dick Van Dyke Show*.) The other was the frenetic vaudeville and nightclub comic Jerry Lester, who hosted on Tuesdays, Thursdays, and Fridays. Amsterdam left the show early in its run, and Lester took over the other two nights. As entertainment historian Stephen Cox reported in his 2002 book *Here's Johnny!* the breakout success of Jenny Lewis, who played a ditsy blonde bombshell known simply as "Dagmar," upset the balance of the show's large cast of regulars and the ego of Lester, who originally hired her. The resulting turmoil led to Lester's departure, an unsuccessful stint by replacement host Jack E. Leonard, and, after a fifteen-month run, the show's demise in August 1951. For Allen, the cancellation would pave the way for a huge opportunity.

SUBBING FOR GODFREY

In the early 1950s, Arthur Godfrey dominated the radio and television airwaves. As a widely popular and charismatic host, he was the Oprah Winfrey of his day, commanding a huge and fiercely loyal following. Folksy, witty, and laid back, Godfrey "had such a vital personal magnetism that it was difficult not to be pleased by almost anything he presented," recalled Allen. "Somehow when Arthur said, 'Well, the weather is certainly nice today,' one felt that the weather was unusually pleasant."

Godfrey hosted *Arthur Godfrey's Talent Scouts*, a top-rated TV forerunner to latter-day talent shows like *Star Search* and *American Idol*. *Talent Scouts* had a contest format in which new entertainers performed their acts on live TV, with the winner determined by an audience applause meter.

In January 1952, Godfrey found his plane locked in by bad weather in Miami, unable to return to New York for that evening's show. A panicky CBS programming exec phoned Allen that afternoon and wondered if he could fill in for Godfrey—tonight. Allen ran right over to the studio. The only thing was, he had rarely seen Godfrey's show and had never studied its mechanics, but he confidently assumed that he could learn them all within the next three hours.

"As it turned out," remembered Allen, "the very fact that I was unacquainted with the production details amused the audience. I got the message at once and proceeded to purposely goof up even more than my ignorance justified. I kept forgetting the contestants' names, and I misread the applause meter and announced that the wrong contestant had won the night's honors."

Godfrey often played his trademark ukelele and did commercials for Lipton in which he made a cup of tea or a bowl of chicken noodle soup on-camera. Allen, who was never known for his dexterity, spilled the tea, combined the tea and soup in a pot, and then poured the concoction into Godfrey's ukelele amid screams from the audience. A master of ad-lib, Allen almost prayed for things to go wrong because it stimulated his imagination and provided him with an instant springboard for humor. "When something on the show goes wrong," he once explained, "all you have to do is let the people in the viewing audience know about it. Immediately it becomes funny, and the laugh helps you over the situation."

As it turned out, Allen himself was scouted by *Variety*, the showbusiness bible:

> Chalk up the first five minutes of Monday's *Talent Scouts* display as one of the most hilarious one-man comedy sequences projected over the TV cameras in many a day. One could have wished that, for the occasion, the *Talent Scouts* format of bringing on semi-pro

performers could have been tossed out the window to permit Allen greater latitude as a stand-up comedian in his own right. . . . The guy's a natural for the big time.

WHAT'S MY LINE?

Also in 1952, Allen accepted game show guru Mark Goodson's invitation to join *What's My Line?* in which a celebrity panel of four interviewed contestants with unusual occupations. The panelists had to guess the occupation from the yes or no answers to which the contestant was limited. It was a sophisticated show, entirely ad-libbed, with erudite panelists such as publisher/author/humorist Bennett Cerf and comedian Fred Allen, along with Arlene Francis and Dorothy Kilgallen and host John Daly. One would think that Steve Allen would feel right at home in this genteel crowd. At first, however, Allen found himself nervous: "Ad-lib shows had always been child's play. But this was not my program; I was not in control. I had to concentrate on the technical business of the game and hope to pick off the funny lines on the fly."

Allen had no reason to be nervous. Jayne Meadows, the red-haired, charming, and glamorous actress who would marry him in 1954 (and who herself starred on another popular celebrity panel show, *I've Got a Secret*), recalled how *What's My Line?* viewers discovered "this young man who was so funny, the youngest person on a panel of much older celebrities." During his yearlong stint, Allen charmed audiences with his ad-lib ability, even coining the catchphrase that still survives today: "Is it bigger than a breadbox?"

In asking that question, Allen wasn't even trying to be funny. He was genuinely trying to determine the size of an object manufactured by a guest. But the audience laughed uproariously. Allen speculated that the breadbox was "such an old-fashioned item, and so the word had the sort of connotation that surrounds phrases like high-button shoes, celluloid collar, or raccoon coat." Soon, the other panelists made the line a running joke. One kitchenware manufacturer even wanted to put a Steve Allen breadbox on the market.

Not only did Allen's initial nervousness vanish, but he reveled in the format that was new to him: "If you can manage to feel at home on a TV panel, it's like stealing money. There's no rehearsal, no memorizing, no emoting, and no physical effort of any kind. You just show up an hour or so before airtime, sit around a dressing room making small talk with charming people, go on the air, play a parlor game, and if you get two big laughs for the evening, people will tell you all week long how funny you were."

Because he was so likable, Allen was able to get away with the kind of casual, offbeat humor that "consisted of merely telling the truth when you expect a polite evasion," as one newspaper writer described. Upon interrogation by the *What's My Line?* panel, a woman revealed that her occupation had something to do with chimpanzees. Dorothy Kilgallen asked if she made the animals' clothes, but she answered no. Although the other panelists didn't dare bring up the woman's eccentric choice of attire, Allen precociously seized upon the opportunity. "Without thinking, I asked if the chimpanzees made clothes for her. It got a big laugh—but it was inexcusable. If I hadn't worked so hard at learning to talk before I know what I'm saying, I never would have said that."

WNBT'S *THE STEVE ALLEN SHOW*

In the early 1950s, NBC was in the process of assembling a local television station in New York City, WNBT (later known as WNBC). Ted Cott, a successful New York radio exec at WNEW, was hired as general manager to create and head the new station, which would cover the New York–New Jersey–Connecticut area. Richard Pack was hired as director of programming and operations. In an *Emmy Online* article written by Pack, in 1953, WNBT was "being clobbered most nights from 11:20 p.m. on because WCBS-TV, the CBS flagship Channel 2, was spending a great deal on movies to supply their new *Late Show* strip." A major local brewer, Knickerbocker Beer, wanted to sponsor a late-night slot to compete against WCBS's movies and a variety program out of ABC's New York station.

Pack decided to drop the mediocre British movies then being aired, "which were so bad they had never played in American movie houses." He recommended that WNBT counter with a variety show. Although Cott agreed, he needed a star and a show. Pack suggested comedian Jack Carter, but Cott approached Steve Allen, who after three years had not seemed to take off at CBS. Not only was Cott a fan, but he knew that, as an ad-lib comedian, Allen didn't need any writers, thus making him financially attractive to a fledgling station with a small staff and budget. Allen would be the star, explained Cott, and whatever he wanted to do would be the show—as long as it had that freewheeling quality that marked his radio show in California. Allen said yes.

Premiering in the fall of 1953, Allen's new program showcased his loose, ad-lib style with its minimal script and guest and audience interviews. Five nights a week, from 11:15 to midnight, there was music from popular trombonist Bobby Byrne's orchestra, Allen on piano, and a seventeen-year-old singer named Steve Lawrence. It was essentially, described Allen, the television version of his old Hollywood radio show: "Only instead of a table, I now sat at a desk. All I actually required on a typical night was a piano, a couple of amusing letters from viewers, a newspaper article that had caught my fancy, an unusual toy that a member of my staff had picked up, a guest or two to chat with, and an audience to interview."

The show was originally titled *The Knickerbocker Beer Show*, which was representative of an era in early television in which sponsors frequently forced their names into show titles; WNBT had managed to sell a full sponsorship to the brewer. What's more, the program would open with the sponsor's advertising pitchman—a costumed medieval friar named Father Knickerbocker—waddling on stage, ringing a town crier's bell, and shouting with gusto, "Hello, Steve!" Allen would obligingly shout back, "Hello, Father Knickerbocker!" Thirteen weeks later, the program would be renamed *The Steve Allen Show*.

If Allen prayed for mishaps, the premiere of his new show delivered more than he bargained for. At the time, Jayne Meadows was dating Allen. (He and Dorothy Goodman had divorced in 1951.) She and her actress sister, Audrey (who would later star as Alice Kramden in *The Honeymooners*), gathered about a dozen friends to go to the studio and surprise Allen in the audience. They arrived at the stage door to wait with the rest of the audience, only to discover that they *were* the audience. "This was early TV," explained Jayne. "It just shows you how little the executives knew in those days. It never occurred to them that, for a man who was famous for working with an audience, they gave him a theater with no audience. Steve met us at the door, and when he saw how many of us there were, he said, 'Thank God, you're here! I have no audience. Will you guys be the audience?'"

This was twenty minutes before air. By that time, Cott realized that someone had forgotten to get Allen an audience, and so a hurry call went out. Allen was a half hour into the show, recalled Jayne, "when they got a busload of thirty, forty old ladies. What they didn't figure on was that Steve *preferred* old ladies. He said, 'They've gotten beyond the self-conscious age of wanting to see themselves on the monitor and how they look. They'll tell you anything.' And some of his biggest laughs came that way."

To compound matters, the show originated from a studio on 67th Street—which, explained Pack, "in the earliest years of TV had been built on the fallacy that directors would want to hide the studio audience from the cameras. The audience had to be seated high up in a balcony, with so many lights in front of them that they could never see the action, except on small, badly-placed monitors." Allen wanted to interview those lovely elderly ladies, but how would he get up there? He could go the conventional way and slip out of the studio, climb a back stairwell, and reappear in the audience. Instead, remembered Jayne, he scaled a rickety ladder perched against the wall, making a joke out of that studio, and got laughs right away: "Nothing made him happier than to climb an old ladder to reach this local New York audience on television."

Johnny Sterns was the show's first producer, but he was unable to adapt to Allen's nontraditional, spontaneous style of comedy and was almost immediately replaced by Bill Harbach, a WNBT director and son of Broadway librettist Otto Harbach (*No, No, Nanette!* and *Roberta*). WNBT management told Harbach that the station's new flagship show needed help, and that only he—with his quick, adaptable, and ebullient personality—could work with Allen better. As Harbach explained, management pleaded with him to terminate his first vacation in two years in order to return to New York and accept the position: "My ego was helped a little because you think you're saving some kind of a ship. So I flew back and had lunch with Jules Green [Allen's manager] and Steve Allen at the Drake Hotel because they wanted to see how our chemistries would be. Steve and I found out that we were both crazy about one very special thing: jazz. I loved jazz and had great friends in it, and Steve is a big aficionado. So we hit it off right away."

According to Harbach, Allen required his producer to be right off camera—next to him at the desk or wherever he would be—because Allen had to "relate" to him. This allowed Allen to remain spontaneous throughout the show. Harbach watched the show for about a week to figure out what "relating" to Allen meant, discovering that "with Steve's way of doing things, you had to be alongside the camera. You couldn't be in the control booth and say, 'Tell Steve to do this,' as the communication would be too slow. He didn't want to have to call the booth and say, 'Tell them I want to go into the audience next,' or 'How are we doing?' He wanted the control of somebody just off camera. You had to be right alongside the camera to look at his eye and run the show to make it work."

Harbach made it work: "I would be behind the camera saying, 'I feel something's not going,' and I'd go like this [*in a shouting whisper, motioning*]: 'Go into the audience!'" Taking Harbach's cue, Allen would get rid of the guest or whatever he was doing, casually remark, "I think it's time we go into the audience," and get up from his chair. In the meantime, Harbach has told director Dwight Hemion, "He's going to go into the audience."

"And when he went into the audience," said Harbach, "he was always pure gold. It was like a great safety net. If anything was dying on the show, *send him into the audience* because he would find something crazy going on, and it would be a riot."

For Harbach, standing right off camera, instead of sitting in the control booth like other producers, made him feel more "like I was part of the show, like I'm out there on the stage, people watching me, and Steve's watching me, and I'm relating to him. It was exhausting, for you're on your feet for the whole show. You're running up to the booth saying, 'Dwight, I think we ought to do this,' and running back out again."

Hemion felt that Harbach was the best cheerleader for the show and Allen: "Billy brought a new kind of enthusiasm. He reacted better than anybody to anything funny that would happen. All you could hear in the audience was Billy laughing all the time. Johnny [Sterns] wasn't that way."

"The loudest guffaw is Bill's," wrote Allen about Harbach in 1960, describing him as "a cheerful enthusiast with a warm and wacky manner of handling people and getting their finest work out of them."

Nearly four decades later, Harbach remained just as warm and cheerful, allowing his interview to be conducted in an examination room at Memorial Sloan-Kettering Hospital in Manhattan, where he had just undergone a regularly scheduled radiation treatment.

Allen's show started with a writing staff of one: himself. No one else was needed at the time, he said, as he only occasionally would write a simple sketch for a guest and himself. That meant that he was entirely responsible for crafting his opening monologue, five nights a week. Explained Harbach, "There was no script, just a routine—a page and a half: (1) Steve opening—he'll do, maybe, three minutes at the piano; (2) read notes from the audience; (3) Steve Lawrence sings song; (4) Steve introduces a comedian; (5) Steve goes into the audience; (6) commercial." New Yorkers would stay up past their bedtimes to see Allen eat and drink, sing, play the piano, conduct weird interviews, present modern jazz, get haircuts, get fitted for suits, and take a swimming lesson.

"We just get an order going and even then, some nights Eydie Gorme or Steve Lawrence doesn't get a chance to sing, or something else gets lost," said Allen in 1954. "We even forget commercials once in a while."

The format was a departure from low-risk, tightly scripted variety shows and dramas of the day. To Doc Severinsen, a young trumpet player in Bobby Byrne's band who had been a staff musician on various NBC shows, Allen's new show "was totally different. This thing here was kind of wingin' it—just do it as you go along," said Severinsen in 2005. "[Steve would] have his normal kind of an opening. Sometimes he'd just open sitting at the piano, playing a tune. And then he'd get up and talk to the audience a little bit about something or other, and then he'd have a guest on. We had a lot of unusual people. And then if we ran out of something to do, they'd open up the back door out onto 45th Street, and Steve would talk to whoever was out there."

Steve Lawrence concurred: "Steve Allen was doing things that heretofore had never been done: walking out into the street, interviewing people, going into an audience with a microphone. He was just wild and off the wall for a guy who looked and sounded as he did: very erudite and bright and witty and very self-educated. He knew a lot about the business because he was brought up in it."

According to programming director Richard Pack, the show clicked, and in its first month it was beating the late movies on WCBS. As its success grew, the budget was increased to add its first and sole staff writer, Stan Burns (who would later write for Carol Burnett, Dean Martin, and the Smothers Brothers).

The media loved the show, too. *Newsweek* mused, "The critics took one long look and fell all over themselves, raving." John Crosby wrote in the *New York Herald-Tribune*, "Allen's 40-minute show on WNBT is the brightest thing to come along in a long time. It deserves a wider audience." Observed Jack Gould: "Mr. Allen has always possessed one of the more nimble wits on the air, and WNBT has wisely given him free reign to amble though music and nonsense." *Variety* declared Allen's show as "successfully invading the domain of the division of the tired old feature pictures."

GOING NETWORK

Despite the failure of *Broadway Open House*, Pat Weaver remained convinced that network programming opportunities existed in early morning and late night. In 1952, he launched a morning show called *Today*, which became—and remains—the network's flagship morning program.

A successful advertising man, Weaver liked to think in slogans. With the success of *Today* in 1952, he wanted to try a late-night entry that could bookend the network's daily programming and to call it *Tonight*. According to Richard Pack, the success of *Today* initially led Weaver to aim for a journalistically news-oriented magazine format, more like a nighttime version of *Today*. But he was never able to assemble the ingredients to build *Tonight* the way he had originally intended.

Pack believed that the success of the local *Steve Allen Show* warranted converting it into *Tonight*. Weaver saw that for himself and, as Bill Harbach recalled, Weaver eventually decided that "that crazy little local show that everybody's flipping over in New York City would be a great show to close the network with every night. The day's over, it's insane, it's crazy, it's fun, it's loose—*loose* is the operative word." Allen had caught Weaver's eye, having proven himself as a panelist on *What's My Line?* as an emergency fill-in for Godfrey, and now as the host of a hit late-night show on NBC's biggest station—emanating from the city where Weaver lived and where NBC's network offices were located.

Bill Allen, Steve's son (by Jayne Meadows) and a former president of MTM Television, pointed out that the kind of show his father was doing was "low budget, not an expensive show to do, so Weaver could try this out in late night and see how it worked. So he told my father, 'I want to put you on the full network, but I want to change the name to *Tonight*.' Dad said, 'Fine!'" (And when *Tonight* finally aired, *Newsweek* would report that it cost only $50,000 a week to produce).

By then, NBC also had a noontime magazine show called *Home*, hosted by Arlene Francis. Now the network would have three signature shows. In July 1954, NBC broadcast a *"Tonight" Preview* sales presentation over a closed circuit to all the NBC affiliate stations, targeting their sales departments, prospective sponsors, and the press. The sales reel featured Dave Garroway, the respected, folksy journalist/host of *Today* (a kind of Charlie Gibson of his generation), singing a lighthearted duet of "Them There Eyes" with Allen at the piano—actually, a parody on the big horn-rimmed eyeglasses that each of them wore. It was a charming bit. Neither was seriously auditioning his singing talents for the NBC affiliates, but the natural rapport between the two, along with their television appeal, was obvious. Arlene Francis also made an appearance to endorse her fellow *What's My Line?* panelist, singling out his "wit and graciousness" as a "rare combination in a comedian, and I know that it will make his *Tonight* program a big success."

Fronting the reel was Weaver, who predicted that *Tonight* would "open up new avenues of sales efforts to an enlarged viewing and buying audience." He went on to explain that it was the goal of such signature shows "[t]o make television more useful to more advertisers, to broaden the base of the medium as old-time radio was never broadened, to attract a wider range of products, and to admit smaller-budget advertisers to big-time television. In this way, we get more money to do shows that we couldn't actually afford to do otherwise. Some of the smaller advertisers are developed by television and its sales power into big advertisers, as we've demonstrated again and again through sales records on *Today*. . . . These new advertisers develop into buyers of more network time and more spot time."

Weaver proudly announced the *Tonight* show's first signed advertiser, the innovative and fast-growing Polaroid Corporation. But beyond Weaver's attractive and slickly pitched sales points, what really sold the affiliates was the stunning sample of Steve Allen's casual and witty exchanges with members of the studio audience of three hundred assembled especially for the program. Allen explained that the program on the reel was "closed-circuit, not at all like my regular program. In other words, the public is not watching this show." Allen paused to reflect on what he had just said. "Come to think of it, it *is* like my regular program!"

Even though *Home* didn't last, legendary writer Herb Sargent (who would soon write for Allen and later for *Saturday Night Live*) was amused by NBC's ad campaign: "*Today, Home,* and *Tonight*: Your NBC Experience for the Day"—or, as Sargent in a 1999 interview irreverently translated, "Get up with us. Have brunch with us. Go to bed with us."

THE CREATION MYTH

For a long time, the popular myth has identified the creator of the *Tonight* show as Pat Weaver. Because most television shows have been created by a writer/producer rather than a star, even many within the industry erroneously saw Weaver as a programming head who actually created the elements of the late-night variety show, named it the *Tonight* show, and cast Steve Allen as its first host.

But that's not what happened. Although Weaver, acknowledged Allen, was a genius at programming, the show "had already been created—with no input from NBC programming people—over a year before Pat and his assistant, Mort Werner, had the wisdom to add it to the network's late-night schedule. The only change was that it was no longer called *The Steve Allen Show*."

In the publicity campaign during the months leading up to the *Tonight* premiere, the Washington, DC, *Post and Times Herald* reported that the new show would be "simply a network extension of *The Steve Allen Show* which has been seen in New York for some time."

Yet that's not exactly what NBC's marketing people implied about *Tonight* when they included it in full-page advertisements for its three signature shows: "Nothing like these programs existed until NBC-TV created them [and] brought together their stars. . . ." However well intentioned, the ad contributed to a process that increasingly obscured Allen's role as *Tonight* creator so that by the time Weaver died in 2002, newspapers across the country headlined his obituary, "Pat Weaver: Creator of *Tonight Show*." In 2005, the Internet Movie Database was still crediting Weaver as the show's sole creator.

"Pat Weaver had put it on his NBC network, but Steve Allen defined the *Tonight* show," wrote television industry journalist Bill Carter in his 1994 book, *The Late Shift*. "It was a nightly mix of comedy, music, and show business chatter. Allen's *Tonight* show had many conventional elements—the familiar celebrity faces, familiar singers singing standard songs. But what started keeping people awake past midnight was the star's high-energy wit and his appreciation for how the emerging medium could lend itself to spontaneous, original humor."

So why did the Weaver myth survive? Bill Allen theorized:

> NBC, in my opinion, allowed that to be the story, because it made their president look even more creative than he was, although he was one of the most brilliant programming executives ever. He conceived of the *value* of a late-night variety show, the title *Tonight*, and it being a signature NBC show that would be the sign-off for the network at night. All of that was brilliant, theretofore unconceived. But he did not create the show. The show was created over several years in radio by Steve Allen and refined over a one-year period in late-night New York television. The show that aired locally as *The Steve Allen Show* in New York on Monday, September 20, 1954, and the one that premiered nationally on the full NBC network as the first *Tonight* show the following Monday, September 27, were almost indistinguishable from each other.

Bill Allen also believed that some execs at NBC were simply nervous about who really owned the format of the *Tonight* show, which originally had been a production of NBC and Steve's company, Bristad Enterprises: "There was a question in those days—when Steve left the *Tonight* show in 1957 to focus on his prime-time comedy series for NBC—as to whether he continued to own some underlying rights as the creator of the *Tonight* format. It's my understanding that Steve never asserted any ownership of those rights, because it was not in his nature to do so. Early on, some at NBC were concerned that Steve might someday try to claim ownership over the Jack Paar or Johnny Carson versions. And so it was in their interest to publicly credit their own executive with the creation of the *Tonight* show."

In so crediting Weaver, not only did Allen's status as *Tonight* creator diminish over the years, but so did his connection to *Tonight* and late-night TV altogether among the general public, as evidenced by this letter published in the *Boston Sunday Herald* TV Q&A column in 1997: "I have a bet with my son, but I can't seem to find an answer. Who have been the emcees of *The Tonight Show?* I know Jack Paar was the first, and I say that Steve Allen was between Paar and Johnny Carson. My son says Steve Allen had nothing to do with the show. Please help!"

In later years, more secure heads of NBC fully credited Allen with the creation of not only the *Tonight* show, but of the late-night comedy/variety/talk format. Rick Ludwin, NBC's current vice president of late night and prime-time series, acknowledged in a 2003 interview: "*Broadway Open House* was a presentational, Milton Berle–style revue. Steve did a different show. He made it more like a cocktail party, where people could come out and they were a little loose, maybe had a little something to drink, and it was conversation and comedy, as opposed to just sketches and proscenium, presentational comedy like a vaudeville show. Now [it] is so commonplace, so much part of the fabric. People should know that it was Steve Allen who brought that to television. He is the guy who invented that form and invented how it was staged. That sort of show did not exist before Steve started the *Tonight* show. He invented the grammar of late-night shows: the desk, the chair, the performance area, the band."

Ludwin noted that this grammar is still observed on the present-day *Tonight Show* and the shows of David Letterman, Jimmy Kimmel, Conan O'Brien, and "on and on and on and on. Don't ask me why it works. It just works! And whenever you try something different, maybe it'll work, maybe it won't. Dick Cavett's late-night show in the late '60s was a semicircle arrangement of chairs without a desk but with a coffee table in the middle. So there are other forms that can work."

Ludwin even pointed to the old-fashioned, pill-shaped microphone on Allen's desk that became a fixture on the desks of Carson, Leno, Letterman, Conan O'Brien, Larry King, and other hosts. On the current *Tonight Show*, that microphone is used only in emergencies, said Ludwin, "because Jay uses an RF mike on his tie. But a few years ago, someone wanted to take the mike off the desk. I said, 'Absolutely not! It's part of the grammar of the show. It's part of what viewers expect to see.'"

"The *Tonight Show* today looks about exactly the way it did in 1954 when Steve first put it on television. We modernize the set and constantly have to reinvent it and give fans new reasons to come back, but certain things won't change."

Carl Reiner, the legendary comedy writer and performer and longtime friend of Allen, agreed: "When you think about the things he started on his *Tonight* show, they still exist. They exist in Letterman. They exist in Leno. Going out and talking to people. The crazy things—dropping things that Letterman does off a building, getting into a tank."

Even the convention of the announcer/sidekick is traceable to Allen, as Ed McMahon acknowledged on *Larry King Live* on the night after Allen died in 2000: "He invented that whole concept for television. And there were followers. Steve Allen had [Gene Rayburn]. Then Jack Paar had Hugh Downs, and Johnny had me."

In another interview for CNN, McMahon also acknowledged, "I was one of those guys who really watched every night of the Steve Allen *Tonight* show. It was the end of my day, and I loved it. I never dreamed that I'd ever be involved in the show. So I had a primer on how to do it from watching him do the sketches and how he developed the family. When Johnny took over, he had that same direction of having a family. We'd do sketches with Doc and Tommy Newsome and use Fred DeCordova in things, and it was a further extension of that. Allen invented all of this. He's the one that started all of this."

Yet, after taking pains to set the record straight, Steve Allen was not entirely comfortable with all the credit that was heaped on him for "inventing" the talk program, which he compared to inventing "—oh, the paper towel. The result is useful, a source of enormous profits, and the world is somewhat better off for it." Even during the height of his success on *Tonight*, Allen shrugged it off, telling the *New York Times Magazine*: "I seem to have stumbled in at the right time in history, where a man who owns a combination of fairly mediocre abilities and wears a clean shirt can do well in a particular medium. A hundred years ago, I'd probably have been an unsuccessful writer."

Indeed, for as much as Allen loved to make audiences laugh, he was ill at ease with adulation. Whereas superstar peers like Bob Hope and Milton Berle would bask in standing ovations at Carnegie Hall, Allen found lengthy standing ovations embarrassing and would quickly wave his admirers to be seated. "And not just at Carnegie Hall, but anywhere he performed during the last twenty years of his career," noted son Bill. Allen himself admitted, "I have a horror of conceit," reluctantly accepting lavish introductions that touted his many accomplishments "as if someone were saying they liked my shoes or my car."

Allen's modesty belies the fact that he created one of the few truly enduring genres in the history of television. In the 1950s and '60s, variety shows hosted by the likes of Jackie Gleason, Sid Caesar, and Ed Sullivan dominated the landscape. So did live dramatic anthology series like *Playhouse 90*, *G.E. Theater*, and *The U.S. Steel Hour*, as well as westerns like *Gunsmoke*, *Bonanza*, and *Maverick*. Also during that era, panel shows like *I've Got a Secret*, *To Tell the Truth*, and *What's My Line?* frequently placed in the top twenty. The 1970s were the decade of blockbuster miniseries such as *Roots*, *Shogun*, and *Winds of War*.

Today, those genres are nowhere to be found in network television. Sitcoms, a popular staple for many decades, nearly disappeared in the early 1980s before being revived by the success of *The Cosby Show*. But the late-night form created by Allen has proven to be the most durable: the only genre to flourish consistently over the past fifty years and the only one that is more popular today than ever before.

Chapter 2

LAUNCHING *TONIGHT*
The Start of Something Big

$\mathcal{T}$he move from the local *Steve Allen Show* to the network *Tonight* show meant an increase not only in exposure but also in the overall scale of the show. Producer Bill Harbach welcomed the move from the small confines of the WNBT studios on 67th Street to the Hudson Theatre just off Times Square on West 44th Street, a large, proscenium arch theater well suited for comedy. Gene Rayburn continued as announcer and Allen's sidekick. Two additional singers—Andy Williams and Pat Marshall—were hired to augment the existing team of Steve Lawrence and Eydie Gorme. The two teams generally rotated so that each appeared twice one week and three times the next. But a network cost-controlling move resulted in the replacement of Bobby Byrne and his band with NBC network music director Skitch Henderson and a group of NBC house musicians.

Tonight! debuted on September 27, 1954 (the ! would later be deleted). NBC in-house documents described the spontaneity and variety of the new show, which had Steve Allen written all over it:

Tonight!: a completely informal and ad-libbed variety program starring comedian Steve Allen. No set format is used on the show—instead, the entertainment revolves around Allen and what he decides to do next. Planning of each night's show is held to a minimum so as to provide for a maximum of elasticity, so that the program can take advantage of any situation that might come up, whether right there in the studio, outside on the street, or in some other city in the U.S. Allen usually opens the program by playing a selection on the piano—then he rambles over to his desk and reads a few notes and comments on whatever strikes his fancy. One or more guests are featured on each program—usual form is a different 10-minute guest spot in each of the three half-hours, but this varies a great deal—from one guest appearing in two spots, with another appearing in the third spot, to one guest monopolizing the whole show, either intentionally or unintentionally.

Allen frequently goes down into the audience and interviews people at random—mostly just folks visiting the city, but occasionally name personalities who have been asked to sit in the studio audience. Guests on the show vary in type from a street vendor to a top concert artist, with material being presented ranging from a comic monologue to a serious discussion on a topic of current interest. A very brief summary of the news, sports and weather is usually given each night around 12:30 a.m. Allen frequently comments on books he has read and plays he has seen, and mobile unit pick-ups from the source of a special event are a regular feature.

THE FIRST SHOW

The premiere show opened with the camera panning live across Times Square. Allen, casually seated at his piano, ominously warned his new national audience: "In case you're just joining us, I want to give you the bad news first: This program is going to go on—*forever*. It's a *long* show. Goes on from 11:30 until one in the morning. We especially selected the Hudson Theatre for this show because it sleeps about eight hundred people."

Mild-mannered comedian Wally Cox (*Mister Peepers* and later *Hollywood Squares*) did a monologue. (He actually stepped in at the last minute when the advertised inaugural guest, Martha Raye, suddenly had to bow out.) Singer Bill Kenny of the Ink Spots sang "If I Didn't Care." Outside, the energetic, smiling Steve Lawrence and Eydie Gorme—exuding a confidence honed from the past year performing together on the local show—strolled down a Manhattan sidewalk, bathed in a spotlight, singing the swinging "Say Hey Willie Mays," while the band, using an elaborate audio hook-up, accompanied them from back in the studio. They arrived at the apartment of the New York Giants center fielder and National League batting champ. Steve and Eydie serenaded the pajama-clad superstar and climbed a ladder to greet him, as he leaned out his second-story window. This was followed by a split-screen conversation between Mays and Allen (back in the studio), each of them holding telephone receivers, about the upcoming World Series between the Giants and the Cleveland Indians.

In the studio, a freshly scrubbed Andy Williams made his network singing debut, somewhat stiff and ill at ease, but executing a powerful rendition of "In the Still of the Night." Allen likened him to "a teenage Noel Coward."

The show cut frequently for local stations to air one-minute commercial breaks but would continue airing in New York. This was a novel practice at the time, and so whenever the network broadcast resumed, Allen would tease his returning national audience by making up great things they supposedly missed during the past minute, such as the entire Notre Dame football team appearing or Clark Gable dropping by to dance with Lana Turner.

The show contained two three-minute newsbreaks delivered by announcer and sidekick Gene Rayburn—who, Allen announced in official tones, was "downstairs, from the NBC Newsroom," but who looked more like he was crammed into a converted backstage closet. The day's big news: a US Senate committee voted to rebuke Wisconsin Senator Joseph McCarthy. Behind Rayburn were illustrative photos primitively mounted on plywood boards that he had to slide into position. He also gave the national weather report, using chalk and a sliding blackboard map.

Later, the show cut to Cleveland, Ohio, where several hundred raucous Indians fans—mostly young guys dressed in the typical traveling attire of the era, business suits—were about to depart to New York aboard a fleet of Greyhound Scenicruisers, complete with a send-off by a Dixieland street band.

There were two spots that Allen filled by playing jazz piano backed by Skitch Henderson's band. After the opening monologue, he did a lively boogie-woogie. At the beginning of the last half hour, he performed an elegant rhumba version of the standard "Imagination."

Allen also spent ten minutes wandering through the audience, which was dressed in the typical television audience attire of the era: dresses for the ladies, business suits for the men. Allen's personal charm was unique—freewheeling and smart-alecky enough to be funny, yet amiable and nonthreatening, so as to make even grandmas giggle and want to pinch his cheek. He asked one of the first people he approached, Mrs. Laffak of Coney Island, if she wanted to wave to the camera at any of her friends watching at home, but noting the late hour of the new show, she giggled and blurted into his hand mike, "Oh, no, they're all asleep." Allen groaned, "Thanks a lot! There goes our four-million-dollar ad campaign out the window!"

Early reviews of the show were skeptical. "Allen's wit might be too New Yorkish," cautioned *Newsweek*. Even comic actor Louis Nye, who had frequently guested on the local *Steve Allen Show*, warned Jayne Meadows as they sat in the audience on the final night of the local show—the Friday before *Tonight* would premiere: "I think they're making a fatal mistake putting us on the network all across the country. Because there's a comedy dell'arte quality to this show, the rest of America is never going to get it. The South, the Midwest, they're never going to understand our humor. We're so New York."

Meadows, ever the optimist, disagreed: "Louis, it's going to be the biggest success ever, and the show will run forever. Because Monday's my birthday—September 27—and that's a good luck omen. You wait and see, you're going to be bigger than ever!"

But the question—Will viewers stay up late to watch TV?—was a new one and real one at that time. Steve Lawrence could still hear the buzz: "Are you crazy? Nobody's gonna be up at that hour of the night watching television." Lawrence said that he and his colleagues were resigned to one logical late-night demographic: "Winos and insomniacs."

These jitters would be proven unfounded, for the show quickly became a critical success, thanks in large part to Allen. "Allen is remarkable for his . . . ability to sidestep the usual stuffy and stilted language of radio and television," wrote the Cleveland *Plain Dealer*.

"A fresher and wittier type of comedy . . . equally appealing to a philosopher or to a Dodger fan" was the assessment of the *New York Daily News*.

"He can do virtually anything that can be done on television and do it surprisingly well . . . appeals to all IQ levels," said the *San Antonio Express* of Allen.

Variety labeled Allen "the best ad-glibber of the medium."

Allen's late-night party revolutionized the habits of entire communities across America. The *Star-Herald* of Kosciusko, Mississippi, wrote: "Night life in Kosy was virtually non-existent less than a year ago. . . . Sidewalks may as well have been rolled in at 6 p.m. But how the picture has changed since a guy named Steve Allen inaugurated a TV program called *Tonight*. . . . Practically all

Kosyans are now sitting up until after midnight. Thus, the traditional custom of going to bed early in this typical Southern community has been forgotten—and because of a fascinating damnyankee at that!"

Even the initially cautious *Newsweek* came around, putting Allen on its November 29, 1954, cover, crowning him "Television's Mr. Midnight" and thoughtfully analyzing his multiple talents: "[T]hough proficient as comedian, musician, actor, and interlocutor, [he] is only great as a combination of them all. He is, furthermore, a man whose humor is quiet in a medium where the most trusted comedy values are the prat fall, the trap door, the elaborate disguise, or [other] slapstick."

In six months, "*Tonight* had replaced old Charlie Chan movies as the midnight TV show of choice," wrote critic Gerald Nachman in his 2003 book, *Seriously Funny*.

The elastic nature of *Tonight*, ballyhooed by NBC, was clearly the essence of Allen's local late-night show. "They keep asking me if *Tonight* is really as off the cuff as it seems—or do we all go somewhere and rehearse it?" Allen wrote at the time. "*Tonight* is even more off-the-cuff than it appears to be. We don't have a script, we have a schedule. We don't even pay strict attention to the schedule. Maybe I've allotted 15 minutes for this, and 15 minutes for that, but if I'm out interviewing in the audience and it turns out to be funny, we drop something else—a song or a piano solo by me—in order to make room. It often does turn out to be funny."

An exchange between Allen and Hungarian bombshell Zsa Zsa Gabor in December 1954 turned into an unpredictable ad-lib fest that was enhanced by her trademark accent:

ALLEN: Zsa Zsa, what is the first thing you notice about a man?
GABOR: I frankly notice his necktie. And you have a very loud necktie on.
ALLEN: Well, I have a very loud neck.

GABOR : It's not so bad. But I sink vhen a man has on sort of a qviet necktie, then he's sort of a nice, qviet guy. But, of coss, I alvez make mistakes—neckties can really fool you.

ALLEN: Yes, especially in the hands of a strangler.

* * * * * * * * *

ALLEN: Do you do your own decorating?

GABOR: I lahv to decorate. I decorate my apartments, my houses, and za men vith whom I go. I tell zem to vehr dark suits, gray suits, navy suits.

ALLEN: They must get pretty warm with all those suits on.

* * * * * * * * *

ALLEN: You have two sisters, Zsa Zsa. Have you ever wished you had brothers?

GABOR: No, I don't sink I vould like to have a brother, because he vould give me hell all za time, and I get enough hell as it is. [*The audience roars with laughter and surprise that Gabor has said "hell" on television, a no-no in those days.*]

ALLEN [*waiting for the laughter to subside*]: Actually, folks, in different parts of the world, different words have different meanings. For example, to a Hungarian, "hell" is probably the word for "Vienna."

GABOR: Oh, you're not allowed to say "hell" on television?

ALLEN [*as the audience roars again*]: If any children are watching, why the heck aren't you in bed? . . . Now I know what men see in you, Zsa Zsa. It's your gay, devil-may-care—uh-oh, there we go with the devil again!

Tonight quickly became the show where stars with big names wanted to appear, as well as rising stars who wanted their names to become bigger. The show's rapid success prompted Allen's manager,

Jules Green, to establish the practice of paying all guests, without regard to stature, the union scale ($265.50 per appearance at the time). And so was born what author Bill Carter dubbed "the highly efficient economics of late-night talk. The star could command a massive salary—Allen got up to about $3,500 a week during his tenure—but the other costs were modest and mostly fixed. The total original budget was $11,000 a week. With the amount of commercial time in a ninety-minute, five-night-a-week show so abundant, *Tonight* instantly set itself up as the champion cash cow in the network pasture."

MORE THAN A TALK SHOW

Allen was quick to emphasize, especially in later years, that the original *Tonight* show was not just a talk show, which it was only on certain nights. Rather, he explained, the show was "very experimental, a canvas on which we could paint anything we wanted," including comedy, dramas, musical tributes, wild stunts, political debates, and special remote segments from around the country. Celebrity guests could not just come onstage, talk, and then leave, or they wouldn't be booked, said writer Stan Burns. "They also had to do a sketch, a song, a 'Crazy Shot,' or something extra," added Bill Harbach. "We'd always work our guests." That's how President Harry Truman's daughter Margaret wound up playing a schoolteacher in a sketch on TV violence and how Charles Laughton got to do "Letters to the Editor."

For the most part, *Tonight* was characterized by what Allen described as its "fraternity house atmosphere" that was well received by audiences and critics alike. "We wanted to keep it as zany as possible," said Harbach. While a choral group sang, "Wait Till the Cows Come Home," Harbach pushed eight live cows from behind the scenery onto the stage. "One cow went up to a Zoomar lens and started licking it. They tore up the set. Brought the house down."

An October 1954 broadcast featured a parlor game in which the show's cast and guests had to pass a grapefruit from one person to the next, without using their hands. Players had to maneuver the grapefruit with their chins and the rest of their bodies to keep it from falling to the floor. Having a particularly enjoyable time throughout all this was nineteen-year-old Steve Lawrence, who was struggling with the alluring siren of the era, actress Kim Novak. For Lawrence, the challenge was to "pry" that grapefruit from where it had become so steadfastly perched—atop the plunging neckline of Novak's dress—using his chin. Lawrence's head seemed buried there for longer than the situation called for, but that apparently didn't matter to the howling audience.

All this variety took a lot of work, Harbach said. "It was fun, but you were exhausted. I mean, five days a week! Every show had to try to hit twelve. Some shows you hit a ten or eleven or nine." In any case, the show did not have a problem finding a studio audience, as long lines of people would queue up outside the Hudson Theatre for as long as two or three hours before air, reminiscent of the lines stretching around the block for Allen's West Coast radio show only a few years earlier.

"[Allen] kind of set the tone of what the *Tonight* show should be," said Ed McMahon in a 2000 NBC interview. "They call it a 'talk show,' but the way Steve Allen did it and the way Johnny Carson did it, it was far from a talk show."

Tonight ran for ninety minutes, but Allen and his company also had to fill an additional fifteen minutes in front of the cameras. Although the new network show effectively replaced the forty-minute local *Steve Allen Show*, the local show was not eliminated completely. At 11:15 p.m., a local *Steve Allen Show*, sponsored by Knickerbocker Beer, continued to air in the New York–New

Jersey–Connecticut area as a prelude to the national broadcast that followed at 11:30.

MOBILE UNIT REMOTES

Tonight was the first late-night entertainment program to regularly feature live, remote broadcasts from outside the studio. While it may be routine today for, say, a Dick Clark New Year's Eve special to feature remotes from several locations around the world, it was an ambitious undertaking in 1954 to do a single remote across town. On a given night, the mobile unit, under the supervision of director Michael Zeamer, would cover a mambo contest at the Palladium Ballroom, skating at Rockefeller Center, or daredevil driving at the Los Angeles Coliseum. On another night, it would enable Allen in New York to interview New York Giants outfielder Dusty Rhodes in Cleveland. There was mobile unit coverage of an October 1954 flood in Chicago. A show in May 1955 originated from the New York *Herald Tribune* printing plant and included a tour of its facilities and interviews with its editors and correspondents.

There were periodic remotes from Hollywood to cover world premiere films and their stars, such as *White Christmas, A Star Is Born* (Judy Garland and husband/director Sid Luft), *The Man with the Golden Arm* (Frank Sinatra, Judy Garland, and director Otto Preminger), *Alexander the Great* (Rod Steiger and Charlton Heston), *The Man in the Gray Flannel Suit,* and *Around the World in 80 Days* (Michael Todd, Elizabeth Taylor, Eddie Fisher, David Niven, Edward G. Robinson, Milton Berle, Shirley MacLaine, and Red Buttons). Dean Martin and Jerry Lewis did their comedy routine in a Hollywood remote on November 11, 1955, eight months before their highly publicized split.

A remote on December 16, 1954, captured the fifth anniversary celebration of the legendary Birdland jazz club in Manhattan and included numbers by Count Basie, George Shearing, Lester Young, and Sarah Vaughan. Allen started the show in the Hudson Theatre on 44th Street, raced out to Birdland at 63rd Street for the remote, and then high-tailed it back to the Hudson for the next segment. Bill Harbach remembered the thrill of doing this live:

> Steve would be at the desk to introduce Steve and Eydie to do a duet. That'd be three minutes. Out of that, we'd go to a commercial. Out of that, we'd go to a station break. And out of that, we'd go to Steve at Birdland. So that's about six-and-a-half minutes. We had a cab outside waiting. Steve would say, "And now here's Steve and Eydie to sing. . . ."
>
> Then, zzzhhhooom-BOOOM! We'd run out, get in that cab, and the traffic—we never missed, but we often came close—run down those stairs to Birdland. The whole audience is there. Count Basie's there. Steve would announce, "Here we are in Birdland, and here's Count Basie." Count would say, "You take this number, Steve." Steve would play with the band.

Allen himself found the experience exhilarating, privately remarking to Harbach: "You play about sixteen bars of blues and the brass comes in, wailing behind you, and it's like being picked up by the back of your coat and carried up in the air!"

"Now we've gotta get back to the theater," said Harbach. "So we'd end it with Basie, and Steve would say, 'The great Count Basie Band! And here's Andy Williams [back in the studio] to sing.' And then, BOOM! Up the stairs, into the cab, into the elephant doors, into the theater. Commercial. Six minutes to get there."

SINGLE-GUEST SHOWS, SINGLE-THEME SHOWS

Under Allen, *Tonight* introduced the single-guest show and the single-theme show, concepts later appropriated and refined by Dick Cavett, Phil Donahue, Charlie Rose, Tom Snyder, and Bob Costas. One essentially single-guest show on December 10, 1954, revolved around Carl Sandburg, the acclaimed poet and Lincoln biographer, although it wasn't originally planned that way. Sandburg was booked for a ten-minute spot. The routine for the remainder of the show was supposed to include actor Charles Coburn in a comedy sketch, jazz pianist Marian McPartland performing a few numbers, and Allen interviewing the audience. Sandburg came on as scheduled, but he started running well over his ten minutes, and Allen found himself thanking the tireless poet repeatedly in polite but vain attempts to wrap up the interview. Without any hint of annoyance, Allen interrupted Sandburg's recitation from his biography of Abraham Lincoln with an aside to the audience: "Twenty minutes or so ago, we threw the schedule out the window." Sandburg, apparently oblivious to the mayhem that his extended visit was causing, continued reciting.

Allen broke into another aside: "Well, we'll cancel something. I don't know what." He then concluded, "This is kind of slipshod, but, oh, well." At no point, however, did he get impatient with the elderly, albeit uncooperative, poet, preferring to take a solicitous approach. As a result, Sandburg felt at home on the Hudson Theatre stage. He finally looked up at Allen and remarked, "I'm surprised at how easy it is here tonight. Somehow, out in the darkness, I feel I have friends."

Allen nodded in agreement. "You and I are taking it easy up here, but there's panic out in the control room."

"Do I have to go?" Sandburg innocently asked. Allen cheerfully let him stay for nearly an hour, and the heralded poet proceeded to play the guitar and sing folk songs with Allen. Later, Allen offered Sandburg his choice of a clock or watch furnished by a sponsor, but Sandburg blurted that he preferred a watch made by another manufacturer. At first, Allen winced but remarked sympathetically, "I'm with you! I think the time is past for sponsors when the mention of another product gives them chills and fever." Toward the end, Allen playfully informed the audience, "This is a new type of program known as shambles. Mr. Sandburg dropped in for a minute about an hour ago."

Reported the *New York Times Magazine* of the genial and adroit Allen that night, "Both Sandburg and the audience adored him audibly." When Sandburg, Allen, and Coburn closed the show with a three-part harmony rendition of "Home on the Range," "it was one of the most thrilling experiences in my entire professional history," said Allen in 1992.

Sandburg's magical appearance almost didn't happen, revealed Bill Harbach. Sandburg agreed to do the show in the first place, in part because of his long-standing and close friendship with Harbach's father, Broadway librettist Otto Harbach. "My father attended Knox College in Galesburg, Illinois, Carl's hometown," Harbach recounted. "He used to come to where we lived and visit Dad overnight. I remember sitting out on the porch and hearing them. I couldn't see, it was so dark. But you could see the two cigars glowing as they would talk to each other about Chicago at the turn of the century. My God, I wish there would have been a tape of that stuff.

"I said, 'Mr. Sandburg, could I ask you to do the show I'm producing called the *Tonight* show?' He said, 'Son, I'd love to!' I called Steve and said, 'Steve, I talked to Carl Sandburg, and I think I've got him!' He got all excited. And the next Thursday, he was going to be there."

That Thursday, Harbach got detained at a weekly network staff meeting at the NBC offices about a mile from the theater. The meeting ended at 6 p.m., the very time he was supposed to meet

Sandburg at the Hudson Theatre. "And I had visions that he was going to be there, and I'm not there, and he'd say to the crew, 'Just tell Bill good luck, and I'll see you soon.' And I was gonna say, 'Steve, I lost Carl. I was late coming down here.'"

Panicked, Harbach "ran through red lights, almost got killed. I got to 45th Street, sweating like hell, saying, 'I've blown it, I've blown it, I've blown it.' I was, like, ten minutes late. And out of the side of my eyes, I saw a beat-up-looking, grey-haired guy with a satchel, paper bag, looking in a little hardware store window. And I went over to him and said, 'Mr. Sandburg?' And he was very dramatic, the way he talked: 'Ooooh, Biiiilll, am I laaaaate?' I said, 'No, sir, I thought I was, sir. We're only a block from there, so we can go now.' He said, 'Oh, yes. But come look into this window.' It was just a window full of hammers and saws. 'Look at that hammer, look at the design of that hammer. And look at how the human hand holds it.' He was describing these mundane things, the poet. I was in a church for about ten minutes."

The topics for the single-theme shows ranged from the serious to the whimsical. There was a Halloween party in October 1954 featuring Steve Lawrence, Eydie Gorme, Andy Williams, and Pat Marshall, all in animal costumes, in a seasonal song-and-dance number, "Trick or Treat." The show on August 10, 1955, was dedicated to the US Air Force in connection with the ninth anniversary of the Air Force Association convention and the premiere of the motion picture *The McConnell Story*, both in San Francisco. In the film, Alan Ladd played Joseph McConnell, the triple jet ace of the Korean War who rang up the highest combat record of any soldier but who returned home after being grounded and was eventually killed while training jet pilots. The show featured an Air Force drill team executing maneuvers above an outdoor parking lot in Hollywood.

One recurring theme focused on the music, cuisine, and traditions of a particular ethnic culture. A Hawaiian night included hula lessons for the cast. A show on Japan included a sword dance demonstration. A show on Switzerland included horn-blowing, yodeling, and a ski lesson for Allen. There were also shows devoted to Cuba and Israel. After sampling Israeli beer on the air, Allen—who rarely drank—began chirping gleefully, "Is-really beer!"

On Monday morning, March 19, 1956, Allen discarded the original game plan for that night's show and feverishly began preparing a tribute to comedian and *What's My Line?* panelist Fred Allen, who had died suddenly over the weekend. Allen idolized the late comedian, a rare philosopher-wit in the tradition of Mark Twain and Will Rogers. Allen gathered recollections of guests live in the studio, via telephone or televised remote or via written statements, including Bob Hope, Jack Benny, authors Bennett Cerf and Herman Wouk, and numerous columnists and celebrities. Allen assembled film clips, kinescope clips, and still photos. In addition, he and his guests quoted examples of Fred's distinctive, incisive wit. On the social value of television: "Everything in TV is so graphic that it leaves nothing for the mind—it's all for the eyes." On diminutive New York Mayor Fiorello LaGuardia: "He was the only man who could milk a cow standing up." On the increasing size of TV screens: "People say that screens are larger today—but they aren't—the audience is small." On Jack Benny accidentally flubbing a recitation of Lincoln's Gettysburg address: "Jack, how could you possibly have misquoted the Gettysburg address when you were there?" And on the many vice presidents employed by NBC: "If the United States could get along with one vice president, I can't understand why NBC needs twenty-six."

To pull together the guests (in the studio, on the phone, and via remotes), the film clips, the statements, and the still shots for a live tribute—within hours of the death of a major politician, sports figure, or entertainer—is a Herculean, stress-laden task. Virtually no one today stops his or her show and devotes an hour to a newly deceased public figure. One exception is Larry King, who has become perhaps the most gifted practitioner of the art of the instant live tribute, a sorely needed alternative to the standard one-minute obituary on the evening news. It was King who frenetically assembled moving tributes following the deaths of Princess Diana, Ted Williams, John F. Kennedy Jr., and numerous other public figures, including former *Tonight* hosts Steve Allen in 2000 (featuring guests Ed McMahon, Carl Reiner, Andy Williams, Steve Lawrence, Don Rickles, Mike Douglas, and Bill Allen), Jack Paar in 2004, and Johnny Carson in January 2005.

GOING ON THE ROAD

On occasion, in an attempt to boost ratings, *Tonight* did for the first time what late-night shows have been doing ever since: It took the show on the road. The entire cast and crew would travel to Miami Beach, Chicago, Cleveland, Dayton, Baltimore, Los Angeles, Niagara Falls, and other destinations for programs designed around these locales.

Allen opened the first road show in January 1955 by jumping into the swimming pool of the Sea Isle Hotel in Miami Beach. *Tonight* spent a week commemorating that city's fortieth anniversary as one of the world's foremost resorts. For the most part, the show originated from the pool and adjoining patio and featured a variety of local and national talent. Comedian Henny Youngman rode with Allen in the pool in a small boat, which eventually capsized. There was a tug-of-war among the cast members, with the losing team being pulled into the pool. A mobile unit remote covered a dog race from the Miami Kennel Club. The cast participated in a "pajama race" in which each team had to race back and forth across the pool, but only after each member first put on a long nightshirt.

Two stunt men known as "The Human Torches," saturated with

gasoline and set on fire, dove into an oil-slicked pool. A porpoise trainer gave a demonstration using a live porpoise swimming in the hotel pool. Jackie Willie wrestled an alligator out of the pool and onto the grass, opening its jaw and then rubbing its tummy to put it to sleep, only to wake it up later in the show by mimicking its mating call. Milton Berle, Debbie Reynolds, Gordon MacRae, and Vaughn Monroe made appearances. The week ended with a beach party, with everybody dancing the mambo in the sand to Calypso Eddie and His Calypso Band.

On another visit to Miami Beach, the show opened with a staged mock military water invasion of Miami Beach—live, at precisely 11:30 p.m. Allen: "Somehow, because of the popularity of the show, we were able to talk a local military unit equipped with a landing craft into providing about forty soldiers, fully armed, though with blank ammunition." Dwight Hemion: "It was late at night, and all of a sudden, we set off these things to detonate in the sand." Writer Herb Sargent: "Guests in the hotel weren't sure it wasn't real and were checking out by the score." Singer Andy Williams: "Lights went on all over the beach in these hotels, and people were frantic." Since this was during the time shortly before Fidel Castro invaded Havana and defeated Batista's reactionary forces, some hotel residents, hearing the gunfire and commotion, believed a Cuban-Communist invasion of the American mainland was underway.

Allen nearly drowned in the mock invasion, as his heavy World War II gear (a full uniform, complete with helmet and rifle) rendered him almost immobile in the tide, which had risen substantially shortly before airtime. Four soldiers had to pull him onto the deck of the landing craft so that he could splash ashore, run up the beach toward the camera, and begin his monologue. Once on the shore, things began to go smoothly for the next thirty seconds, but then Allen stepped on a nail-ridden board hidden in the sand and had to continue his monologue with a minor but painful puncture wound in his foot.

Instead of taking it easy after these elaborate and sometimes dangerous openings, Allen instead opted for something even more ambitious: landing on the beach in a helicopter. "It was a daring thing to open a live TV show by flying the host in over the ocean at night and having him land right on the beach, only a few feet from the breaking waves, right in front of the then–brand new Americana Hotel on Miami Beach," marveled Bill Allen.

Allen's helicopter touched down without a hitch, but as he stepped victoriously onto the beach, "the downdraft from the large propeller suddenly blew his glasses off, and he couldn't read the teleprompter," once he made his way up the beach to the cameras, remembered David Pollock, a high school–age Allen *Tonight* fan who would later write and produce Allen's shows in the late '60s and early '70s. "Whoops—I lost my glasses, folks!" Allen exclaimed, and he proceeded to march back toward the chopper and the ocean, desperately searching for his glasses in the sand. "Sure, everybody's laughing," sighed Allen in mock exasperation, "but I really need those glasses!"

Jayne Meadows had arranged for her father, who had been ill, to stay with her and Allen in their Miami Beach hotel suite for a week of peaceful recuperation in the sun. "And just as we walked into the suite," recalled Meadows, "the body of a man falls from the top of the building right down in front of our window. And this is why my father, who was so desperately ill, came to Florida for a week? Nobody had told me that it was one of the gags that they were rehearsing to do on the show that night—that a man was going to jump off the roof of the hotel and land in the swimming pool. I don't remember my father's reaction, but my own was terror for Dad!"

Terror of a different sort marked an April 1956 broadcast from the fairgrounds at Fort Worth, Texas. Bill Harbach had decided that Allen was to make his entrance on horseback. The entrance worked flawlessly during rehearsal with a handsome, docile palomino. But during the actual broadcast, the horse got spooked by the blaring band of twenty and the rowdy audience of five thousand—neither of whom had been present at rehearsal—and started charging toward the audience. Miraculously, the horse jerked back, but then it suddenly stood up on its hind legs, "Hi-ho, Silver!"–style. Allen slid down the back of the horse onto the ground, unharmed. Mishaps like these instantly and permanently altered the lives of composer Cole Porter and actor Christopher Reeve. Ironically, this nearly disastrous accident made Allen—an admittedly inept horseman—appear the masterful equestrian to all except three expert horsemen who had been watching. Their hearts, Allen recalled, "had been in their mouths."

Conductor Skitch Henderson remembered a less-harrowing aspect of that incident: "The horse left the area and deposited its feelings right beside the orchestra."

In the dead of winter 1955, the show braved five-below-zero temperatures in Dayton, Ohio, where it played to a full house at the NCR Auditorium. Allen entered on an NCR locomotive and then pedaled down the aisle on a Huffy bike. According to a local reviewer, Allen looked tired from the trip to Dayton, but that didn't affect his sharp performance or energy. He even stayed for the post-show cocktail party for the press that began at 1:30 a.m. and jammed on the piano until past 5 a.m.

But some of Allen's best ad-libs occurred off-camera during the warm-up with the audience. One person asked him if his wife had come along, to which he answered no. A woman then said to him suggestively, "I have something for you."

Allen quipped, "It's a good thing I didn't bring Jayne."

Seconds later, a director approached Allen and whispered in

his ear. Allen turned to the crowd and said: "This show has just been canceled."

POLITICAL DIRECTIONS, SOCIAL RESPONSIBILITY

Besides his freewheeling sense of humor, it was Allen's conscience that drove the *Tonight* show, said writer Herb Sargent. Decades before spirited debate-style programs like *The McLaughlin Group* and *Crossfire*, *Tonight* under Allen would occasionally swing in provocative political directions. "Steve had a grasp of everything that was out there," said Steve Lawrence. "He was one of the early, great libertarians. He spoke out with regard to all kinds of injustices. He was a great liberal in the true sense of the word *liberal*."

One show from June 1955 covered McCarthyism—a topic that "people just didn't talk about on television," said Lawrence—and involved a panel debate on AWARE, Inc., a self-appointed organization dedicated to rooting out those whom it had decided were Communist and leftist actors. "*Red Channels*, a book of every suspected member of the Communist Party" or its affiliated organizations, explained Sargent, "was circulated among all the networks. It was a little bible. The people who were in it couldn't work. Mostly actors, a lot of writers."

The panel consisted of two in favor of AWARE, AWARE president and Fordham University law professor Godfrey Schmidt and *Red Channels* author Vincent Hartnett, and two against AWARE, actress Faye Emerson (then wife of Skitch Henderson) and *New York Herald Tribune* radio and television critic John Crosby. Crosby had written a column that catalyzed the debate, asserting that "the blacklisting racket, which has simmered down quite a bit in the motion picture industry, still flourishes openly in television."

As an example of the practice, Crosby described how actor Leslie Barrett had received a letter from Hartnett stating that he had a photograph of Barrett marching in a 1952 May Day parade and asking if that accurately reflected Barrett's present sympathies. Failure to respond to the letter would create the presumption that Hartnett's contentions were true. Barrett, however, had never been in a May Day parade or been a Communist sympathizer.

According to Crosby, Barrett tried unsuccessfully to enlist help from his union, the American Federation of Television and Radio Artists (AFTRA). Even the FBI, though sympathetic to his plight, maintained that it was helpless. Other actors got blacklisted for having foreign names or for having appeared in plays written by Arthur Miller.

Crosby reported that AFTRA eventually took a stand condemning AWARE and its blacklisting practices, in part as a result of a speech Barrett had made about his ordeal. Allen himself took a stand and became among the first to book blacklisted talent. "We wanted to put on Zero Mostel, Jack Gilford, and others who did stand-up," but they were blacklisted, Sargent remembered. "And Steve said, 'Let's book 'em.' The network said no. Steve said, 'Then good-bye. I want them on. Forget what the network thinks.' So they did get on. That gave me a big charge."

The show on October 3, 1956, contained a forty-five-minute panel discussion, "The Pros and Cons of Exposé-Type Magazines," with the publisher and editor of *Confidential* magazine debating two newspaper columnists.

Allen spent the first half hour of a February 1955 program discussing the police capture of murder suspect August Robles the previous day in an East Harlem flat, which ended in Robles's death. Allen personally witnessed the incident and went through the flat afterwards. He was appalled by how many in the crowd, especially children, seemed to glorify Robles, forty-one, who had been in trouble with the law since he was fourteen. Allen described the scene in the flat—bullet riddled, a foot of water on the floor, with Robles lying dead on the floor, his undershirt bright red with blood. Allen was also disturbed by the unruliness of the crowd that had gathered outside, which hindered police and firefighter efforts and required the dispatch of additional forces to control the mob.

There was an April 1955 program devoted to drug abuse, featuring the director of New York's Health and Welfare Commission, a display of drug paraphernalia, and interviews with former addicts. "Steve did a magnificent, moving, dramatic job of presenting the problem of narcotics addiction . . . a subject most TVers would be scared stiff to touch and utterly incompetent to deal with tastefully," wrote *Chicago American* columnist Janet Kern. Later that week, Allen featured a representative from the National Safety Council discussing drunk driving and demonstrating a Breathalyzer device.

Former First Lady Eleanor Roosevelt appeared to promote a May 24, 1956, civil rights rally to be held at Madison Square Garden.

Many of these efforts were supported by NBC brass, and Pat Weaver even sent Allen a memo encouraging the inclusion of such thought-provoking material. "That memo ought to be reprinted and sent to everybody in the business about once a week," Allen wrote in *Hi-Ho, Steverino!* (1992).

ALLEN'S BRUSH WITH THE MOB

Even before *Tonight*, Allen was developing his social conscience as well as a sense of obligation to share it with his viewers. He came across an article in *Life* magazine about a Northlake, Illinois, milkman who was beaten by mobsters because he had spoken out at a Lutheran church meeting against the installation of pinball games in a candy store near a neighborhood school. "They were careful not to hit him above the neck so he wouldn't lose consciousness," Allen told the Cleveland *Plain Dealer*, "but they broke every bone in his body and in the magazine there was a picture that listed every broken bone. The picture made me very angry and the next day, on my afternoon show, I had the cameras stay on the picture for five minutes while I let off steam."

Allen began to develop a keen interest in organized crime and sought to devote one night of his local *Steve Allen Show* to the corrupting influence of organized crime in New York City. At Allen's request, WNBT granted an extra half hour of air time for him to write and produce a seventy-minute documentary. Allen spent several weeks working with the New York City Anti-Crime Committee, digging up photos and film clips of top gangsters, assembling a panel of experts on organized crime, and writing a script about the ownership of many garment firms by racketeers.

As the August 31, 1954, air date approached of the controversial program, titled "The Tenth Commandment," "strange obstacles were thrown in my path," recalled Allen. One panelist, a former state prosecutor and author of a book on the same subject, called Allen to back out of his appearance. The panelist explained that after reading the script, he had decided that, in his current position as an attorney in private practice, he couldn't afford to antagonize so many powerful men. The panel ultimately consisted of William Keating, staff counsel for the Anti-Crime Committee; John O'Mara, chief investigator for the Anti-Crime Committee and former FBI agent; Victor Riesel, labor columnist for the New York *Mirror*; Sol Marks, assistant deputy district director for the INS; and George White, supervisor-at-large of the US Narcotics Bureau.

Later that day, Allen received a call from one of the biggest figures in the clothing industry, who, coincidentally, also had read the script. "I didn't ask him how he'd gotten a copy," mused Allen (twenty-five mimeographed copies of the script had been sent to various people on the show), "but it seemed that the most likely source was the attorney who had just begged off." The caller, recalled Allen, was seeking to "'offer a little friendly advice: Don't do it.'" The caller asked whether Allen realized that doing the show could do a great deal of harm to himself. When Allen stood his ground, the caller asked if Allen could at least refrain from referring to one of the documentary's subjects—Benjamin "Benny" Levine—by name because he has been straight for many years now. To resurrect his unfortunate past would be "'a terrible blow to him,'" said the caller, according to Allen.

Allen said he would reconsider his decision only if the Anti-Crime Committee had erred in its assessment of Levine. The clothing exec then asked Allen if he'd like money, special business contacts, a new car, or powerful friends. "I don't want anything, except a better city," Allen told him.

Allen then checked with Keating, who responded, "'Levine is now a wealthy and powerful garment manufacturer, but he was an important member of the Lepke-Gurrah gang and went to jail for extortion. He was an advance man for the mob back in the thirties, the guy who could make the proper labor contract when a strike was getting too rough. He's also mixed up in the Algam Corporation which owns the land and buildings at Yonkers Raceway. Don't believe the stories that he's now sweet as a rose.'" In 1938, Levine had surrendered to then–District Attorney Thomas E. Dewey, who described him, according to the *New York Journal American*, as "second only to 'Lepke' Buchalter and Jacob 'Gurrah' Shapiro in the operation of garment center rackets that took in millions of dollars a year." Levine served a one-year prison term in 1942.

When Allen told the clothing exec that the facts on Levine were accurate, the exec continued to warn Allen that he was making a big mistake. Still later that day, Irving Gray, manager of Allen's friend Milton Berle, called from Las Vegas, where Berle was completing an engagement at The Sands, one of the town's biggest gambling operations. Gray said he was "speaking for one of the most respected members of the garment industry" and urged Allen to not to use the name of "'Mr. L.' Apparently, he was afraid to say the name on the phone," Allen said. Gray suggested that Allen, a clean-cut, thirty-two-year-old entertainer, leave this matter to the professional journalists. But Allen refused, explaining, "It's too late to change my plans now. I think it's time somebody said these things out loud anyway. That's one reason the mob is so powerful in New York—people are afraid to speak up."

A second caller said he represented Levine's "partner" and hoped that Allen would delete the name from the script. Allen refused. Three minutes later, Allen received another phone call from a gentleman who "asked me to cancel the show." Allen refused again, but the caller "offered to pay me twice as much as I was getting to leave out any 'reference' to 'Mr. X.'"

The next day, Allen was summoned to WNBT's executive offices to meet with an attorney sent by International Ladies Garment Workers Union President David Dubinsky. The attorney asked to study the script for a couple of days in order to ensure the factual correctness of any references to labor. According to newspaper reports, the attorney requested deletion of the following line from the script: "Gangsters could not operate if it weren't for the lethargy of union officials." A number of deletions were reportedly made, and the reference to ILGWU became only an oblique one. NBC spokesmen expressed amazement that scripts seemed to turn up "strangely and suddenly" in the hands of both the ILGWU and friends of Levine.

WNBT station manager Ham Shea told Allen that he had been receiving inquiries and "suggestions" about the forthcoming broadcast. Knickerbocker Beer sponsored *The Steve Allen Show* three nights a week, but the night of the controversial broadcast was not one of them. Nevertheless, the station's switchboard was flooded with calls demanding that Allen be taken off the air, apparently as part of a campaign to have him fired. Levine's business associate continued to call him. "The close tie-ups between mobsters, politicians, and union leaders in New York are notorious," thought Allen, "and I was afraid that pressure was going to be exerted upon the station to prevent the show's broadcast."

Allen faced a dilemma: insist on keeping Levine's name in the script and risk having the station cancel the show or agree to delete his name to ensure broadcast of the rest of the program. Of particular concern to Allen was that his successful local show would be giving way in four weeks to *Tonight* on the full network; if WNBT decided to cancel the anticrime broadcast, he didn't think he would have the opportunity to do a similar show on the network.

Allen chose the latter option because even though Levine had often been linked to *Murder, Inc.*, an early 1950s book by Burton Turkus and Sid Feder about organized crime, no actual reference to his name could be found in it. For that reason, a network spokesman reportedly said that the deletion of his name seemed a "simple enough favor." Ultimately, said Allen at a postbroadcast press conference, "The decision to delete the name was mine and mine alone."

Although Allen would omit Levine's name, he added a risky twist of his own. During the broadcast, at the point where he would have read Levine's name on the teleprompter, Allen departed from the script, instead saying, "Ladies and gentlemen, for reasons that I will not go into, I have deleted from tonight's script the name of a very powerful man in the garment industry. But even though I will not mention his name, I think you ought to know about his evil influence. So I will tell you his story but will refer to him only as Mr. X."

Allen's teaser strategy worked. Public interest in the identity of the mysterious Mr. X skyrocketed. Sure enough, the next day, the *New York Journal–American* broke the story revealing Mr. X as

Levine. "But by that time, all hell had broken loose," said Allen. Even though Knickerbocker Beer had not sponsored *The Steve Allen Show* on the night of that broadcast and had no connection with it (a fact that Allen felt compelled to point out at the beginning of the show), "hundreds of saloons in Brooklyn and along the water front had refused to accept deliveries of their beer." The tires on Allen's car, parked right outside the theater, were slashed. On the positive side, NBC tallied 350 phone calls to its switchboard about the broadcast, 345 of which were favorable. Assistant District Attorney Alfred Scott, chief of the Rackets Bureau, questioned Allen about the pressures he had encountered beforehand, and Allen acknowledged that he had "reluctantly" promised not to divulge the name of "Mr. X." Threats were made against Allen and Jayne Meadows, who were given police protection for the next two weeks, accompanied by a pair of detectives wherever they went.

Two weeks later, shortly after the show went on the air at 11:20 p.m., stink bombs erupted in the second balcony of the theater. (Levine was reputed to have used stink bombs against factories.) Allen, watching all this unfold from the stage, smelled an opportunity for humor, began sniffing the air, and quipped, "This may be the straight line of the year, but this place stinks!" It was "one of the funniest shows we had done in months," according to Allen.

The local and national publicity that these incidents attracted could not have come at a better time, just weeks before the premiere of *Tonight*. A headline in *Variety* read, "If Steve Allen Wasn't 'Pressured,' What a Buildup for 'Tonight'!" A number of newspaper reporters, however, dismissed the entire episode as "just another publicity stunt." This incensed Allen, who branded their attitude as "jaundiced" and wondered how they "would assume I worked for weeks on a story, tackling nothing less than the murderous Mafia itself, placing myself in serious physical danger and my career in jeopardy as well, purely for the purpose of getting publicity."

Allen told the Cleveland *Plain Dealer*, "My motive for doing the program was no more mysterious than that of the man on the street who wonders about crime and says, 'Isn't that terrible!' It wouldn't mean anything if I went on the air and said the same thing, so I sat down and wrote a script, with the help of the New York Anti-Crime Commission."

As a result of the program, Allen was named Young Man of the Year by the New York Board of Trade.

Allen revisited the ordeal in a March 20, 1956, *Tonight* broadcast. He reviewed a new book about the beating victim that mentioned Allen's controversial documentary. One of the authors of the book—*The Man Who Rocked the Boat*—was the same William Keating with whom Allen had worked on the documentary two years earlier. Nearly three decades later, Allen's brush with the mob would form the basis for a subplot in the 1982 comedy film, *My Favorite Year*, which was set in the world of early 1950s television. One of the film's screenplay authors told Allen that, although a principal character was based on comedian Sid Caesar ("King Kaiser," played by Joe Bologna), the antagonism between New York Mafia gangsters and Bologna's character was actually based on Allen's troubles with the mob.

Allen pointed out that in June 1958, the *New York Times* reported in an article headlined "Seventeen Arrested Here in Narcotics Raid; Top Racketeers Among Those Held on High Bail": "Also held on $35,000 bail was Benjamin Levine, 63, who owns a $150,000 home at Atlantic Beach, Long Island. Levine, a one-time confederate of the garment racketeers Louis 'Lepke' Buchalter and Jacob 'Gurrah' Shapiro, was said to have planned the financing of the narcotics traffic."

"I sent a clipping of the *Times* story to Levine's clothier friend, among others," Allen added.

"THE GREATEST FRIEND JAZZ HAD IN TELEVISION"

Jazz critic Leonard Feather dubbed Steve Allen "the greatest friend jazz had in television" because he featured a formidable number of jazz greats on *Tonight*, at times turning the show into a living jazz museum. In October 1954, the American Jazz Society recognized Allen, along with Lionel Hampton, for their contributions to this uniquely American musical form.

A jazz lover and competent jazz pianist himself, Allen saw *Tonight* as a dream-come-true vehicle to present many of the jazz artists that he first admired and saw in local Chicago spots such as the Panther Room in the Hotel Sherman and the Blackhawk. These performers had sparked his fascination with jazz: "After all, the 1930s, when I was going to high school, were years of the golden era of jazz music. Benny Goodman could almost have run for President," Allen told *Redbook* magazine.

"I am now able to meet, and have on the show and also know socially some of the same performers I used to go to watch when I was in high school," Allen wrote in a 1955 essay for *Ebony* magazine. "Louis Armstrong was an idol of my youth. Years ago in Chicago, when I was a kid, I used to see him once in a while. I think he's just the best. The one thing about his playing that has always appealed to me is that he plays with humor. There are certain people who can sell insurance, or whatever they do, and they have a way of pleasing the people who watch them. Louis has always seemed to me to have that, even when he is playing something sad at any moment, he can make a crowd laugh, just by looking at them in a certain way or by singing a note a certain way."

Tonight viewers were treated to performances by Armstrong, Count Basie ("April in Paris" and "One O'Clock Jump"), Dave Brubeck ("The Trolley Song"), Earl Hines ("Honeysuckle Rose"), Teddy Wilson ("Airmail Special" and "Lady Be Good"), and numerous other greats. It was not unusual for an artist to do three, four, or more numbers in a single appearance.

But Allen did more than just present these performers in Ed Sullivan–esque fashion. He recognized that the public might not readily accept jazz, particularly in its more progressive forms, and he felt the need to enlighten his audiences and enable them to cultivate an appreciation for it. He told the respected jazz magazine *Metronome* in 1955: "I just like to give them a little background— you might call it sort of a reason for our presenting jazz. When Brubeck was on, I did an introductory eight-minute bit on the history of jazz piano playing, which led us right into Dave's music." Allen also chatted with the stars (Dizzy Gillespie, for example, discussed his goodwill tour to Iran and Pakistan), and he often recognized seldom-credited soloists, reflecting his knowledge and appreciation of their musicianship.

"TV can do more to convert people to an appreciation of jazz," Allen told the jazz musicians' magazine *Downbeat* in 1954, "than, let's say, a record album of the same music. An old lady hearing jazz on the radio is likely to turn it off if she doesn't dig it, but if she's a fan of a particular TV show she may stick around to watch. If I say, 'I have something that may interest you,' she'll stay with us."

Tonight during the Allen era found itself in the middle of a musical cold war between Dixieland and modern progressive schools of jazz. Allen refused to take sides and instead urged "tolerance": "When a Dixielander says, 'That's just a lot of noise Dizzy Gillespie is playing,' it seems to me about as silly as the comment you hear from old ladies who say, 'I don't like jazz,'" wrote Allen. "It surprises me when an important musician criticizes progressive music. I can enjoy Louis Armstrong and also Miles Davis, who is very modern. Their trumpet styles and ideas differ strongly, but they always have something interesting to say."

The roster of jazz artists appearing on *Tonight* during the Allen era included:

Louis Armstrong
Chet Baker Quartet
Count Basie and His
    Orchestra
Art Blakey and His Jazz
    Messengers
Dave Brubeck and Quartet
Cy Coleman Trio
Eddie Condon
Wild Bill Davis Trio
Wild Bill Davison
Duke Ellington
Maynard Ferguson Jazz Band
Ella Fitzgerald
Erroll Garner
Stan Getz and His Jazz
    Quartet
Terry Gibbs Quartet
Dizzy Gillespie
Lionel Hampton
Coleman Hawkins
Neal Hefti
Woody Herman
Eddie Heywood
Earl Hines

Billie Holiday
Jackie Kane and Roy Krall
Stan Kenton
Gene Krupa
Shelly Mann
Marian McPartland Trio
Carmen McRae
Modern Jazz Quartet
Thelonius Monk and Trio
Red Norvo
Oscar Peterson
Tito Puente
Buddy Rich
Bud Shank Quartet
George Shearing and
    Quintet
Bobby Short Trio
Horace Silver
Art Tatum
Billy Taylor Trio
Mel Tormé
Bobby Troup
Sarah Vaughan
Teddy Wilson
Lester Young

Allen, who at the time also wrote a column for *Downbeat*, periodically jammed with his heroes on the air. "He would actually bring in these people from everywhere," recalled Eydie Gorme, "so that he could be right there with them in person and watch how they did it." Allen never hesitated to ask his guests to show him what they were doing: "I think that every musician can learn from other musicians. It would be silly, for example, to take a man like

Chet Baker and, because you worship him for the wonderful way in which he plays, to think that he couldn't learn something from Louis Armstrong. In the same way, Louis could learn from Chet. Every musician has something to give, and every musician has something to learn."

The next day, Eydie and Steve Lawrence would overhear Allen trying to repeat the piano licks that he had heard the guest do the night before. It was more than a passing attempt. According to cabaret pianist/singer Bobby Short, Allen loved Earl Hines's recording of "Boogie-Woogie on the St. Louis Blues" so much that he "took it upon himself to not just learn it, but to record it, note-for-note."

A SHOWCASE FOR ARTISTS OF COLOR

Allen launched what was perhaps the country's first network television platform to regularly showcase African American talent, including singers, musicians, actors, and athletes. Viewers were treated to Louis Armstrong singing "Mack the Knife," Erroll Garner playing "I've Got the World on a String," Leontyne Price singing "Summertime," Carmen McRae singing "Bewitched," and Billie Holiday singing "Nice Work If You Can Get It." Sammy Davis Jr. made the audience laugh by doing a lighthearted lip-synch of one of his own records. On a more serious note, Allen discussed the status of race relations in the major leagues during a February 1955 broadcast with Brooklyn Dodger Jackie Robinson, the first black Major League Baseball player.

The roster of African American guests whom Allen booked on *Tonight* included:

Louis Armstrong	George Kirby
Pearl Bailey	Joe Louis
Count Basie	Willie Mays
Art Blakey	Carmen McRae
Cab Calloway	Thelonius Monk
Thelma Carpenter	Oscar Peterson
Dorothy Dandridge	Leontyne Price
Sammy Davis Jr.	Jackie Robinson
Duke Ellington	Bobby Short
Ella Fitzgerald	Horace Silver
Erroll Garner	Art Tatum
Dizzy Gillespie	Sarah Vaughan
Lionel Hampton	Dinah Washington
Coleman Hawkins	Ethel Waters
Earl Hines	Mary Lou Williams
Billie Holiday	Teddy Wilson
Lena Horne	Lester Young
Bill Kenny	

This roster is even more impressive considering the racist attitudes then prevalent across America, including in the entertainment industry. The civil rights movement was just dawning. When *Tonight* premiered in September 1954, the United States Supreme Court's landmark decision in *Brown v. Board of Education* was fresh in the headlines, and it would be more than a year before Rosa Parks refused to give up her seat on the bus.

"Think about the plight of black people in the 1950s," said Bobby Short, whom Allen booked to appear on *Tonight*, in an interview conducted one month before Short's death in March 2005. "Many of them could not vote, went to inferior schools. There was this high degree of poverty, and they were being abused right and left. And they were looked down upon.

"It was long before the Civil Rights Act, and it was awfully hard to find a black person on television. The whole idea was that television was a new, intimate kind of medium. Suddenly, you turn the switch on, and there were people in your home. You sat there and watched them in your pajamas, and they were a part of your lives. There were great precautions being taken by the people in charge. People had great prejudices, and perhaps they were not so pleased to have a black person suddenly on the screen in their home.

"It was all about fear. The fear of offending the viewer because if Pepsodent toothpaste would sponsor a show that was going to feature black people, and black people are anathema to three-quarters of the viewers, that's not going to work very well, is it?"

Legendary performer Eartha Kitt observed, "If you were a person of color, it was not that easy to get on television in any form or fashion." In 2005 she recounted the time she wanted to get the title role in *Salome*, a 1950s television production of a biblical story. "I asked one of the guys at the agency to get me on that program, and he said, 'Eartha, don't you know what color you are?' which made me either cry or laugh at the same time." Determined, she successfully lobbied the director of the production for the part herself.

"But Mr. Paley, the head of CBS, was in the studio when we did the dress rehearsal," Kitt continued. "During the part where Salome takes the brother and throws him down the stairs and says, 'Get me the head of John the Baptist,' Mr. Paley came in and had a meeting with us afterwards on the set and said, 'You can't do that. We can do that to you, but you can't do that to us.' Salome was not black or white or pink or green. She was a biblical subject. The director was forced to cut those scenes. I remember looking at the director, who also had some tears in his eyes because it was so stupid."

In the 1950s, the challenges were compounded for performers who were both black and female, recalled Diahann Carroll, Tony Award–winning actress and singer, in a 2005 interview:

There were so many terrible practices, such as "We've had our three black artists for this month, so we have to forgo Sammy Davis Jr. this month." As a young, black woman, I was so aware when I was in the presence of sexual innuendos. The difficulty, the discomfort one felt when you had to deal with someone's male ego was always a nuisance for me. A sexual innuendo on the air from a male host was not unusual. It was certainly acceptable to the public. Women were used to being treated as little dolls—"Isn't she cute?" Oh! I had to try to hold on and remind myself that that's not who I am. That's what they projected me to be—not to fall into that trap, to try and step around it. So many other places that I went, I was subjected to it.

Allen did not consider himself a civil rights crusader. To him, it was simpler than that. In "Talent Is Color-Blind," a 1955 essay Allen wrote for the respected national black magazine *Ebony*, he explained: "[Talent is] a gift not a commodity, and those who have it ought to be treated as the VIP's they really are. On my television show I use a lot of talent and it is all talent that, to me, has no color tag. It just so happens that a pretty high percentage of the guest performers on my show are Negroes. It's not a planned thing. . . . With me, it's basically a question of my accidentally doing what I guess is the right thing. I just hire the best singers and piano players and trumpet players, and it just happens that a very high percentage of them are Negroes."

"We've been let completely alone in the matter of presenting jazz artists," Allen told *Downbeat* in 1954. "I've done shows in the past where the sponsor, the station or the agency would say go easy on jazz—or someone would pull something stupid like telling us not to have too many colored performers."

Allen further explained that, growing up in a tough Chicago neighborhood, equality with African Americans was not something he had to learn: "I don't remember any anti-Negro feeling at all. So it was never a particular problem in my early years. My first contacts with Negroes were usually kids at school. . . . The first Negroes that

I got to know socially were chiefly musicians because I would play with them on little jobs, and since they were always better musicians than I was, my only feeling was the same as if they had been white and better musicians than I was. . . . The issue of color just seemed to never come up." Allen regarded black pianists like Teddy Wilson, Erroll Garner, and Art Tatum among his chief musical influences.

Kitt, who performed on Allen's shows, observed that Allen did not make color an issue. "He was one of the people who was the first to hire you as an artist, rather than as a person of color. He cared about you as a person. He didn't care about me for what my color was; he cared about the artist, and he wanted me to feel welcome in my endeavors," Kitt said.

Carroll, whom Allen also booked on his shows, agreed: "You were allowed to keep your dignity in a manner that didn't happen on so many of the other television shows at that time. His sense of each person's dignity, just because they were a human being, was something that shone through for Steve more so than for everybody else. That's just who he was. His thought process was on a different plane, and it permeated everything that he did. It was a joy to be in his presence. He did not play games."

Furthermore, Carroll appreciated Allen's respect for the dignity of women performers. "Steve didn't have any male chauvinistic qualities. He was without innuendo. We worked. I had the comfort of knowing that I was going to be treated very well, allowed my artistry, to rehearse properly, to do whatever it was that I had to do with great comfort and great respect."

Although Lena Horne had established herself as an esteemed star of stage, screen, nightclubs, and records during the 1930s and '40s, her career suffered a temporary decline during the Communist scare of the early 1950s. "I did very little TV because I was blacklisted. I had been named in *Red Channels*," recalled Horne in 2005. She had been targeted as a result of her associations with civil rights activist W. E. B. Du Bois and actor-turned-black-liberation-activist Paul Robeson and her support of civil rights causes. Nevertheless, Allen booked Horne to appear on *Tonight* (on September 28, 1954) and on his pre-*Tonight* local late-night show in 1953.

Allen recalled being asked whether he was consciously striving to make a favorable impact on minority groups. He denied that booking a large number of black guests was an early form of affirmative action: "I'm not directing messages to special groups in my television audience. My show is for everybody."

Moreover, Allen "shared his dignity of spirit with everyone," said Carroll. "Everyone in the black community was aware that he was a special human being who felt that if you had a gift, he wanted to help you find a showcase for it."

"I think that is the wonderful thing about people like Steve Allen," said Kitt. "They did it because they knew it was the right thing to do, not because they had to."

For the most part, remembered Short, Allen went about booking black artists "in a quiet fashion. I don't think he meant it to be a big to-do. He simply did it." But Carroll pointed out that "he was certainly devoted to it, and we were well aware of that. The black community—because we've been brought up in the culture that taught us that we couldn't think, and we couldn't 'this,' or we're not 'that'—the sensitivity of someone like Steve did not go unnoticed. He was assuredly one of the most respected people on television, as far as the black community was concerned."

During the *Tonight* broadcast on March 14, 1956, the *Kansas City Call*, an African American newspaper, presented Allen with its John Russworm Award, named for the nineteenth-century Jamaican commentator who in 1826 became the second person of African descent to graduate from a US college. The award recognized outstanding achievements, democratic principles, and high ideals in the American way of life. *Call* spokesman Donald Davis said that the award is given to people who "stop talking and really do something." Allen modestly deflected the honor. He noted that about seventy-five other people also work on the show, that he presents the facts as he sees them, and that talent is booked "without thought of race, creed or color."

Allen might not have considered himself a civil rights crusader, but he did speak out against prejudice on several occasions. In his *Ebony* essay, he criticized the exclusion of African Americans from television, as well as the industry's attitude that to include them would be unprofitable: "Television needs the Negro performer and benefits by his contributions to the medium. I consider it unfortunate that this idea is still not generally accepted by the television industry. Certain producers or performers feel that if they use a high percentage of Negroes that perhaps viewers in the South or elsewhere might object. This always seemed to me to be ridiculous thinking. I don't hold with it. And as proof that it is ridiculous, I think I have gotten about two letters or cards that could be said to represent that kind of negative, evil thinking."

Allen might not have been trying to send messages, but some things that came naturally to him sent pointed messages to certain segments of his viewership. Like kissing Lena Horne at the end of her song. "To me," recalled Allen, "it was just the old, traditional, almost meaningless Hollywood kiss. You know, the 'Hi, sweetheart!' kind of thing at a cocktail party. Nowadays, nobody notices it because it's so common. But in the '50s, it drove Southern racists crazy."

Before Bill Harbach ever got involved in Allen's local late-night show, he came to the studio to observe the show for himself and see how it was run. It was there that he witnessed Allen reading a letter from a viewer on the air. "Dear Steve," Harbach recalled Allen reading aloud, "I thought I liked you. The other night, you had Lena Horne on the show, and you kissed her on the cheek. How dare you do a thing like that on television!"

"My mouth opened up," said Harbach. "The audience was still. And then Steve put the letter down, looked into the camera, and started saying, 'This is an absolute bigot. If anybody knows him, he's sick. He should go to a hospital.' And then he did a diatribe on bigotry. I said to myself, 'This guy's for me for the rest of my life,' because this is exactly the way I feel about things."

"The letter made me so angry that I carried it around in my pocket all day and I kept reading it," wrote Allen in a 1955 issue of *Ebony*. "I finally read it on the air and it created a little bit of fuss. The fellow signed himself 'An Irish American,' and I would not have read it except that I am Irish-American myself. I said if this guy would come down to the studio I would be happy to belt him one right in the head. I also said, 'If I find out you're *not* Irish, when you get up I'll knock you down again for signing your letter that way.'

"I lost my temper," Allen later admitted.

Allen's color-blind stance continued beyond *Tonight*. Boxing champ Sugar Ray Robinson, in a rare display of his dancing talent, appeared in a production number on a December 8, 1958, Allen prime-time comedy-variety show. During rehearsal, a network lackey noticed that the choreography of the song-and-dance number, "Mister Success," had Robinson nimbly weaving his way in and out of a line of white and black female dancers. This prompted the man to complain to Harbach, "You can't have him dancing with a white girl." Incensed, Harbach reported the exchange to Allen, who fired back, "Who do they want him to dance with—a plaid girl?"

Beyond Allen's sense of social responsibility, Kitt respected him for his sheer intelligence and genuine interest in other artists. "He didn't ask me dumb, stupid questions. He'd ask things that were meaningful. That manner in which he'd ask the questions gave me the feeling that he cared, which was very stimulating," she said. "This is different from today's shows, where they ask questions such as, 'What was your last album?' They don't think in terms of anything that is profound or of substance. Steve was able to ask more substantial questions to you on the air because he was interested in what you were all about *as well as* what was going on in [show] business."

Horne agreed: "Steve didn't have a dumb show. I liked him. People should know that [he] was a bright, talented, likable guy whose show was smart, funny, and for grown-ups."

Carroll regarded Allen as "an absolute humanitarian and so brilliant that he was humble. There are some people that take in so much information that they understand that there is something special about them, but they don't wish to flaunt it. I think of Steve that way.

"Recently, we lost an incredible human being, Ossie Davis. The feeling that was evoked by his passing was almost the same as when we lost Steve. When you were in their presence, it was spiritual, and you were very fortunate to be here at that time that they were here. I truly felt that way. I was very moved to see that President Clinton was at the Ossie Davis memorial. He touched so many peoples' lives. Steve was exactly the same way. We were privileged to have known Steve Allen. Ossie was a humanitarian, and Steve was the same."

MUSICAL TRIBUTES

Because Steve Allen was himself a musician, singer, and composer, it was no surprise that the *Tonight* show under his watch would introduce the first television musical tributes. Leading composers would appear to showcase their best work. The grand piano would be in the center of the stage, surrounded by bar stools for Allen and the four house singers. For an entire show, the composer—Richard Rodgers, for instance—would play his own music and accompany the singers, telling the story behind how he wrote this song or that song. Allen and conductor Skitch Henderson would also play piano.

The atmosphere was intimate, like having these legends in your living room. Allen noted that "there were no tricks, no production numbers. There was nothing rehearsed, we weren't working off a script, and there were no cue cards. The sheet music was right there on top of the piano. The guys would open it and start to sing whatever song it was."

Other tribute guests included Harold Arlen, Hoagy Carmichael, Burton Lane, and Johnny Mercer. There was producer Bill Harbach's dad, Otto Harbach, lyricist for *Roberta* ("Smoke Gets in Your Eyes"), *Desert Song*, and *No, No, Nanette!* One show was devoted to lyricist Billy Rose. There was also a memorial tribute to George Gershwin featuring his friends and fellow composers, including Oscar Hammerstein; the four *Tonight* singers sang twenty Gershwin classics, Skitch Henderson played a five-minute passage of "Concerto in F" on the piano, and Edward G. Robinson read the eulogy he had read at the composer's funeral in 1938. In addition, said Henderson, there would be "film tributes where we'd do film songs, and then we'd just use the singers and Steve would narrate or play, or I would play. We'd try anything that was thematically musical."

In addition to these tributes, Allen conducted serious panel discussions about musical topics. On a March 1955 show, following Leontyne Price's stirring rendition of "Summertime," Allen led a discussion on the new book *The Agony of Modern Music*, in which its author, Henry Pleasants, argued that modern serious music is neither "modern" nor "music," not enduring, and that the music of Gershwin, Rodgers, or Kern is more valuable. Joining Pleasants on the panel were three other music intellectuals expressing somewhat unexpected viewpoints. The classically trained Skitch Henderson opposed Pleasants's thesis, as did celebrated twentieth-century composer Aaron Copland ("Appalachian Spring"). Concurring with Pleasants was Eric Leinsdorf, the world-renown classical conductor of the Boston Symphony who frequently scheduled Copland's work.

The mere prospect of having a guest of Leinsdorf's stature appear on late-night television would be the equivalent of having the late Chicago Symphony conductor Sir Georg Solti appear on a latter-day *Tonight Show*. Other serious performers were welcome on *Tonight*, including pianist Oscar Levant, who performed Gershwin's "Concerto in F," and Leonard Bernstein, who played selections from "On the Waterfront."

Henderson brought then-unknown pianist Van Cliburn on *Tonight*. At the time, Cliburn was still attending Julliard, and he would not capture the gold medal at the International Tchaikovsky Competition in Moscow until 1958. Henderson admired his artistry. But an NBC ultimatum required that a classical music number not last more than four minutes. Henderson found the perfect solution: He had Cliburn play Gershwin preludes.

During a December 1954 New York newspaper strike, Broadway theaters were desperate to get any publicity for their shows. Harbach remembered being offered the cast of *Kismet* (starring Alfred Drake), fully costumed, to come in on their first anniversary and sing. "I gave them the whole show," said Harbach proudly, "an hour and twenty minutes on *Kismet*, 'cause the show was so hot, and ticket sales the next day went gangbusters."

SHORT-LIVED NETWORK TINKERING

Although NBC programming chief Pat Weaver abandoned his original vision of *Tonight* as the nighttime version of *Today* and its newsmagazine format in favor of Allen's looseness and zaniness, that didn't stop him from injecting elements of his vision into the Allen format. Each of these "service features" (as a network ad for the *Tonight* premiere touted), however, "left those of us who were actually creating it night by night open-mouthed with astonishment,"

said Allen. "Weaver, it bears repeating, was a gifted network pro-
grammer, but that profession has no necessary connection at all
with the actual creating and production of programs. A programming executive simply decides which programs he will carry, and
secondly where they will be placed in his schedule." The results of
the network's suggestions were panned—and for the most part, to
NBC's credit, short-lived.

First, the network insisted on interrupting the middle of the
show with a summary of news, weather, and sports, thereby killing
the momentum generated by the comedy, music, and spontaneity. It
was apparent from the beginning that the compliance by Allen's
team was nominal. Gene Rayburn was stuffed into a broom
closet–sized "NBC Newsroom," sliding graphics mounted on plywood boards and drawing on primitive blackboard weather maps.
The reporting tended to be weighted in favor of the eastern United
States. Critic Janet Kern of the *Chicago American* tartly wrote:

> If viewers stuck with *Tonight* long enough to get the news and weather
> reports, then they might have tuned out with ire in their hearts, after
> hearing a bearded genius report the nation's weather thus: "Rain all
> over the East Coast." This he inscribed in large letters on the New
> York–New England portion of the map. So far as he was concerned,
> the Midwest, West and South could sing for their local weather
> prospects. Then came the "news": "The baseball season opens
> tomorrow. Well, I guess it opened officially today . . . where did I put
> the scores? Oh, well, I know the Cubs and Washington won."
>
> Sometimes, in fact most times, New York TV's love affair with
> New York and its blithe assumption the whole country feels that
> nothing happening west of the Hudson is worth thinking about,
> strikes me as the eighth and greatest wonder of human civilization.

Second, the network mandated nightly reports on skiing conditions around the country. "When Bill Harbach told me about this,"

Allen recalled, "I laughed heartily, as if he'd just said, 'the fellas think we should have a segment every night where we tell people how to cast voodoo spells.' The really funny thing is that the NBC people were absolutely serious."

According to Bill Allen, there might have been some logic in the network's thinking, albeit faulty: "Weaver lived in New York, he probably liked to ski, and he probably saw that these reports worked on the *Today* show. Skiing is also a sport for upscale people, and networks always want to sell advertisers on the fact that they have an upscale audience watching them, which, in turn, commands a higher price for advertising."

Gene Rayburn was stuck with the unhappy task of filling a long and painful five minutes by diagramming weather and ski conditions on a blackboard map. Eventually, the bosses came around. "To the credit of the programmers," wrote Allen, "they came to realize that it was pointless to force us to inform our millions of listeners around the country that there was light snow at Stowe or poor conditions in Aspen. The segment was, after a very brief period, dropped and forgotten."

Third, the network wanted to add a serious drama critic, Robert Joseph, to a cast that emphasized comedy and music. He would review all the new Broadway plays. Allen told his bosses: "(a) a tiny fraction of one percent of our audience would be interested, (b) most of them would live or die without ever having seen a Broadway production, and (c) most plays with unknown actors in leading roles were failures." Allen also noted that Joseph, a personal friend and able critic, "was not exactly a walking bundle of charisma, so that even if some such regular segment could have been justified, he was far from ideal casting for the assignment."

Such tinkering from the top is not unusual, observed Hal Gurnee, who directed the *Tonight* show under Jack Paar and later went on to direct David Letterman's daytime and late-night shows.

At the beginning of a show's run, "the network is in the driver's seat," said Gurnee in 2005. "The network executives get credit for the show's successes at the start. Only when the show isn't getting good numbers, they suggest ways to improve the show. Once the show becomes successful, the executives disappear; they want to stay in the background.

"I remember in the early days of Dave's morning show, the numbers weren't good and people were saying, 'What the hell is this kid doing on a show for housewives?' And we would have to do cooking segments. We realized that we had no idea what we were doing. We'd sit in these meetings, pretending to take notes, and then go out in the hallway and laugh our asses off, because we were so completely against the whole idea of it!

"The funny thing is, if we had listened, and the show had become even slightly successful with housewives, Dave's career would have been over. He would've been doing game shows, and he'd be gone by now. It was the very fact that he resisted that made him successful. We did the cooking segments—and Dave still does them today—but he would introduce Velveeta cheese into every conversation. He would ridicule the cooking. The ones who understood this—especially Martha Stewart—and could deal with Dave's nonsense were the most effective guests."

As the so-called service features suggested by NBC for Allen's early *Tonight* programs were eventually tossed overboard, at least one critic expressed relief and delight: "Allen presumably knew that the keynote to late-night programming is informality, as evidenced by the success of his show when it was telecast only in New York. NBC braintrusters, however, seemed to feel that on the network it should be a nighttime version of Dave Garroway's early-bird *Today*. Steve was burdened with so many gadgets, gimmicks and multiple station breaks that most of the fun vanished. Now, fortunately, Allen runs the show as much as possible like his old local program."

THE GENIUS OF THE STUDIO AUDIENCE

Despite the wealth of comedy talent in front of and behind the *Tonight* cameras, Allen never forgot the genius of the studio audience, with whom he made sure he continued to interact. After mentioning, say, the strawberry festival in Genesee, Wisconsin, in his opening monologue, he might introduce the members of the Fireman's Auxiliary of Mineola, Long Island, sitting in the audience. "What does a fireman's auxiliary do?" shouts Allen to the balcony.

"We make coffee for the firemen," someone shouts back.

"Isn't that an expensive way to put out a fire?"

Another audience query: "Do they get this show in Rochester?"

"Lady," Allen deadpanned, "They *see* this show in Rochester. I don't think they *get* it."

When Steve asked an audience member what he did for a living, the man answered, "I'm an undertaker." Steve shot back, "Are you here on business or pleasure?"

When another man asked, "Why did I have to wait outside for an hour to get in tonight?" Steve quickly responded, "I guess it's because you got here an hour early."

Allen would read letters from the audience. One viewer wrote, "Once I tune in to *Tonight*, I'm dead. I've lost an hour's sleep, but I can't turn it off and I never miss it," to which Allen commented, "We're the only show that comes under the Federal Narcotics Act."

"I like to use mail," Allen told an interviewer. "It makes for a note of reality and believability. The more a person believes what you're saying, the easier it is to make him laugh."

Sometimes the mail got out of control. One Friday night, at ten minutes past midnight, while doing a live, one-minute commercial for the Broil-Quik Super Chef rotisserie oven, Allen casually invited viewers to mail in their names and addresses to become eligible for a drawing to win one of five Broil-Quiks. Within days, 137,831 letters and cards came pouring in. To the sponsor's delight, the drawing required a small swimming pool and a Boy Scout up to his knees in mail.

Upon wandering all the way to the top row, Allen asked a young lady where she was from. "I'm from Seattle," she answered. "And I'm going home tonight," she added with unintended urgency.

The lady's tone struck Allen, as well as the audience, as funny. "Could you give me just a minute or two?" he pleaded. The lady and the audience erupted in laughter. This perhaps exemplifies Allen's gift: Whereas the viewer might sense other hosts in similar situations straining for a punch line, or trying to top what the visitor just said, Allen never had to work that hard—the humor of any situation, any sentence, any silence struck him. Instantly. Effortlessly. The audience would relax, and so would the visitor being interviewed.

"The very first time I saw him on television, I watched him create the art of conversation," observed Dick Clark, veteran TV host (*American Bandstand*) and producer. "He sounded like an ordinary guy, even though he wasn't. He was extraordinary. But he sounded like he was talking just to me. And I stole that, and I used it for years and years. I can't fathom the mind he had. He was superior in every way. But I noticed that when he talked to me or to anybody, he was so kind. He didn't lord that superiority over you."

One night, Allen came upon three elderly women who introduced themselves simply as "reindeer." When pressed to explain exactly what it is that reindeer do, one lady answered, "We pay sick benefits." It was an organization, it turned out, named "The Reindeer." But when Allen inquired what the organization stood for or what else it did, no one seemed to know. No one, it turned out, had ever received any sick benefits. Every woman in the group—about twenty-seven scattered throughout the studio audience—had become a member because some other woman asked her to. Perhaps, thought Allen out loud, the group was not a social club but an

111

insurance company that either insured the healthiest group of women in the United States, or enjoyed an extremely large treasury. "There must be at least one member of your group who has been laid up with something or other," said Allen. "I'd like to speak to the treasurer of your club. Where is she sitting?"

"She's not here with us tonight," the lady on the aisle said.

"Oh? Where is she?" Allen asked.

"She's home sick."

Wandering into audiences night after night, Allen frequently ranted about how mentions of cities and towns command instant audience ovations. An audience will sit on its hands when, for example, a woman says she has borne thirteen children, but people will clap like crazy when she adds that she lives in Brooklyn.

The audience interviews frequently ended with Allen presenting the participant with a sponsor-furnished gift: a record album, a toaster, a watch, a KitchenAid food mixer, a lei flown in from Hawaii by United Airlines, or more whimsical items, such as a three-foot slab of Hebrew National salami. If the gift seemed not quite right, Allen would gently remind the recipient, "This is a new type of give-away program: *Take What You Can Get.*"

On another night, after interviewing others in the audience, Allen eventually came to a lady and announced, "Ladies and gentlemen, this is Mrs. Sammy Snead, the wife of the famous golfer." Everybody applauded very respectfully. Allen asked her, "Did Sammy have any superstitions when he plays golf?" She answered, "Yes, before each game I kiss his balls."

The camera went on Allen. "He just didn't change the expression on his face," recalled Steve Lawrence. "And the longer he stayed with it, the longer [director] Dwight [Hemion] stayed on him, and the audience got hysterical. Tears were coming out of [Dwight's] eyes. The audience got hysterical laughing, and of course, they didn't stop for about two minutes. And Mrs. Snead realized what she said and blurted, 'I mean, his *golf* balls!' Which made it even worse. It was one of the funniest deadpans that I've ever seen on live television."

Bob Costas, who hosted a late-night talk show, *Later with Bob Costas* on NBC, observed, "One great strength that Allen had was that he could simultaneously be performer and audience. He could be an excellent audience, and therefore the larger audience itself could take its cue from him, with that very distinctive sort of rat-a-tat laugh that he has. That poker-faced look of, 'What's going on here now?' or that almost says, 'There's nothing I can add to that,' or lets the audience think along with you like, 'I'm digesting that now,' or 'I'm digesting that and aren't you trying to figure out what I'm gonna say next?'"

"No one actually brought the audience into it like Steve did," believed Michael Feldman, the witty host of NPR's long-running live audience radio program, *Whad'Ya Know?* "He did a kind of stream-of-consciousness that I related to. I thought he was funniest going off on a tangent with something that he found amusing or interesting. And to me, it's all about tangents—they really aren't tangents. The tangent, to me, is sort of where it's at, where it's funny. The tangent's what it's about!"

But not everyone who came to sit in the *Tonight* audience was hoping to be seen on national TV. There was one night when Allen, mike in hand, approached a man, whereupon the woman standing next to him made a mad dash away and into the crowd. "Where's she going?" Allen asked.

"Oh," the man said and shrugged, "she's just afraid my wife will see me with her."

Chapter 3

THE MOST IMITATED MAN
IN TELEVISION

In attempting to entertain an audience for ninety minutes every night, Steve Allen and his innovative Tonight *team created a template for their many successors. Not only has the general format of the show been successfully appropriated for the past five decades, but even specific elements and actual routines have been "borrowed" by many of Allen's successors. Much of what has succeeded on late-night talk shows was introduced, in some form, during the first three years of* Tonight, *the New York–based late-night* Steve Allen Show *that preceded it, or the Sunday night prime-time or syndicated nightly* Steve Allen Shows *that followed it. Even the roaring "WHOA-OH!" whoop from the studio audience that greets most late-night hosts to this day was started by Allen's trombone player, Frank Rosolino, and picked up by the entire band and audience of the original* Tonight *show.*

Stan Burns, Allen's first writer on Tonight, *once wryly suggested that the home video compilations of Johnny Carson's* Tonight *years should be retitled* The Best of Carson AND Steve! *In a 1995* Comic Relief *salute to Allen's prime-time show, Whoopi Goldberg described it "as the most widely imitated TV show ever. You've seen elements of it on very successful talk shows, variety shows, magazine shows, and even lately on the news."*

"AND THE QUESTION IS . . ."

"*A*nd now, ladies and gentlemen," proclaims Ed McMahon, "I present to you . . . Carnac the Magnificent!" Amid the band's ceremonial fanfare, enter Johnny Carson, dressed in a swami robe and a bejeweled turban. He bumbles his way across the stage and takes his seat at the desk. Ed presents him with a sealed envelope, the contents of which, he makes abundantly clear, have been seen by no one. Johnny solemnly holds the envelope to his temple. After careful concentration, he divines a sentence, a phrase, or a word— often something out of pop culture, such as a movie title. Ed repeats the set-up line for emphasis. After the two exchange a series of pseudoserious looks and asides, Ed continues the ritual: "And the question is?" Johnny tears open the side of the envelope, squeezes it open, blows into it, pulls out a card, and reads the question. The question is the punch line.

Johnny and Ed etched "Carnac" into America's consciousness during nearly thirty years of broadcasting this routine, but it was Steve who introduced the concept to television in two forms. First, there was Allen's "The Question Man," which originated on the Allen *Tonight* show and became a staple on his 1956–60 Sunday night prime-time series. An announcer, usually Tom Poston, would feed Allen, as the omniscient but eccentric Question Man, an answer consisting of sentence, phrase, word, or even a telephone number, often flashed on the screen. Allen, sporting a fake mustache and old-fashioned swallow-tail coat, his dangling, greased hair parted down the center, would repeat the set-up line for emphasis. The announcer would ask, "And the question is?" Allen would divine the punch line:

ANNOUNCER: Butterfield 8-3000.
STEVE: How many hamburgers did Butterfield eat?

* * * * * *

ANNOUNCER: Mad Hatter, White Rabbit, Cheshire Cat, Dormouse and the Queen of Hearts.
STEVE: Name a lousy poker hand.

* * * * * *

ANNOUNCER: A loaf of bread, a jug of wine, and thou.
STEVE: What's on a cannibal's menu?

* * * * * *

ANNOUNCER: Go West.
STEVE: What do wabbits do when they are tired of wunning awound?

* * * * * *

ANNOUNCER: The Los Angeles Dodgers.
STEVE: How would you describe pedestrians in Southern California?

* * * * * *

ANNOUNCER: Daisy Mae.
STEVE: Do you think Daisy will?

* * * * * *

ANNOUNCER: The United States Steel Hour and the United States Missile Program.
STEVE: Name a dramatic program and a comedy program.

117

A second Allen routine was "The Great Swami Allen," a sort of mystic Ann Landers, which had Allen dressed in a swami's robe and turban. Announcer Gene Rayburn would read a letter containing a question, usually seeking advice, and Allen would deliver the punchline:

> ANNOUNCER: My husband passed away twenty-five years ago. But when I go into the living room, I can still see him sitting there by the fire. What should I do?
> STEVE: Bury him.

Not long after Allen introduced "The Question Man," a Los Angeles radio comic, Bob Arbogast, contacted Allen and informed him that he had thought of the Question Man idea several years before Allen and his team did. "When I satisfied myself that this was indeed the case, I promptly told Arbogast that I would be quite willing to either immediately stop doing the routine or else give him both money and public credit every time we did it." Arbogast opted for the latter. It was a smart move. Allen continued to do the routine for several decades, both on television and in concerts, and Arbogast himself periodically contributed material. A collection of routines from the show formed the basis of the 1959 best-selling book, *The Question Man*, in which Allen credited Arbogast in the foreword.

In his 1992 autobiography, *Hi-Ho, Steverino!* Allen wrote: "*The Great Carnac*—as scores of journalists have observed—is a precise copy of *The Question Man* with a funny hat." Dick Cavett, who hosted a late-night talk show on ABC (1969–72), wrote in his autobiography, "Steve Allen's Question Man went into swami drag and became Johnny's Carnac." Whether deliberate or not, *Carnac* reflected elements of both Allen's *Question Man* and *Great Swami Allen*. Compare the following examples of *Carnac* from 1989 and 1972, with "The Question Man" from 1958 (the season during which Carson made his first two appearances on the prime-time *Steve Allen Show*):

Carnac (1989):

ANSWER: A nail, a board, and an S&L customer.
QUESTION: Name something that's hammered, something that's sawed, and something that's screwed.

Question Man (1958):

ANSWER: Khrushchev, pistol, clarinet, Lincoln Highway, and carrot.
QUESTION: Name a red, a rod, a reed, a road, and a root.

* * * * * * *

Carnac (1972):

ANSWER: Around the world in 80 days.
QUESTION: What can a flight from L.A. to San Diego turn into?

Question Man (1958):

ANSWER: Around the world in 80 days.
QUESTION: What was the slogan of the airline that went out of business?

Even the infamous curses that Carnac would occasionally offer up ("May a desert scorpion seek shelter in your shorts!") bore an uncanny stylistic resemblance to the following curse inflicted by the Great Swami Allen on his straight man, Gene Rayburn, on the March 8, 1956, broadcast: "May the time-honored bones of your fat, greasy ancestors remain untouched by human hands throughout the everlasting dynasty of the great freem in the sky!"

Allen reported that Arbogast did try to stop the Carson *Tonight*

Show from doing the routine, but he "never received any acknowledgment from the show of his attempt to protect his creation."

"THE LATE SHOW PITCHMAN"

Carson also popularized a character named Art Fern, a fast-talking pitchman who hosted afternoon movie reruns peppered with the forerunners to today's tacky infomercials. The recurring routine was called "The Tea-Time Movie with Art Fern" and became one of Johnny's best-known recurring routines, featured at least three times on *The Ultimate Carson* DVD collection released in 2001.

On his *Tonight* show, Allen originated "The Late Show Pitchman," in which he played a fast-talking host of a late-night movie program who subjected his viewers to high-pressure commercials. In those days, many local stations ran old movies late at night, and announcer-hucksters on these shows, called pitchmen, would hawk slicer-dicers, broil-quick tabletop ovens, blenders, hair tonics, and knife-sharpening sets. Allen spoofed health insurance with "the Double-Cross Hospital Plan." He cheerfully extolled the amenities of "Mother Finster's Resort," a dubious vacation spot: "You'll have breakfast in bed . . . because the dining room is filthy!"

Allen found the similarities between his "Pitchman" and Carson's "Art Fern" uncanny, "right down to the showing of old film clips and Art Fern's wearing of a dark wig and mustache. In fact, the word *fern* itself was one of the original *Tonight* staff's standard double-talkisms, with Louis Nye as the originator."

Compare the following excerpt from an "Art Fern" sketch from 1982 (pitching a knife) with one from a "Late Show Pitchman" sketch from 1956 (pitching spot remover) and another from 1959 (pitching a swimming pool):

"Art Fern" (1982): "Friends, you can own the GIPSU (knife) not for $9.95, not for $7.95, and not for $5.95, but only $134.38."

"Late Show Pitchman" (1956): "Don't forget the price of Spotto Cleaner—only $1.50—and you also get a Spotto Cleaner rag, all at that low price of $4.75! . . . This is strictly a TV offer. You can't buy it at your local store, because it's been banned by the Better Business Bureau, and the price is still a measly $35.69! We give you two weeks to try it in your own home—just time enough for us to get out of town. What do you want for only $78.23?"

"Late Show Pitchman" (1959): "Now here's the good news. You can get a complete Barracuda Pool for the low, low price of $1,600. That's what I said, $2,000. Imagine that, only $7,500. Why, where else could you get a swimming pool like this for $15,000? And friends, once you've paid $22,000 for a Barracuda Pool, you'll *know* you've been *soaked.*"

Both Fern and the Pitchman had dubious real estate to peddle. In 1986, Fern was offering "The San Andreas Village Estates": "At our home sites, friends, there are lots of fun outdoor activities, such as quicksand jogging." But nearly thirty years earlier, the Pitchman was offering "Shamble Acres": "When you actually see these fine homes, you'll be anxious to get settled in one. And it won't take you long to get settled, because each home is built on *quicksand.*"

Allen took pains to deny an Allen-Carson feud: "Since the news media thrive on controversy, it is probably inevitable that these observations, though entirely factual, will somehow be taken as justification for some sort of Allen-puts-down-Carson stories. If only to forestall that possibility, I will set down here, once and for all for the record, my opinion that Johnny Carson has done an absolutely superb job of hosting the *Tonight Show* during his years at the helm," wrote Allen in his 1992 autobiography. "I enjoyed his work long before he had had experience at talk show hosting and used to occasionally book him to do his own always clever routines on my prime-time NBC comedy series. Unlike some popular comedians, Johnny has always written a certain amount of his material and has deservedly become a national institution due to his over quarter-century of experience as America's king of late-night TV."

Following his retirement from the *Tonight Show* and professional entertainment in 1992, Johnny Carson declined nearly all requests for interviews. When asked to do one of the first interviews for this book, his personal assistant, Helen Sanders, wrote politely but firmly that he was declining to participate. When asked again a year later, Ms. Sanders replied that he was declining to provide even written comments, but she did acknowledge that her boss respected Allen's talent and conveyed his best wishes for the success of the book.

In February 2005, a few weeks after Carson's death, Ed McMahon, who had spoken warmly and publicly about Allen on many occasions (including Larry King's panel tributes to Allen), agreed to be interviewed about Allen for this book. But before a firm date could be scheduled, McMahon changed his mind, citing his desire to save his comments for a book he was planning to write about his life with Johnny.

FROM STEVE ON THE STREET TO JAY WALKING

Jay Leno's popular "Jay Walking" is descended from one of Allen's favorite *Tonight* routines in which he would open the back door of the studio, point a camera outside onto the sidewalk, walk out into the night, and try to engage passersby in extemporaneous conversation. One night, Allen dressed up in a policeman's uniform and began stopping traffic on live television. "Sorry, sir," he said to the first motorist who slowed down, "but this is border patrol and we're making a spot check for contraband."

"What band?" asked the befuddled driver.

"I just wanted to know if you're smuggling any fruits or nuts."

"No. Absolutely not!" Back inside the theater, the audience roared.

"Drive on," Allen instructed, "and remember, the life you save . . . may not be worth it."

In his later shows and specials, Allen would walk the streets asking passersby a serious question, only to receive the dimmest answers. In a "Steve on the Street" segment from the early 1980s, he asked, "If a person running for the presidency of the United States was an acknowledged *heterosexual*, could you vote for him or her?"

"No. No way!" adamantly declared one woman.

"I'd vote for *her*," specified one man. "Not for *him*."

After a lengthy, thoughtful pause, another man answered, "Yes," in a noble, open-minded tone of voice. Rising to the occasion, he continued: "Every person is entitled to his own beliefs, his own way of life. You judge a man on his capabilities, not on his private life."

"Head-over-sexual?" wondered a lady named Josephine.

When a raspy-voiced older woman with a thick Brooklyn accent immediately blurted yes, Allen asked if she had ever voted for a heterosexual. "Oh, no, no, you're talkin' about sexual?" she asked, now scandalized by the question. "No, no, no. I'd nevah vote fah *that*!"

Years later, on a typical "Jay Walking," Jay walks the streets. At a college commencement reception, he asked one of the cap-and-gown-clad graduates if she knew anything about the Gettysburg Address. After hemming and hawing, she responded, "I don't know the *exact* address." And then there was this exchange with two giggling coeds on spring break:

JAY: If you were going to the UK, where would you be going?
COED NO. 1: The Ukraine.

COED NO. 2 (laughing at COED NO. 1): No, wait. The United
   Kingdom.
JAY: And the United Kingdom is where?
COED NO. 2: Disney World.

As Jay later explained to his *Tonight Show* audience in a tribute to
Allen in 2000, "[Steve] would go out in the street and talk to people
and bring them in, which is essentially what we do now on 'Jay
Walking.' He was there first. He did it. That's from watching Steve
Allen as a kid."

ZANY STUNTS

There were assorted one-time stunts that cultivated Allen's reputation as a brainy prankster. One stunt had him opening the show by
frying hundreds of eggs in a thirteen-foot-diameter frying pan on the
sidewalk on 44th Street outside the Hudson Theatre, while another
show found him hawking frankfurters to passersby. One night, Allen
flagged a taxi in front of the Hudson Theatre. "Where to, chief?"
asked the driver amiably.

"Just take this to Grand Central, and hurry!" Allen instructed,
opening the rear door and flinging a giant salami onto the backseat.
The driver immediately sped off into the night, and "the audience
laughed so loudly that they sounded like a football crowd," recalled
Allen. "We never heard from the driver after the show, and I have
often wondered why he shot off down the street following such an
insane order."

Some other stunts included Allen playing piano while sitting in
a swimming pool, a tire-changing race in the street outside the
studio, and a helium demonstration by Mr. Wizard (Don Herbert)
that raised the voices of the *Tonight* regulars to chipmunklike

octaves, as well as Allen getting lessons from kooky teachers in bird calling, hula dancing, and cigar rolling.

A hypnotist appeared one night and threw Gene Rayburn into a trance, balancing his body between two chairs. "He was perfectly straight," remembered singer Pat Marshall, "and the hypnotist sat on Gene's stomach—with no support! The next day, we were on the plane leaving for Florida; the whole show went to Miami Beach. Gene was not feeling good. His muscles were sore."

The idea for another stunt, obviously designed to underscore Allen's "Everyguy" image, was born when Bill Harbach's brother Bob appeared one night on the show. According to writer Herb Sargent, people noticed an uncanny resemblance between Harbach's brother and Allen—same tall frame, side-parted black hair, and dark horn-rimmed glasses. So, for the next two weeks, it was announced that only young men who looked like Steve Allen would be admitted to the theater on a certain date. Sargent and fellow writer Stan Burns were able to fill the studio with four hundred look-alikes—with Allen himself sitting anonymously in the audience.

These and other stunts on the *Tonight* show set the stage for more classic stunts on Allen's post-*Tonight* programs in the '60s in which Allen would leap into vat of Jell-O; get outfitted as a human tea bag and hoisted into a vat of water; clumsily fly in a wire harness over the streets of Hollywood as a Superman wannabe; attempt to become airborne while strapped to an eight-foot kite, facing a powerful industrial turbo fan; bathe in a tub perched above the theater marquis; get outfitted in swim trunks and pasted with dog food immediately before a herd of friendly but hungry dogs was unleashed on the stage; and mud-wrestle with one tough female opponent.

These shows blazed the trail for Allen's most devoted follower, David Letterman, who regularly staged stunts in the Allen tradition on *Late Night with David Letterman*. On the night Allen died, Letterman reminisced with his audience:

When we started doing the morning show on NBC in 1980, we needed a show to do, so what we would do on that show and later on the old *Late Night* show—we would steal all of our ideas from the old *Steve Allen Show*. He had a lot of good ideas because in those days in television, they had plenty of time and no money, and he was terrific because he was endlessly resourceful and gifted and had a great mind for stuff to do on television.

And so we just said, "Well, heck, let's just steal all of those great ideas!" And we did. And to our credit—and this is the only thing for which we deserve credit—when we did that, we would say, "Here's something Steve Allen used to do."

In a direct nod to Allen's "Human Tea Bag," Dave was slowly deposited into a water tank, emblazoned from his shoulders down with hundreds of Alka-Seltzer tablets. There was Dave sprawled out in an oversized glass cereal bowl, while three vats of milk were poured on him. In another Allenesque stunt, Dave and bandleader Paul Shaffer engaged in a rolling chair race in which their desk chairs were propelled backward by fire extinguishers that each held to power and steer his chair down NBC's long hallways.

In May 2005, Dave was continuing to entertain audiences with wild stunts on the street outside his theater, including throwing an assortment of things off the roof of his building and hoisting eighty-year-old film legend Paul Newman high over the streets of Manhattan, suspended by more than six thousand helium-filled party balloons.

Allen's audiences were also conscripted for stunts. For his Hollywood-based early '60s talk/variety series, writer Stan Burns recruited a hundred volunteers for a tug-of-war match—against a live elephant. The goal was to pull the poor elephant over a white line. The audience tugged valiantly, the elephant took two effortless steps backward, and everybody went flying over the line.

That might have been the end of a cute stunt, except then the elephant broke loose and stampeded down the street. "This is at midnight," Burns recalled. "It was live, and people were opening their windows, and they see this crazy elephant thundering down the street. The biggest thing in the world. A little drunken jockey, a small guy, sees the elephant." Instead of scrambling out of the way, the little guy stops. "He goes out to the center of the street and holds up his hand, and then the elephant stops *right in front of him!* Unplanned. And this was just another night on the show."

Another night saw what Burns dubbed "the largest pie fight in the world." Unsuspecting audience members were given plastic raincoats to put on. Next, the cast did a pie bit on stage. The action moved into the audience. Soon, everybody was getting in the mood for pies, and two hundred people began throwing pies at each other. "We did these things," said Burns, "and it was not only funny, but it was so offbeat that people would watch. They'd ask, 'What's going to happen tomorrow?'"

Unpredictability, according to Burns, was one of the few qualities that Allen's *Tonight* shared with Jack Paar's *Tonight*. Paar, Allen's first successor, is credited with narrowing the *Tonight* format into mainly conversation. "Paar didn't do anything but talk, which was fabulous because he was such a neurotic character. So people would stare at him. What's he gonna do? Is he gonna quit? Is he gonna throw up? That's why they watched him. And he had great guests. That was a *talk* show. We did a *variety* show."

FUN WITH NEWSPAPERS

In Allen's radio and early television shows, he gravitated to reading funny items in the papers. On *Tonight* he developed a satirical variation called "Letters to the Editor." Allen and his guests would take turns reading aloud overheated, angry letters that actually appeared in newspapers such as the *New York Daily News*. Explained Allen, "Letters like these are written in anger and should be read the same way." And that's exactly what he and his guests did, peppering their recitations with angry emphasis, eliciting growls and catcalls from the audience.

The twist, however, was that the readers would change the authors' names to something incongruous to the text. A letter decrying the rise of rock-and-roll was read as having been signed by Elvis Presley. A modern-day letter, suggested Allen, might go something like this: "It's an absolute disgrace the way young women are dressing these days, baring their bodies to excite men to lust! Signed, Madonna." The routine became so popular that guest stars like Jerry Lewis, Milton Berle, and distinguished dramatic actor Charles Laughton volunteered for the chance to get screaming mad.

Jay Leno continues the tradition by regularly mining newspapers for humor in his popular "Headlines" routines, where he reads and shows strange headlines submitted by viewers. "The headlines that we do," Leno told his audience in 2000, "are Steve Allen picking up the *Daily News* or the *Post* or whatever paper it was at the time and reading the letters to the editor."

AUDIENCE TIGHT SHOTS

Allen and his writing team invented a running sketch that became unique to the live television studio audience format. They would take tight shots, or close-ups, of the faces of preselected audience members, give them fake names, and script routines around them, usually in the form of "The Missing Persons Report," "The FBI's 10 Most Wanted," or the summation of an ongoing soap opera saga like "As the Stomach Turns" (a title that *Tonight* writer Stan Burns would use again for a running soap spoof he developed for *The Carol*

Burnett Show fifteen years later) or the more frequently used title, "The Edge of Cancellation." The latter was a parody of the title of a popular soap of the day, *The Edge of Night*. Allen first introduced the sketch by warning viewers to prepare for "daring exposés that will set your TV on fire."

The humor sprang partly from the writing, but the laughter was catalyzed by the reaction of the unsuspecting person, startled to suddenly see himself on the studio monitor as the unsavory character Allen had just described. The person might laugh, cover her face, look shocked, become self-conscious, or—after several seconds— become the last person in the audience to discover her face in the monitor. Here's a taste of an early routine from a 1954 *Tonight* show:

[CLOSE-UP OF A NICELY DRESSED WOMAN IN AUDIENCE]

STEVE: This woman's face was feared by three major networks.

[CUT TO TOUGH-LOOKING MAN IN AUDIENCE]

STEVE: This man's past was a mystery. Why did he have his hand to his face? Why was he smiling? He came out of nowhere to the head of the ticket line. His seat was saved by the woman in black. What strange power did he hold over the fourth row?

These sketches required quick, nimble moves shortly before air. During the warm-up, Allen and his writers would size up the audience for faces matching the characters called for in the sketches. He would read his writers' first draft of the sketch, while director Dwight Hemion would take separate shots of the visitors.

At airtime, as the routine unfolded, ad libbing was still necessary. For example, a woman, startled to see herself on the studio monitor, might suddenly cup her hand over her mouth in embarrassment. This would prompt Allen to ad-lib, "Freda can, of course, be recognized by her tendency to clutch at her upper plate in moments of emotional stress."

Allen continued these sketches throughout his era of *Tonight* and in his 1960s and '70s *Steve Allen Shows*. Eventually, he heard from fans and writers that these routines were continually being appropriated by Johnny Carson, or that Carson was being credited for creating them. In the 1992 book, *Here's Johnny!* for example, author Stephen Cox recounted *The Edge of Wetness*, a running soap opera spoof in which a camera took tight shots of audience members whom Carson introduced as residents of that sordid town, Sludge Falls, and about whom he read the most embarrassing exploits. According to Cox's sources, the bit was originally a television routine written in 1964 by comedian Pat McCormick for Jonathan Winters, and it was Carson who adapted it for his own *Tonight Show*. It is a fact, however, that a good ten years before McCormick, an Allen fan himself, ever wrote his routines for Winters, Allen and his *Tonight* team had already established audience tight shots as a successful running gag, complete with a title parodying *The Edge of Night*.

Allen wrote a letter of protest to Carson's *Tonight Show* producers. "The response to my letter—alas—was a blank-faced denial of plagiarism and a claim that their own writers had thought of the idea independently. Even in the unlikely event that they had, the simple fact that our show had repeatedly done the sketches starting more than 20 years earlier would have settled the issue, had the matter been taken to court, or even to Writer's Guild arbitration," Allen wrote in his 1992 autobiography.

CRAZY SHOTS

"Crazy Shots" emerged as Allen grew bored with the seemingly limited number of ways he could be photographed playing serious piano numbers. So Dwight Hemion shot Allen playing from offbeat angles, such as a close-up of Allen's left eye. This evolved to a series of quick-cut, cartoonlike, visual non sequiturs—incongruous, illogical, and humorous. One scene might show a woman yawning and closing her eyes, revealing another set of wide-open eyes painted on her eyelids. Another scene might be set in a cemetery, revealing two empty milk bottles next to a tombstone, one with a note sticking up; a milkman would enter, look at the note, and replace the empty bottles with full ones. There'd be five seconds of fish swimming around in an office water cooler. "There'd be unusual shots of Steve playing the piano," Bill Harbach said. "Or we'd go through Steve's glasses and dissolve. We'd do about twelve shots a number."

"It was Steve's idea to go away from the piano," said Hemion, who found it unusual but refreshing to leave the star performer out of the shot. The "Crazy Shots" concept of non-sequitur blackouts was eventually appropriated on *Rowan and Martin's Laugh-In*, starting with its premiere telecast in 1967. "Dan Rowan, Dick Martin, and [producer] George Schlatter were personal friends," said Allen, "and they were always kind enough to acknowledge publicly that they had borrowed the routine from our repertoire."

Decades later, the concept would become embedded in the entertainment subconscious. Rick Ludwin, NBC's current senior vice president of specials, variety programs, and late night, brought up "The Staring Contest," once a regular bit between Conan O'Brien and sidekick Andy Richter, in which Richter, distracted by something he was seeing over Conan's shoulder, would always lose the contest: "They're doing 'Crazy Shots'! I bet they don't even realize what 'Crazy Shots' is. That's a direct example of a bit that would have been right at home on Steve Allen's show. There's no question that the style of comedy was influenced by what Steve did. Conan's love for comedy is for the cartoony and the absurd. He was definitely influenced by Steve Allen in the sense of not only admiring him personally, but also the kind of anarchistic comedy that Steve began in the mid-'50s continues today on the Conan O'Brien show."

REAL PEOPLE: FROM ECCENTRIC AND
OFFBEAT GUESTS TO "STUPID HUMAN TRICKS"

As evidenced by the success of such modern-day departments as David Letterman's "Stupid Human Tricks" and "Audience Show-and-Tell," real people were ultimately more integral to *Tonight*'s success than guest stars, contended writer Stan Burns:

> If you had Henry Fonda on, and he did a sketch, it was okay—but it was *normal*. The sketches weren't that important except for "Man on the Street," which was very good because we had our own characters every day, every night. The guest stars came on just for the rating and the idea of having guest stars. But the main thrust was Steve Allen, audience participation, and offbeat guests that made the show.
>
> I would come to Steve and say, "There's a guy that can pick up a table with his teeth, and he's got the strongest ears in the world." And people would tune in just to see if he could do it.

The guy's name was Joe Interleggi, a cheerful, young Italian immigrant. Allen greeted him at the curb outside the Hudson Theatre and watched as the diminutive Interleggi affixed ropes to his ears with clothespins and began hauling a truck that was hitched to the ropes by crawling backwards on his hands and feet.

As Allen congratulated him following the stunt, the ebullient Interleggi mustered the nerve to ask "MistaSteveAllen" (as he always called him) if he could sing a few songs. Allen, startled by the request, said there was no time (there was another act waiting to go on) but invited Interleggi to return another night. Interleggi, however, mustered even more nerve to plead for just one song—in Italian.

Allen relented: "Cancel the next act," he said, as he and Interleggi reentered the stage through the open elephant stage doors. Without a musical cue, Interleggi broke into a spirited rendition of

"A Compare." Skitch Henderson and the band began improvising to match the key of their impromptu singer. Allen began clapping to the beat, and the street crowd that had gathered around the open elephant doors began clapping, too, as did the audience in the theater. Allen and Gene Rayburn broke into an Irish jig. For someone who didn't audition, Interleggi could carry a tune, and charmingly at that. It was a brilliant moment, with all the makings of a scene from a Broadway musical.

Except none of it was planned.

Interleggi became a popular *Tonight* guest, whom Allen dubbed "the Human Termite" because he "ate" wood, or at least could bite holes into any piece of wood. "MistaSteveAllen," he would say, "I wanna thank you for havin' me here. MistaSteveAllen, you a good guy. MistaSteveAllen, we all love you. MistaSteveAllen, I will now lift a kitchen table with-a my teeth."

On another occasion, Interleggi dangled a large woman sitting in a chair three feet above the stage, using only his teeth and a clothesline tied around her waist and the chair. While suspended in midair, the woman let out a nervous squeal, which, Allen recalled, "apparently unnerved Interleggi so much that he let the rope slip from his usually mighty jaws," causing the woman to come tumbling onto the stage. To complicate matters, Interleggi had carpeted the floor with crushed glass for dramatic effect. Fortunately, the understandably upset woman escaped with lacerations on her kneecaps.

Stan Burns observed that modern-day late-night shows do the same thing. "They hire a 104-year-old guy who stands on his head. They hire animal people. We did that. Carson did that, too. But we started with the offbeat people. That's what Letterman and Leno do every night. They get the oldest person, the youngest person, the person who stayed underwater for three days. We did that. We had people come in from all over, such weird offbeat people, which we didn't embarrass, but they went along with the laughs. 'Good sports,' as Steve would say."

The Allen *Tonight* show also regularly featured novelty guests, which usually made for entertaining interviews. There was Max Conrad, a songwriting pilot who had recently flown solo across the Atlantic. There was Blanche Scott, the first licensed woman pilot. There were Washington Dodge and Katherine Manning, two survivors of the *Titanic*. There was eighty-four-year-old Mme. Inga Christensen, the world's oldest concert pianist.

Then there were the eccentric and offbeat guests who were, well, way out there. Bill Harbach liked to describe them as "out in left field." There was Marie Mann, the Hat Check Queen, and Miriam Silverman, a weight guesser. There was Mrs. Sparrow, a palmist also known as "The Wish Bone Lady," and George Ito, a fire eater who did a live demonstration. There was Prince Robert, also known as The Prince of Hobos, as well as a man who hoarded five tons of chicken bones.

Long before Joan Embery and Jim Fowler brought their exotic animals from the San Diego Zoo to visit the Johnny Carson *Tonight Show*, Ripp Murray brought his collection of scorpions, lizards, and tarantulas to share with Allen and his viewers. Evelyn Curry did a lion-training demo. Bill Esenwein did a rattlesnake demo without protection. (Program notes attempted to reassure that he had never been bitten in five years.) Another snake handler, Bill Haast, brought in an eight-foot king cobra. H. S. Gatchell brought his dog, Kid, who could understand two thousand words. Mr. Trowbridge, a worm-farm owner, brought his worms with him. Professor Wilner hypnotized animals.

It was apparent that Allen understood the fun of having live creatures onstage. Jim Moran was a publicist who would bring exotic animals on the show. One night he brought a kinkajou, a raccoon-like mammal. Steve Lawrence: "He walked on, Steve greeted him, and they shook hands. Steve asked him what the animal did, and seemingly on cue, the animal peed. Without missing a beat, Steve asked him, 'So what does he do for his next trick?' This was live television." (In post-*Tonight* talk shows in the late '60s, he would do bits with live tigers, elephants, seals, and camels).

Mr. Drapo made ladies' dresses in thirty seconds. With great flourish, he would quickly cut a generous amount an elegant fabric from a roll and mold it into a high-style dress—live, onstage, right on the body of a beautiful, slip-clad model. The fact that so glamorous an outfit could be concocted in just thirty seconds was a comment on popular fashion. Then it was Allen's turn to try his hand at high-speed dressmaking, but the results were not exactly chic. While Skitch and the band played "Flight of the Bumblebee" in the background, Allen awkwardly and hilariously found himself bundling his model in excess yards of fabric.

Jack Walsh demonstrated his weight-lifting skills by lifting an elephant and supporting a truck. Bill Pacarro was a "shoe sitter," someone who breaks in the new shoes of hotel guests. Leona Anderson demonstrated how she acquired the title of World's Worst Singer.

Reflective of the era, there were several beauty "Misses," such as Miss Human Christmas Tree, Miss National Can Opener Queen, Miss Foam Bedding of 1956, Miss Peach, Miss Chip Dip, Miss California Grapes, and—perhaps the most imaginatively named—Miss Cheese Cake Made of Corn.

Shannon Bolin read Allen's ears to determine his fortune. Rochelle Forrest did the same thing by reading Allen's palms and feet.

There were daredevil-stunt artists like Garrett Cashman, who parachuted from the eighth floor of a Miami Beach hotel into the swimming pool, and The Amazing Randy, who hung from a crane sixty feet in the air by his feet.

Still other guests for Allen to interview included a snake charmer, an inventor, a spiritualist, an authority on spaceships, an eighty-year-old bicyclist with a long white beard, and a lady woodchopper.

By popular demand, Mrs. Diehl and her laughing parrots made repeat appearances. Her parrots imitated laughing sounds and repeated them relentlessly. One of the shows that aired from Miami Beach closed with an extended taste of this laughter.

David Pollock, a writer and producer of Allen's late '60s and early '70s-era shows, attributed the success of these spots to two requisite elements: "The guest had to be sincere and completely on the level, and Steve could not know what was going to happen. His own instinct for the absurd would immediately take over as he was instructed how to play oriental gongs with vegetables, wrap a huge tobacco leaf into the shape of a cigar, or perform exotic Hindu dances. Steve just made these segments happen."

The studio audience was also a gold mine for found humor. A couple of college-age girls had sent Allen a note during a station break saying that they were Irish lasses from Brooklyn who wanted to demonstrate Hawaiian hula dancing, which had become a national minicraze in the years leading up to Hawaii's admission to the Union in 1959 as the fiftieth state. Allen called the girls, who identified themselves as "Dressy and Spicy," to come up. Once onstage, dressed in their un-Hawaiian-like western sweaters and skirts, they kicked off their shoes and launched into a spunky, jitterbug-tinged hula. It just so happened that Woody Herman and his big band were behind the curtain, setting up for their formal spot later in the show, and they backed the girls with an impromptu version of "The Hawaiian War Chant," an appropriately high-energy hula number.

Studio Audience Regulars

While wading through the audience one night, Allen found Carmen Mastren, a short, stocky, middle-aged man with a thick accent of undetermined origin. Carmen regularly attended the *Tonight* show, and whenever Allen came to his seat, he would ask to sing.

STEVE: And what song would you like to do for us?
CARMEN: "Ev'rybody Doin' It."
STEVE: In what key?
CARMEN (*authoritatively*): A.

An unsmiling, no-nonsense kind of performer, Carmen proceeded to "sing," but chanting rapidly in a monotone was more like it: "Ev'rybody doin' it, doin' it, too. Ev'rybody doin' it, doin' it, too."

"He thought he was singing," observed Jayne Meadows charitably. The band gingerly started to chime in. After a few bars, Bill Harbach instructed director Dwight Hemion to get a tight shot of Allen's completely deadpan face staring straight into the camera. The audience started howling. Carmen kept going, oblivious to the reaction around him. Allen kept his straight face.

Allen's brilliance was in making small moments like these funny. It was "found comedy," which Rick Ludwin, an NBC senior vice president, described as something "you couldn't write. It would never be funny if you tried to write it. It would never be funny if it were phony. The only reason it was hysterically funny was because it was real."

"The thing was Steve's reaction," explained producer Bill Harbach. "The audience would roar, watching Steve watching that. Not watching that, but watching *Steve* watching that. Dwight would have a camera tight shot on Steve's face. In the middle of an interview in the audience, someone would do something really ridiculous. Steve would just look straight into the camera, deadpan. Bang! Bring the house down. Like Stan Laurel."

Ludwin noted the importance of how Allen treated people: "[Steve] was never cruel or nasty to people. He was having fun *with* people versus making fun *of* people—it's a subtle but crucial difference."

Carmen's appearances were a popular *Tonight* feature for several weeks, making him, for a time, "one of the most popular singers on television," mused Allen. What Carmen and other amateurs began on *Tonight* evolved into "Stump the Band," a regular *Tonight* feature under subsequent hosts, where the more uninhibited members of the audience would perform songs that no one had ever heard of, and the band would have to invent something to catch up with them.

Carmen was an example of a frequently recurring type of guest: the studio audience regular. Regulars, wrote Allen, were "hardy souls who seemed to have no purpose in life but to spend every waking moment—and some sleeping ones—at radio and TV shows." Regulars appealed to Allen, unlike other hosts who kept them at arm's length and away from the cameras. "I'm constantly on the lookout for the eccentric and for extroverted people who are willing to talk, and this is a good description of a regular."

One regular who showed up almost every night was an elderly lady of modest means, known simply as Mrs. Sterling. Allen and his audiences loved her, and her love of Allen was surpassed only by her love of whatever free gifts she could take home with her. (She would usually ask for a Polaroid camera, which she invariably pronounced "Pomeroy.") Their exchanges often went like this:

STEVE: Good evening, Mrs. Sterling. How are you this evening?

MRS. S: Mr. Allen, you're wonderful.

STEVE: That may well be, Mrs. Sterling, but I didn't come over here to listen to your compliments again, flattering as they are.

MRS. S: But I just want everybody to know what an angel you are, Mr. Allen. I hope you're feeling well.

STEVE: But Mrs. Sterling, I—

MRS. S: You're not working too hard, are you?

STEVE: Up until now I wasn't, no.

MRS. S: That's fine. Say, I'd like to have one of those Pomeroy cameras.

Wrote Allen, "I don't recall whether I ever gave Mrs. Sterling a camera, but we did lavish a wide assortment of stockings, record albums, salamis, wrist watches, perfumes, furniture, and electric appliances on her. Whether she used these articles, sold them, or stored them away on the Collier brothers' plan remains a mystery.

"Not content with demanding things for herself, Mrs. Sterling usually demanded seconds for 'my daughter.' Several people on our staff suspected there was no daughter, but nevertheless we gave Mrs. Sterling two of this and that from time to time, so that her daughter might not be disappointed."

Another regular known only by her first name—Lillian— faithfully but mysteriously found a front-row seat for nearly every broadcast, no matter where. "Wherever we went, she showed up," recalled Allen. "When we did the *Tonight* show once at Niagara Falls, there she was, smiling up from the front row seat. And she followed our circus to Havana, to Hollywood, and to Texas. We never knew how she got her tickets, how she managed to get a front row seat, or where she stayed in the various cities to which she followed us. But she was always there."

THE LOST SHOWS

Allen cherished his years on *Tonight*, not only at the time, but also throughout the rest of his life. In his 1960 memoir, *Mark It and Strike It*, he wrote, "It was tremendous fun to sit there night after night, reading notes from the audience and trying to think up funny answers to them; reading angry letters . . . introducing the greats of comedy, jazz, Broadway, and Hollywood; welcoming new comedians in the business . . . or singers. . . . The *Tonight* show was never really hard work. Since it was largely ad-libbed, there was no rehearsal problem."

As much as Allen cherished his *Tonight* years, he was equally pained that little recorded evidence of those years survives. In a 1997 interview at his Van Nuys, California, office, he lamented, "My four years of the *Tonight* show were burned, if you can believe it. And on purpose, not that they were deciding to burn *Tonight* show things. But the idiot who was in charge of the network storage facility in New Jersey—he decided that he was running short of shelf space. That was his rationale."

Bringing up the *Tonight* kinescopes would cause Allen to become visibly agitated, as if an old wound had been reopened. "It's such a pity. No matter how long I live, I'll never get over the *dumbness* of destroying all those shows. Some of them were glorious. Priceless."

Like that magical show where Carl Sandburg played the guitar. Incinerated.

Allen wasn't alone. The majority of Jack Paar's *Tonight* shows and nearly all of the first decade of *The Tonight Show with Johnny Carson* suffered a similar fate. So did other Golden Age shows. "That doesn't surprise me," said Paar director Hal Gurnee. "There's only a handful of Paar programs. He had control, and he'd have his pieces on two-inch tape, and he'd just throw the tape away! People ask, 'How could they do that?' Well, it was a different time. Television didn't have the place it does now. It seemed like a temporary phenomenon, and then you'd just move on to the next show. I never thought it had any lasting value. Until that special that [director Dwight Hemion] did with Barbra Streisand, I never took television very seriously."

Sid Caesar, an NBC prime-time headliner of that era, was lucky. "NBC destroyed all of the *Your Show of Shows*," he said. "But I have 'em, 'cause in my contract, I said I have to have a copy of every show. And I have all the shows—450 hours."

About the continuing demand for copies of Allen-era *Tonight* kinescopes from documentarians, merchandisers, and fans, Allen sighed: "Generally, no matter what they ask for of the *Tonight* show, we don't have it. We did four years, and all we have is about twelve shows. It still [hurts], after all these years. Some of the nights, I would have burned myself, 'cause even good shows are not great every night.

"But when it was good, it was *giant*."

⋆ ⋆ ⋆ ⋆ ⋆

In 1994, Jay Leno personally invited Allen to appear on the fortieth anniversary broadcast of *The Tonight Show*, where he paid tribute to Allen: "When you started this program, there was nothing to fashion it after. You were the first guy to take the cameras into the street—I guess what they call 'found comedy'; just go out there and see what's out there on the street. We do those stupid headlines that people mail us, and I used to do *What's My Beef?* on Letterman all the time, and I do it on this show once in a while. And I sort of patterned it on when you would come on and put the hat on and read the angry letters to the editor. Oh, man, those were great!"

As a guest on David Letterman's morning show in 1980, Allen was treated to an equally warm and personal testimonial: "I want to ask you about *The Tonight Show*. You started the whole thing. You're the reason we have a desk here. You're the reason that talk shows are what they are today. One of the things that I remember vividly, and one of the things that I just loved—and, in fact, we did a version of it here one day—you put a camera outside and you just looked at the folks walkin' by, and you did that first, didn't you?"

"Yeah," replied Allen enthusiastically. "In fact, we did it last Saturday on a comedy [special] I'm doing for NBC right now, and I loved your version of it, which was brilliantly creative, when you shot the people on the street—and then referred to it as a *fashion* show. That was really funny, great stuff!"

"I remember him saying to me that he was grateful that David Letterman always acknowledged the genesis of some of Letterman's stuff being Steve Allen," said Bob Costas, who once hosted his own late-night talk show on NBC, *Later with Bob Costas* (1988–94), where he interviewed Allen twice. "Letterman made himself into a giant Velcroman and threw himself onto a wall and stuck there, and he went out into the street. Letterman was always quick to say that the person who had first done this was Steve Allen. Allen respected that."

Doc Severinsen, who played in the Allen *Tonight* band and later directed the band for twenty-five years under Johnny Carson, witnessed the evolution of the show from his unique vantage point:

> When Steve showed up, there had been *Broadway Open House* [with] Morey Amsterdam and Jerry Lester; they didn't have anything as specific. Steve came in there and just really gave the show its form, even with the set—how the show was to be done—just by simply doing it. There was nothing there, and he created it out of thin air. The desk, the announcer Gene Rayburn, and the bandleader Skitch Henderson. The guys in the band would play along or do bits, or be expected to do things like that. The actual form of the show really developed with Steve.
>
> Also, what helped was the fact that there was no writer writing a full script for a show. That would've been impossible, because we were on the air for an hour-and-a-half. And so you had to have a guy who could really stand up and talk on all kinds of subjects, and Steve was really the first guy that came along and did that. Steve had the set and the whole thing that is still there today.

The more formal, general acknowledgments offered by Carson and some in his camp were, by comparison, restrained. Upon Allen's death in 2000, Carson issued a three-sentence statement calling Allen "a most creative innovator and a brilliant entertainer" and recognized that all *Tonight* hosts "owe a debt of gratitude to Steve Allen." *The Ultimate Carson* DVD collection recites in its "History of the Show" bonus feature that Allen was the show's original host, and it goes on to describe "the standard for late-night television, a recipe that most all other late-night shows follow with little variation. A desk, a couch, a band, an announcer sidekick, and an emphasis on conversation with the guests." Allen's contribution to that standard, allowed the Carson history, was that he "helped develop" it.

Ed McMahon, in his 1998 memoir, *For Laughing Out Loud*, further minimized Allen by regaling a retreat to Ft. Lauderdale in the summer of '62 that Ed went on with Johnny, his producer and director, and his writers, not long before Johnny would make his *Tonight* hosting debut. It was at this retreat "where we sat around the pool and planned the show. . . . Johnny Carson didn't just show up to do the show; that was my job. He created and produced it. He wrote jokes for the monologue, worked with the writers, planned the sketches. I don't think viewers ever realized how completely the show was a reflection of his personal vision."

As McMahon would have it, it was Carson who conceived his own *Tonight* format. "During that Florida trip," he wrote, "some of television's most wonderful characters—*Teatime Movie* host Art Fern, Aunt Blabby, the great mentalist El Moldo, and the seer from the East, Carnac the Magnificent—came to life."

This is the same Ed McMahon who professed on *Larry King Live* two years later to watching "every night of the Steve Allen *Tonight* show . . . so I had a primer on how to do it from watching him do the sketches and how he developed the family. . . . Allen invented all of this. He's the one who started all of this."

The Ft. Lauderdale retreat also came up in Paul Corkery's 1987 biography of Johnny Carson. He reported that one of the attendees, Herb Sargent, was to become Johnny's head writer but did not mention Sargent's extensive experience as one of the two principal writers on the Allen *Tonight* show, as well as on the prime-time Sunday night *Steve Allen Show* that Allen did for four years after he left *Tonight*. Sargent said in 1999, "I worked for Johnny for less than a year, but we got along very well. He called me when he was going to do the *Tonight* show because he didn't know any writers. I had met him, because he had been on Steve's show at least a couple of times. He said, 'You know that show. You've done it. Will you come work for me?'"

Corkery was specific in setting out the format that the Carson team came up with, even designating the source for each segment in parentheses: "a fifteen-minute monologue followed by guests from the entertainment world (a regular *Tonight Show* feature); sketches and skits (something borrowed from the Allen format); stunts in which Johnny would participate (an idea borrowed from *Who Do You Trust?*); guests who were eccentric or offbeat but not well known (also borrowed from *Who Do You Trust?*); adventures into the audience (also from the old *Tonight* show); and guests with books or ideas to discuss (from the *Today Show* version of *The Tonight Show*); and musical acts (a segment borrowed from all versions of *The Tonight Show . . .*)." Inasmuch as the format of *Tonight* under Carson's immediate predecessor, Jack Paar, had narrowed during the preceding five years into primarily conversation, it would seem apparent that Carson—having personally recruited Allen's longtime staff writer—had decided, deliberately or not, to revive the Allen format. All of these conventions had been instituted during the Allen years, predating the Carson-McMahon years of *Who Do You Trust?* It is therefore curious that Corkery would strain to avoid mentioning Allen by name, except in connection with sketches and skits.

Doc Severinsen remained loyal to his longtime boss: "I don't think [Johnny] ever said, 'Gee, Steve did this or that; I think I'll copy that.' Johnny was pretty much his own man," he said, two and a half months after Carson's passing in January 2005. To his credit, Sev-

With June Foray (*center*) and Wendell Noble on *Smile Time* (1946–48), a daily comedy program on the Mutual radio network that gave Allen his first nationwide exposure.

Hosting *Breaking All Records* (1943–50) on CBS Los Angeles radio affiliate KNX. Later renamed *The Steve Allen Show*, the program was a cult hit on which Allen experimented with celebrity chats, ad-lib audience banter, and other elements that would eventually light up late-night television. The studio audience numbered as many as a thousand.

Steve pioneered the grammar of today's late-night shows, including mining the audience for comedy gold.

BUTTERFIELD 8-3000

Steve as "The Question Man," pondering the question to the answer flashed on the screen. (He would divine the question: "How many hamburgers did Butterfield eat?")

Finding humor in newspapers and magazines was something Allen did on radio and carried with him into his local late-night show and *Tonight*.

In "Letters to the Editor," Steve and celebrity guests would read actual letters to the *New York Daily News* in angry, overheated tones, poking fun at the rhetoric by changing the authors' names.

Philadelphia cigar store owner Octavio Leon teaching the fine art of rolling cigars, but Steve apparently thought he was learning the fine art of rolling pretzels.

With Rayburn and Madlyn Rhue, Miss California Grapes. Numerous spokesmodels visited *Tonight*, including Miss Peach, Miss Chip-Dip, and Miss Cheesecake Made of Corn.

In a sketch with announcer/sidekick/straight man Gene Rayburn. "Steve had [Gene]. Then Jack Paar had Hugh Downs, and Johnny had me," said Ed McMahon.

Allen and wife Jayne Meadows were assigned round-the-clock police protection after he spoke out on a 1954 broadcast against organized crime and became subjected to death threats, a tire slashing, and a stink bomb erupting in the Hudson Theatre.

Kicking around ideas for that night's show with writer Bill Dana (*left*) and producer Bill Harbach (*right*).

Working out a musical arrangement with Skitch Henderson, the first musical director of *Tonight*.

Eydie Gorme rehearsing with Doc Severinsen, who got his late-night start playing in the original *Tonight* band.

With Steve Lawrence, Eydie Gorme, and Skitch Henderson. Allen, Henderson, and the singers would periodically stage tributes to great popular composers such as Harold Arlen, Hoagy Carmichael, and Richard Rodgers (*below*).

With Richard Rodgers, the American musical theater's preeminent composer, whose works include *The Sound of Music, Oklahoma!, South Pacific,* and *Carousel.*

L.A. Stylin': During rehearsal at the Ambassador Hotel with (*left to right*) Steve Lawrence, Jayne Meadows, and Andy Williams.

Laughing with comedian George Gobel. "Steve was that thing that all really, really good entertainers are: a good audience," said Larry Gelbart.

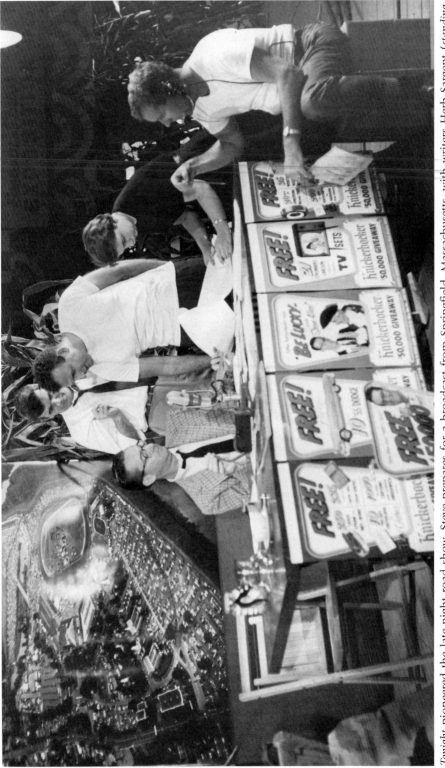

Meadowlane Enterprises, Inc.

Tonight pioneered the late-night road show. Steve prepares for a broadcast from Springfield, Massachusetts, with writers Herb Sargent (*standing, wearing necktie*) and Stan Burns (*standing, in T-shirt*).

The entire *Tonight* cast flew to Los Angeles to spend the summer of 1955 so that Allen could film *The Benny Goodman Story* and continue hosting *Tonight*—without taking a single day off.

Arriving at the Buffalo, New York airport with (*left to right*) Eydie Gorme, Andy Williams, and director Dwight Hemion.

With pianist Mary Lou Williams, once hailed as jazz's greatest female musician. Allen quietly used *Tonight* to showcase artists of color during an era when they seldom were permitted to appear on television.

With Louis Armstrong, who recorded Allen's Christmas jazz classic, "Cool Yule."

With Sammy Davis Jr. performing "I Could Have Danced All Night." A few bars into the number, Davis would leap to his feet, suavely toss aside his cigarette, and dazzle the audience by dancing atop the piano, while Steve continued to accompany him.

Wrapping up a duet with Lena Horne. Producer Bill Harbach (*standing in background*) admired Allen's on-a r condemnation of a bigoted viewer who had written to chastise Allen for giving Horne a friendly kiss on the cheek.

With comedian Henny Youngman, who was never without his trademark violin, even in the life raft in the pool at the Sea Isle Hotel in Miami.

Sharing a laugh at the *Tonight* desk with Ernest Borgnine and Jayne Meadows.

Meadowlane Enterprises, Inc.

Allen (*left, on clarinet*) jamming with (*left to right*) Sol Yaged, Lou McGarrity, Urbie Green, Benny Goodman, Buck Clayton, and comedian Sid Caesar on saxophone.

NBC/Globe Photos, Inc.

On a typical night, crowds line 44th Street in front of the Hudson Theatre to see the Allen *Tonight* show.

TV's first King of Late Night.

erinsen did not dismiss or underrate Allen's contributions. Instead, he offered an earnest comparison of the two hosts: "I think Johnny, his feelings about what the show should be as far as relationships— it was even stronger with Johnny. Steve was more freewheeling. Johnny had more form. His announcer became more prominent. It was a lot like the old Jack Benny [radio] show," pointing to the good-natured banter that characterized the relationship between Benny and his announcer [Don Wilson] and bandleader [Phil Harris]. "Johnny's style was different. Johnny was a stand-up comic, among other things, and a magician. In college, Johnny majored in logic, so he had a lot of advantages. Also, he had a lot of years getting ready for that, in that he did other television shows."

Entertainment Weekly critic Ken Tucker advocated on Allen's behalf: "[Steve Allen] invented the late-night TV talk show as we now know it. The whole megillah was Allen's creation—the desk, the band, the opening monologue, the wacky skits, the going up into the audience to answer questions, the guest chatter," he wrote in a two-page tribute to Allen in 2000. "You think Johnny Carson created Art Fern, the sleazy huckster? Allen did it first, with his Late Night Pitchman character. Think David Letterman invented nutty stunts like the Velcro suit? Allen was jumping into giant vats of Jell-O before Dave was in long pants."

Although former *Tonight* host Jack Paar warned in his 1983 memoir, *P.S. Jack Paar*, "There are many false stories about the history of the *Tonight* program," the purported clarifications he offered seemed to be the very tales he was warning about. He claimed that the "first" *Tonight* was "a variety show of music and skits that starred Steve Allen, not unlike Jerry Lester's *Broadway Open House*." As Rick Ludwin stated in chapter 1, the shows had nothing in common with each other: "*Broadway Open House* was a presentational, Berle-style revue. Steve did a different show."

Then Paar confessed, "[I]f you are referring to the late night program that became the most imitated show in television and that consisted mainly of conversation and personalities, then I am guilty." But, again in chapter 1, Ludwin described Allen's *Tonight* as "conversation and comedy. People should know that it was Steve Allen who brought that to television." To be sure, Paar narrowed Allen's variety format into one of purely talk. That was natural, given that Paar was not the actor, musician, singer, composer, or comedian that Allen was. Paar's gift was in engaging his guests in compelling conversations.

But for Paar to dismiss Allen's format as mere variety and comedy sketches is also false. The "variety" Allen offered was a mix of different elements, but not every night. On many nights, Allen engaged in provocative conversations on serious subjects (like blacklisting, the mob, civil rights, and drug abuse) with serious guests (like Eleanor Roosevelt, Aaron Copland, Tennessee Williams, James Michener, and Gen. Omar Bradley).

Paar also claimed that his "show discovered and presented for the first time to a national audience" Shelley Berman and Louis Nye—both of whom had previously appeared on the Allen *Tonight* show. Nye, in fact, had appeared frequently on Allen's *Tonight*; through his Gordon Hathaway character in "Man on the Street" sketches, he had become one of the hottest regulars on the prime-time *Steve Allen Show*, which premiered in June 1956, well over a year before Paar began his *Tonight* hosting stint.

NBC network logs generated contemporaneously with the broadcasts reflect that Berman debuted on *Tonight* on February 20, 1956. At the time, Berman was an actor who had never done stand-up comedy, although he had submitted an unsolicited comedy sketch that, to his delight, Allen performed on the show. This led to Berman being invited to write material that he could perform himself. "But I'm not a comedian, I've never been a comedian in my life, and I don't want to be a comedian!" Berman insisted to Allen's staff, but he eventually decided to give it a shot. "So I wrote a little phone call thing for myself," recalled Berman in 2005. It would be the first of Berman's signature telephone routines. "It scored on that show. I would later revise it because I didn't think it was very good in the first place. But Steve liked it!"

Paar even congratulated himself for having the first televison program to allow black performers to sit down and speak with the host: "I suddenly realized that in our year or more on *The Tonight Show*, while there were black performers on, I had not actually sat down with one and talked. This may seem a strange thing to say now, but I do it only in the historical context. It just had not been done on any program or panel show that I knew of. And so I asked the next black singer to sit with me and talk."

To the contrary, as detailed in chapter 2, Allen had already booked numerous black artists for his *Tonight* show and interviewed them, often with them sitting next to him. In fact, a photograph of Allen sitting next to pianist Mary Lou Williams at the *Tonight* desk appeared in an *Ebony* magazine issue from September/October 1955, a full three years before Paar purported to invite black guests to sit with him.

How did Allen respond to these attempts to minimize his creative contributions to the show's long-term success? "Dad was certainly frustrated, particularly because he considered Johnny, Jack, and Ed his friends and enjoyed their great success," said Bill Allen. "He would never have filed a lawsuit or sought Writers' Guild arbitration. He was too busy performing, writing and creating new material, and directing his energies toward social causes of greater consequence like civil rights, the death penalty, and vulgarity in entertainment to want to spar over who originated the concept behind a particular comedy bit.

"But, as a principled man, it troubled him if somebody else was trying to claim credit for something that he or any other artist had originated. He felt terrible that Johnny Carson had so frequently appropriated Jonathan Winters's 'Maude Frickert' character in his 'Aunt Blabby' that Jonathan himself couldn't use his own character as much, as time went on. He found it incredulous for Johnny's people to claim that they created 'Carnac' independently of 'The Question Man,' when Johnny himself appeared on Dad's show twice during the 1958–59 season, and 'The Question Man' was by then an established and very popular segment on *The Steve Allen Show*.

"All Dad wanted—and deeply appreciated—was a simple nod his way, like Jay and Dave so graciously did, in recognition of what he and his colleagues on the *Tonight* show rightfully created. It made him feel like a proud grandpa. He was genuinely touched when they acknowledged his influence and delighted when they showed him how they had taken his creations to another level."

"Johnny Carson sent me the most beautiful personal note when Steve died," Jayne Meadows warmly recalled. "In it, he expressed his profound admiration and respect for Steve as an innovator, as an entertainer, and as a man." She added quietly, "I just wish he would have said those things while Steve was still alive."

* * * * * * *

Perhaps the hippest and most telling nod to Allen occurred in a 1993 episode of *The Simpsons*. One of the producers of that episode was Conan O'Brien, the host of *Late Night with Conan O'Brien*, the anointed future host of *The Tonight Show*, and a Steve Allen fan. (Allen's portrait is one of four portraits of O'Brien's heroes that hang in his studio; the other three are David Letterman, Johnny Carson, and Jack Paar). In "Krusty Gets Kancelled," Krusty the Clown's beloved daily afternoon show is knocked off the air by a new but slimy children's program starring Gabbo, a ventriloquist's smart-alecky dummy. As Bart and Lisa Simpson are sitting at home in front of the TV, Gabbo announces, "And now it's time for another patented Gabbo crank call!"

BART: Oh, I can't believe it. He stole this bit from Krusty!
LISA: Well, Krusty stole it from Steve Allen.

Back on the set, Gabbo gets an unsuspecting Krusty on the line and makes a crank request. As Krusty proceeds to make a fool of himself over the phone, he hears the laughter of the studio audience at the other end of the line and realizes that he's being humiliated on live television. Indignant, he screams, "If this is anybody but Steve Allen, *you're stealing my bit!*"

Chapter 4

WRITING FOR AN
OFF-THE-CUFF HOST

STEVE ALLEN: Stan, is this joke you wrote funny?
STAN BURNS: No, but you've gotta lot of guts!

Like Jonathan Winters and Don Adams, Stan Burns (1923–2002) discovered his talent for comedy while serving in the Marines. In 1953, Steve Allen hired him as the sole writer for Allen's new local late-night show (where he remained when the show went network the following year as the Tonight *show), and he continued writing for Allen's subsequent network and syndicated programs. In the 1960s and '70s, he wrote for Dean Martin and the Smothers Brothers, as well as Carol Burnett, for whom he crafted the trademark informal opening spot with her audience and the soap opera spoof, "As the Stomach Turns."*

Before The Steve Allen Show, *Burns had written for* Broadway Open House *with Herb Sargent (1923–2005). When Allen's local show went network, Burns recruited Sargent to fill the opening for a second writer, and the two formed the writing nucleus behind the Allen* Tonight *years. In 1962, Johnny Carson personally recruited Sargent to write for the inaugural year of* The Tonight Show with Johnny Carson. *Sargent went on to write for Bing Crosby, Milton Berle, Burt Bacharach, Paul*

McCartney, Dan Aykroyd, and Dennis Miller. *After he won an Emmy for his work on a 1973 Lily Tomlin special, a co-writer on that special—Lorne Michaels—recruited him to serve as writer and script consultant for a new NBC show,* Saturday Night Live, *on which he worked for twenty years and for which he earned four Emmys. In 2002, Sargent served as writer and script consultant for NBC's gala, star-studded, three-hour seventy-fifth anniversary special.*

In late 1956, Burns and Sargent recruited Bill Dana as the third Tonight *writer. Dana became best known for his creation and portrayal of Jose Jimenez, whom he debuted on a 1959* Steve Allen Show. *In addition to helping launch other comic greats such as Don Knotts, Jackie Mason, and Jim Nabors, Dana won an Emmy for writing an episode of* All in the Family *("Sammy Davis Visits Archie Bunker") that ranked number 12 in a* TV Guide *poll of the "Best 100 Episodes" in the history of television. Dana's other recent projects have included writing for* Matlock *and a recurring role as Uncle Angelo on* The Golden Girls.

Burns was interviewed in 1997 in his wood-paneled home office in the Los Angeles suburb of Woodland Hills. He was still writing—on his electric typewriter—and his robust and good-natured manner and irrepressible humor offered a glimmer of the zaniness he contributed to the early Tonight *days. Sargent sat for his interview in 1999 at an imposing thirty-seat conference table in the Manhattan offices of the Writers' Guild of America, East (for which he served as president from 1991 until his death in May 2005), his low-key, sardonic humor intact. Dana phoned in his interview, richly colored with accents and characterizations, in 1998 from his home in Hana, Hawaii.*

PASSING THE COMPATIBILITY TEST

Stan Burns first saw Steve Allen hosting game shows and an afternoon talk show on CBS in the early '50s: "I didn't know him, but I watched him. I thought, 'This guy is too clever!' I liked his style. I didn't know we were going to get together."

In the fall of 1953, a few weeks after the local *Steve Allen Show* premiered in New York, Burns, at his agent's urging, approached Allen. "He met me," recalled Allen, "as I was having a sandwich across the street from the studio at 67th Street. Said he'd like to write for me. And I said, 'I won't stop you. C'mon across the street.' And so we talked to Bill Harbach." Hired as the show's first and only staff writer, Burns recalled how elated he was to discover that he and his new boss shared the same level of humor: "It happened so seldom. You come in, and how do you know you agree with the guy? It just happens, and you're lucky. My whole life was very visual and offbeat, things that have never been done, and Steve loved that style."

Even shortly after he started, Burns recalled giving Allen a joke he had just written. "Steve asks, 'Is this funny?' I say, 'No, but you've gotta lot of guts!' And I knew I could get away with that with Steve because he loves humor."

Burns would arrive at the studio at 9 a.m. and return home at two the next morning "for a year, by myself," he remembered proudly. Besides, "I loved it so much. I was always dying to get to work because it was too much fun. My life was ad-lib craziness-fun." Each night's program would be prepared mostly that same day. "We worked at that speed, typing, getting the stuff out. If I had a sketch for Thursday and it was Tuesday, that would be fine. But I was only thirty years old!"

Burns denied feeling pressured by the grueling pace, explaining that all the torture he endured while in the Marines must have inspired him to become a comedy writer. Allen once observed that although Burns was forever jovial, he specialized in sick jokes about "death, Hitler, accidents, and national catastrophes. He was the originator, for example, of that much-quoted sick classic, 'Remember, folks, —— Airlines is the airline of the stars: Carole Lombard, Grace Moore, Will Rogers. . . .'"

When the local show went network in September 1954, an opening arose for a second writer, and Burns thought of his former writing colleague on *Broadway Open House*, Herb Sargent. The two had also written one-minute, one-joke sketches for an NBC summer series, *So You Want to Lead a Band?* "Each sketch would contain a clue which would be answered by somebody in the audience," recalled Sargent, "and if they answered it correctly, they'd get to conduct this band."

Sargent had been impressed with Allen's local show. "He wasn't like any other comedian, so that was refreshing. He didn't have an act, a monologue that he prepared to do regularly in theaters. It was a different kind of talent."

Burns had Sargent talk with Allen, and the two hit it off immediately. Allen once fondly described Sargent, "Given to wearing tweed sports jackets, he has the Connecticut haircut and grizzled Ivy-league look of men in cigarette ads. While lost in thought he may stand in the middle of a room, arms held out from his sides, shrugging his shoulders and quietly flapping his fingers."

BONDING WITH THE STUDIO AUDIENCE

One element of *Tonight's* continuing success has been the audience participation aspect of the show, which Allen developed and refined. To achieve this, it was essential for host and audience to bond. "The audience is trained by television just to sit and watch," said Burns. "They want to be entertained, but they have to *like* the person. If the person comes out, doesn't open his mouth to say anything, and they already like him, then he's a winner. That's what happened to Steve Allen."

Allen himself was keenly aware of his likability factor. He had been closely studying TV in its earliest days and noticed how close the audience felt to the performer. This convinced him that it was important for the performer to be liked: "If they like you, they'll be happy to laugh at you. They'll like whatever you do. You don't even have to be very funny. In television, a likable face is more valuable than money in the bank." *Newsweek* noticed the same thing: "[Allen] is also an ad-glib commentator who can make intelligent conversation without being pontifical and make light conversation without descending to the Stygian pleasantries of fake folksiness. It is this rare combination of good qualities—or, perhaps better put, the lack of offending ones—that make Steve Allen TV's 'Mr. Midnight,' a fellow whom audiences really like."

As a *Broadway Open House* writer in 1950, Burns remembered host Jerry Lester as a wild man, doing audience bits and running around. Steve Allen, however, "had more of a classy look to him," said Burns. "He was like an Everyguy. The glasses made him. He was not just a stand-up comic. He was so versatile, and he was so intelligent. The audience loved Steve for his talent, and they weren't intimidated by him. So when he went in the audience, they felt comfortable with him. He made them laugh without insulting them. They respected him. If you get respect from people, they'll go along with you.

"Then, all of a sudden, *he's* doing crazy things. They didn't expect this of a guy like that. He'd sit down at the piano and play, and then, all of a sudden, he's wrestling a boa constrictor. That combination is so amazing to people. They knew how clever he was in books and songwriting, and then they'd see him in a vat of Jell-O."

Burns pointed out another ingredient: Allen's rare ability to ad-lib. "He would just ad-lib, and that was his world, and that's what made it easier for me. You were sure that he could cover anything in comedy. There was no failure with him. And we did it live!"

Allen and his team nurtured his bond with the audience by constantly finding ways to reach out to them. One way was by having them submit written questions on index cards before the broadcast for him to answer on the air. Burns and Sargent would quickly review the cards, select the best questions, write snappy answers for Allen to fire back, and put the cards on Allen's piano. Allen would flip through the cards and say, "Yeah, that's good. Naah, I don't like that one. That's good. That's good." The entire process would take place within ten minutes of airtime. Allen retained the last word, occasionally changing answers, discarding questions, or ad-libbing altogether. The questions had to be real, and the answers priceless. Some examples:

1. Would you show me how to put lipstick on the right way?
   ANSWER: First, let me take it off the right way.

2. I've come 1200 miles to meet you. Do I have a chance?
   ANSWER: Where are you? (FIND MAN IN BACK OF AUDIENCE) Oh, I see . . . you're 50 feet short.

3. Steve, we have seven children—4 boys, 3 girls. What do we do now?
   ANSWER: What have you been doing *up to* now?

4. Where does Jayne get all her pep?
   ANSWER: Well, she gets up every morning, exercises, and eats a hearty breakfast. Then, she gets out of bed.

5. Have you ever mistaken Jayne for Audrey Meadows?
   ANSWER: I'm not sure.

6. If you wore a bikini to the beach and it fell off, would you pick it up?
   ANSWER: If I wore a bikini to the beach, *I'd* get picked up.

7. I have the best-looking legs in town, but I'm not sure anyone knows it.
   WRITERS SCRATCHED OUT THE CARD WRITER'S NAME, Angela Maxwell, AND SUBSTITUTED, "Fred."

8. Is $145.00 at Forrest Lawn a discount price, or are they taking us?
   ANSWER: They'll take you either way!

Another technique was to involve individual audience members in sketches and bits. In one example, the audience was asked, "How many here have a fantasy of being a stand-up comedian?" Two women and three guys raised their hands and were told, "Okay, you're going to do stand-up." They would read cue cards: "Good evening, ladies and gentlemen, it's good to be here," and then they'd read the jokes. It was stand-up comedy from ordinary people. "The audience was the most important thing in our lives," noted Burns, "because we're using real people in situations, and they reacted wonderfully."

Burns could not understand why latter-day shows with audiences seemed reluctant to involve real people this way, especially since most programs are taped, and anyone who bombed could always be edited out of the final cut. In contrast, the Allen *Tonight* years were live, and there was no opportunity to scrap a flat performance. "We didn't care," said Burns, "as we were just having fun. Each time we picked somebody from the audience, they never failed. They were hysterical. It always worked for some reason."

What was that reason? Burns credited part of the success to his own comedy instinct. "I'd say to Steve, 'Do you see that guy in the third row? He'd be perfect for the bit.' That's why I was hired and lasted so long because I knew with my instinct what would go. That's the specialty. I knew exactly what the audience would do. I'd go outside while they're waiting in line, and I'd just look at them. The way he stands, the age, the look. That's all. It's a gamble, but it paid off every time because of Steve. Steve knew how to handle people."

And the people responded with great affection by sending Allen an avalanche of letters and cards (some eight hundred a day), along with countless unusual gifts, including alpaca overcoats, noodles shaped like stars and sprinkled with sequins, gold-plated toothpicks, frozen tuna fish, poems, a bottle of Japanese beer, and maracas made out of three beer cans joined together. One fan sent Allen a breadbox (referencing the "Is it bigger than a breadbox?" catchphrase Allen coined on *What's My Line?*) with instructions to autograph and return it so that the fan could appear on another panel show, *I've Got a Secret*. Although Allen often made an entertaining show of opening the gifts on the air, just watching the gifts arrive at Allen's office was perhaps a show in itself. At four thirty one afternoon, a production assistant knocked on his door: "A present for you, Steve. Silver mink bow tie, silver mink cuff links, silver mink boutonniere."

Allen laughed. "Crazy. I'll wear them on the show tonight."

Of course, there were some people that not even Allen and his fun-loving team could please. There was a night when they planned to take shots from the roof of a nearby building, so they ran TV cables up a building from the back of the Hudson Theatre across 45th Street. "This is eleven thirty, twelve o'clock at night, live," said Burns. "All the lights were on. And some people in the building got angry because they couldn't sleep, and this woman cut the cable. That was too funny. The show was still on. She cut some cable! One of the cameras went out. That was all ad-lib and funny and spontaneous and live."

ADVENTURES IN MIAMI BEACH

Allen periodically took the *Tonight* show to Miami Beach, a popular destination for NBC's morning signature show, *Today*. In January 1955, both shows were staged at the Sea Isle Hotel during the same week. Local station WTVJ scored big by getting both shows to stage their broadcasts there that week. The station beamed the programs daily to NBC, and the City of Miami Beach paid the cable costs incurred. At the time, reported *Broadcasting-Telecasting* magazine, WTVJ quoted a basic charge of $1,000 for each show, which included full crews for eight hours. The Sea Isle, the Miami Beach Kennel Club, and Hialeah Race Course helped defray these costs, with the hotel also furnishing accommodations and amenities for the seventy-two-member casts and crews of both shows.

Sargent recalled, "We were on live at night, and so I had to go up to one of the top floors and struggle with a dummy that was supposed to be [*Today* host] Dave Garroway—trying to wake him up—and then throw him out the window so he'd hit the pool." Unfortunately, the bespectacled Garroway dummy bounced unceremoniously off the pool's edge. "Steve was very upset: 'You goofed!' I said, 'I can't aim from twelve stories up!'"

Having the cast, crew, and staging equipment for two network programs in the same hotel created commotion among the hotel guests, who, as Sargent recalled, "were always complaining because they were awakened by the *Today* show production and kept up at night by the *Tonight* show."

"Dave would start rehearsing at four in the morning, and we'd get through at two the following morning," said producer Bill Harbach. "We had guns going off, fish in the swimming pools. We killed the hotel."

"But the hotels liked the exposure and didn't care about the guests," said Sargent sardonically.

At the hotel next door, one of the guests turned out to be the Shah of Iran. "So Stan and Steve and I walked down the beach to the next hotel and asked him if he could be on our show," said Sargent. "He's in the cabana by the pool. There were no bodyguards, he was just there with his family. He said he couldn't. He was water skiing every day."

The show's first trip to Miami in January 1955 marked the first time that the cast, staff, and crew traveled and roomed together. Burns, then thirty-one, was paired with Steve Lawrence, then nineteen. Up until then, explained Lawrence, "we were in the office laughing, having a good time. Now, I'm living with the guy." At 6 a.m., Lawrence was awakened by repeated, intense, loud grunting. "I'm too frightened to open my eyes," he recalled. "The man—he's a sex lunatic, he's got an ax, he's gonna kill me. Finally, I open my eyes, and I see him pushing against a wall, and I ask him, 'What the hell are you doing?'"

"Isometrics," replied Burns, nonchalantly, "every morning." At six-foot-two, the strapping ex-Marine was engaging in his daily morning exercise ritual.

The bantam Lawrence, still in shock, jumped out of his bed and began banging Burns in the chest. "Why didn't you tell me?" he yelled. "I had a heart attack! I thought you were going to rape me!"

"Rape you?" Burns said, flashing a grin. "You're not my type."

DISHING IT OUT AND TAKING IT

"It was Steve's sensibilities that drove the *Tonight* show," said Sargent. "More of a free-for-all sense of humor." Allen appreciated clever, good-natured ribbing from his staff. One December, he issued a memo imploring them not to give him anything for Christmas. "I was surprised," recalled Allen, "when on December 24th I found a beautifully wrapped gift from Stan and Herb on my desk. Opening it,

I could see that it was a framed object of some sort, perhaps a special portrait or a historic document. It was a document all right—the fellows had given me a tastefully framed copy of my memo."

Allen, too, could dish it out in unlikely situations. One night, recalled Sargent, Allen asked him and Burns for a favor: to drive his car home for him from the Hudson Theatre. "Steve had the biggest, ugliest car I'd ever seen," said Sargent, smiling and shaking his head. "A big Chrysler, I think, with terrible colors—like a green car with a purple top. But it was new. Good condition. He had an apartment on 80-something Street and Park Avenue, so we drove through Central Park. I think Stan was driving. He thinks I was driving. Went through a stop sign. It was late at night. They were patrolling the park. We were pulled over, and the police made us follow them to the station in the middle of the park at 86th Street, the Central Park Police Department. And they took us inside and we said, 'That's Steve Allen's car.' They said, 'Call him.' So we called him at home. He came over, and he walked in and said, 'I've never seen these people in my life.' And—for a moment—we thought, 'He's gotta break this joke.' Which he did."

FINDING A GUEST HOST

In August 1955, after spending eight weeks filming his starring role in *The Benny Goodman Story* (without taking a single night off from his *Tonight* duties), Allen finally decided to take his first two-week vacation as *Tonight* show host. This actually bewildered Burns, Sargent, and producer Bill Harbach because in two years, they never had a guest host. An early candidate was Mickey Rooney. But they nixed the idea, according to Burns, when Rooney tried to assure them, "I can do everything, don't bother."

Burns lobbied for comedian Ernie Kovacs. Harbach approved

and instructed Burns to see Kovacs and set things up. In introducing himself, Burns said to Kovacs, "I'm one of the writers, and we're available to help you."

Ironically, Kovacs also declined their help. "No," he politely responded. "I do all my own writing." And he did. In his two-week stint as guest host, Kovacs debuted his brilliant, crazy routines, including now-classic bits like The Nairobi Trio, before a national audience. "He was so offbeat, different from Steve Allen's approach to comedy," said Burns. "And that's what attracted him to people, because he was strange. He did surrealistic-type things. That's what caught on."

In 1956, Allen accepted NBC's offer to host his own Sunday night prime-time comedy-variety series opposite Ed Sullivan. The network's original vision was for Allen and his production team to handle the new weekly show plus *Tonight* five nights a week. This proved more than Allen and his team could handle, and so Allen cut back his involvement in *Tonight* to three nights a week, Wednesdays through Fridays. Beginning in October 1956, Ernie Kovacs began hosting and producing *Tonight* on Mondays and Tuesdays. Kovacs later became a serious contender to succeed Allen permanently when he left the show in January 1957, although the nod ultimately went to Jack Paar.

ADDING A THIRD WRITER

For most of the show's network run under Allen, *Tonight* was written mainly by Allen, Burns, and Sargent. As the show's success blossomed, one of Sid Caesar's writers, Woody Allen, approached Burns for a job and handed Burns his material. Burns replied, "It's very clever, but we don't have a budget. Thank you." Burns, however, held on to the material and claimed to still have it at the time of his interview in 1997.

But as Allen's Sunday show got off the ground, doing *Tonight* even for just three nights a week began to drain the two writers. In order for Burns and Sargent to devote more time to the Sunday show, *Tonight* would need to add a third writer. The two took notice of Bill Dana, who had been writing wildly funny routines for comedian Don Adams, a recurring *Tonight* guest. Recalled Dana, "Stan and Herb made a strong suggestion to Steve that he hire me, the guy who had written the material for Don Adams, and I had to do a couple of sample sketches."

Dana had capitalized on Adams's talent for doing impressions, including that of William Powell as the Thin Man ("There's your man, Inschpectah!" mimicked Dana in character). The solo routines had Adams portraying a defense attorney, a football coach, "Mister Baseball," and the British in India. Dana had written a joke that was the original "Would you believe—?" that became Adams's catchphrase as Maxwell Smart on the '60s secret-agent spoof, *Get Smart* (whose writers included Steve Allen *Tonight* alumni Buck Henry, Leonard Stern, Arne Sultan, and Dana).

Dana described the *Tonight* show environment as a "marvelous comedy college." For his first two weeks on the show, however, the writing department of this "college" consisted entirely of Dana himself. Burns and Sargent had been diverted to the Sunday show. Dana remembered "my baptism of fire—it felt like forever, but it was probably ten days or two weeks. So I had to write a sketch a day and handle all the bits and pieces."

Dana lived up to Burns and Sargent's recommendation. He wrote a joke for guest George Gobel, who was supposed to own a ranch; Dana says he has since seen the joke in several textbooks:

ALLEN: What's the name of your ranch?
GOBEL: The name of my ranch is The Bar Nine Circle Z Walking O Flying W Lazy R Happy Four Bar Seventeen Parallelogram Five Ranch O.

ALLEN: Do you have many cattle?
GOBEL: No, not many survive the branding.

Peter Lawford once told Dana that "Jack Kennedy's favorite joke was a joke I had written for the Question Man. The answer was 'Chicken Teriyaki,' and the question was, 'Give the name of the oldest living kamikaze pilot.'"

In addition to writing, Dana found himself recruiting new talent for the show, most notably Don Knotts, who guested three times on *Tonight* and eventually joined the cast of the prime-time *Steve Allen Show*. Despite the breakneck pace, Dana found his experience on *Tonight*—and later on the Sunday prime-time show (where he frequently appeared doing his most famous character, Jose Jimenez)—exhilarating: "I couldn't wait to get to work, and I hated to leave at night. Symptomatic of those days was the fact that I would walk from 44th and Broadway where we had the Hudson Theatre to my apartment at 52nd and Second Avenue at three in the morning and never think about it. It was a good two-mile walk. The New York City of the '50s was a nice, safe, lovely place." Reflected Dana in 1998, "Steve, as a writer himself, is a very supportive guy. That's one of the reasons why the show developed so much talent. Steve—it takes one to know one—he recognizes all sorts of major talent, and he supports it; he doesn't compete. You'd see that in his interviews when he talks with funny people, he lets them get their laughs, and he was the best audience, the best public laugher there ever was. He's gone down in history with that marvelous cackle.

"The original *Tonight* show and Steve Allen—simply the template for everything else that came after it. Historically, if you're first, you can't help but have an effect on other people that follow."

WRITING AND RATINGS

In today's age of five hundred cable channels and cutthroat ratings wars, it seems hard to envision a simpler time when neither existed. "We didn't cater to any age group," remembered Burns. "We just did our shows. We didn't know who was watching and why. Nobody ever came to us and said, 'We're only aiming at the so-and-so range.' Nobody ever bothered you. And we got the ratings!"

Not that they even kept track of ratings. "We didn't do what they do now, which is get the overnights," said Sargent. In recent decades, ratings have become such an integral reflection of a show's success that everybody's daily morning ritual now includes scanning the overnights. "And even the writers do, not just the production company."

In Burns's heyday, comedy writers like him and performers like Steve Allen were too busy having fun to become self-conscious or to foresee the power and future potential of television. They were just working five days a week to get a show out. "It was fresh, and television was just starting," Burns recalled. "We didn't sit down and say, 'Now, I'm going to do this, because in forty years people are going to say that was the greatest show in the world.' We would like that, but we didn't think about it. We just wanted to get on and have fun. That was the whole thing. We loved laughter, and TV was an outlet for that."

Allen agreed: "Another reason we early-birds had not the slightest sense that we were making television history is that most of us were much too busy to indulge in such introspection. My co-workers and I just didn't consider our shows a big deal. Bob Hope and Bing Crosby were important stars; we were just a bunch of young guys having a hell of a time."

Among contemporary hosts, Burns found David Letterman to be most akin to Steve Allen in style, drawing comparisons to "the wild things and monkey cameras and going outside and dropping watermelons on people. He used exact bits that we did, but he told the audience that it was Steve's show that started him off on this. Letterman is almost like Steve in a way, with all the crazy things. When you're doing a late-night show and people stay up, they want to see something crazy, just to get their minds awake. What is television, anyway? Adults are running around like kids doing crazy stunts. And what are they doing it for? To attract an audience and get laughs."

Burns could not understand some of the changes in modern late-night television writing. First, the shows employ what seem to be a platoon of writers, something that amused Steve Allen in 1997: "Here's a point that always gets a laugh from those of us who worked in television in the '50s," noted Allen. "If you watch a TV awards show, and they say, 'And the winner is . . . *The Tonight Show!*'—this is for comedy writing—everybody applauds, they play the theme, and forty-eight people get up. I exaggerate, but sometimes twenty or more writers get up, and each gets a little gold statue. The reason that strikes us funny is, guess how many writers I had when the late show started? Zero." The show would function for most of its run under Allen with two writers, Burns and Sargent. Allen joked that when David Letterman's show won an Emmy for best writing one year, it appeared that half the audience stood up to accept the award.

Why so many writers today? "I don't know," wondered Burns. "I never worked with Letterman or Leno, but they want security. They want ten thousand writers, so they have more material to pick from." Sargent agreed: "It's insurance. They have to do it every day and have good material. And they hire new writers, young writers they find in college."

"Steve didn't really depend on the writers," said Burns. "He was an ad-lib star. That's what made him. He would come in and say, 'Who's on the show tonight? What are we going to do?' I'd say, 'Here's an idea, what do you think?' The ad-lib feel was the key to the show's success, especially with a guy like Steve, who can ad-lib his way into and out of any situation.

"I know these guys, like Letterman: 'What do you mean by this joke? What do you think of the writers?' Oh, God, I couldn't take that! I'm an ad-lib type guy."

"There was always the perception that Steve had arrived just minutes before the show and was experiencing it at the same time I was," recalled writer David Pollock. He remembered watching *Tonight* as a kid and noticing Steve "constantly flipping through papers, calmly trying to determine what was supposed to happen next. '. . . Do we introduce Eydie Gorme's song now or do the sketch?'"

"Working with Steve was the best experience I've ever had in television, including my days working at *Saturday Night Live*," professed Sargent, who went on to write and serve as a script consultant for *SNL* from 1975 through 1995 ("Weekend Update," "Schiller's Reels," and "Mister Bill"). In fact, the *Internet Movie Database* credits Sargent for giving the young *SNL* cast the moniker "The Not Ready for Prime Time Players." Sargent continued:

> The *Tonight* show—I know it was a short time, but it was the best. It was one of a kind, and it was the first of its kind, which was great. Steve was a new face then. And he inspired you to get loose. He could be calling it "silly." He was a good writer. It was mostly Steve, and a great part of it was all those people who worked on it; they were all smart, all terrific. And to collect them all in one production, you're lucky. Different from *Saturday Night*, which is another kind of show. *Saturday Night* is all about writers. So much material. And an original cast [rotating through] a couple of generations. But after twenty years, I outgrew it. It had changed. By that time, they had become what the original group used to kid about.

One contemporary show that Sargent enjoyed was *The Daily Show* with Jon Stewart, which he found to be "100 percent better since the days when Craig Kilbourn was host. Kilbourn interfered too much with his own idea of his own personality. Jon Stewart is seriously good and funny, a little crazy and can do anything. The writing is very good. It's every day, four nights a week. And they're right on top of the news of that day. And I think it has a lot to do with the fact that it's New York and not California. Which, in turn, has a lot to do with the audience that comes to that studio. In California, it's tourists. Here (in New York), it's people who want to see the program. Tourists don't get a lot. Not that they're stupid, it's just the references are beyond them or delayed."

THE CENSORSHIP PENDULUM: PUSHING THE ENVELOPE

Censorship standards were strict in the '50s, recalled Sargent. "NBC's network censor would send out a monthly newsletter talking about the scripts he had reviewed, things he had turned down, and the reasons why. He was well known in broadcasting as a very responsible, literate censor. And funny, too." Nevertheless, warned Sargent, "you had to watch out for the church. Anything that suggested children in trouble. Profanity, scatological humor. [Producer] Billy Harbach was even taking raps for Jose Jimenez."

And not just for Jose Jimenez, recalled Harbach: "I remember NBC saying, 'You can't call 'em "Crazy Shots." Call 'em "Funny Shots"' because they were worried that insane asylums would be offended."

Dana offered a more critical assessment. During the 1950s, he observed:

> This country was so uptight sexually that you couldn't show a close-up of the stork on *Zoo Parade*. We were in a cultural prison. The censors were all over the place. They called them "Program Practices" or whatever the euphemism was. You couldn't say, "damn" or "hell." You couldn't have two people in the bed at the same time. There was no way you could suggest pregnancy. You couldn't use the word *pregnant*. Yet we were just as funny during

that period as anything today. And given that license, things today should be a lot funnier.

Television has become such a swamp under the heading of really brilliant work. The references to masturbation and every possible body function on the brilliant shows like *Seinfeld*—you wouldn't have thought of being able to do anything like that [in the '50s]. If you sneaked it onto live television, you'd be in prison the next day.

Mae West was scheduled to appear. Burns and Sargent had been assigned to write a *Call of the West*–style sketch about the Yukon. Sargent recalled West requesting, "'Make sure that every line I have is one sentence, and it's a joke.' She was the Yukon Belle. Steve was supposed to be drinking in this saloon. And she says, 'How ya' doin', Big Boy?' He says, 'You're the Belle of the Yukon. Whaddya say, Belle?' She says, 'Ding dong.' She approved the script, but it never got into rehearsal because NBC didn't want her on. We already had her booked! NBC said, 'We can't have Mae West on. The image is too suggestive.'"

It became a running gag that writers could sneak things in on the censors, said Dana, who later wrote and produced a summer series for Spike Jones on CBS. One of the sketches centered around the lazy days of summer, with Spike lounging in a hammock. Dana recalled the joke:

"It was so hot down in the South that the cotton pickers couldn't pick, and the chicken pluckers couldn't pluck. It was the *hottest, cotton-pickin', chicken-pluckin'* day in the South." Now a censor shows up in rehearsal: "You can't use that line. You know what the reference is." We had used "cotton-pickin' chicken plucker" on the old *Tonight* show, so I just lost it. And I screamed at this guy. And we got to do it, but that's how bad it was. He didn't want us to do "cotton-pickin' chicken plucker" because "pluck" had a "u-c-k." I've never met a network censor with a sense of humor—I guess that wasn't an M.O. for that job."

169

Although Sargent and Dana assail the strict broadcast standards of the '50s, NBC's current vice president of late-night and prime-time series, Rick Ludwin, pointed out that certain kinds of ethnic and other characters widely embraced in the '50s would be absolutely prohibited today. Take three memorable characters from Allen's prime-time series. Dana's hugely popular Jose Jimenez, a Latino character that he wrote and performed, could not be done today, "at least not in the form that it was done," said Ludwin. "The malaprops, the misunderstanding, the seeming slowness of wit, lack of intelligence, and stereotypical slurs—performed by a *Caucasian*—would be completely unacceptable today." So would Pat Harrington's recurring Italian character, Guido Panzini, who appeared as a surviving officer of the Andrea Doria or a pro golfer. Even Tom Poston's character from "The Man on the Street"—the man who couldn't remember his name—might offend today's viewers as ridiculing people afflicted with Alzheimer's disease, Ludwin thought.

Ludwin gave other examples of popular characters from shows of Allen's era that today's broadcast standards people would veto: Foster Brooks, who played the lovable lush on *The Dean Martin Show*, and Hal Smith, who played Otis Campbell, the amiable town drunk on *The Andy Griffith Show*. "Now, if you were given permission to depict a drunk," explained Ludwin, "you would have to show the consequences of drinking too much. Even when we did *Cheers* in the early '80s, there was a lot of hand wringing about people drinking in a bar. First of all, you never saw anybody get drunk in the bar, but there was definitely pressure when the show first went on: 'How dare you depict people sitting and drinking for hours, days on end, being barflies!'"

Burns neither understood nor accepted the vulgarity that pervades modern television comedy, especially on cable. Add to that the cynicism and in-your-face edge, approvingly known as "attitude." "Yeah, that's what's today," Burns lamented in 1997. "They have Drew Barrymore take off her sweater in front of Letterman. So that's more news than any comedy bit in the world. Nothing is clever about that.

"Blue material is the dumbest thing in the world. They're just doing it for shock, speaking of Howard Stern. But that's the world today. The kids love it. You train them. That's all they look for, really. Jerry Springer. Now, you know, those shows are so obscene, but nobody stops them, and he's getting ratings.

"It's tough enough to sit down and write comedy sketches and make sure that it's right, and then put it on and get laughs. The easiest thing is to come out and drop your pants. Or have a filthy joke or a dirty word, which they use like crazy on cable. That's what drives me crazy: 'Well, we can do those things on cable, so that's why we do cable.' That's dumb!

"Steve never resorted to anything like that, and that's because he has that mentality and class, and we all were in the same bank. Why can't you go out there without those four-letter words and see if you can get laughs? That's *class*. Every show I was on was a success. *The Carol Burnett Show*—the biggest, cleanest, nicest writers, fun people. Then I went to Dean Martin, same thing. Smothers Brothers, same thing. I even did Flip Wilson, and he was very nice."

Today, noted Ludwin, "it's a different world, and the truth is, we're not allowed to bore the audience. And the audience has embraced things like *Sex and the City* and *The Sopranos* and given Emmys and other awards to those shows. Clearly, it's a broad-based audience that wants to have that kind of entertainment. So you can't do any hard and fast rules like, 'We will not discuss sex. We will not depict sex. We will not depict violence.' Violence and sex have been a part of literature and entertainment for two thousand years. The Bible is full of those things. So it is in the way you do it that is the measure of how good a writer or producer or director or performer you are. I would think that Steve was lamenting those who go for the cheap laugh and not necessarily that sex was being discussed."

Indeed, when periodically asked what he thought about sex on television, Allen would crack, "Well, I think you'd have to be awfully careful of the antenna."

Jerry Seinfeld prided himself in doing subject matter that in different hands would have been vulgar and offensive. Ludwin, who supervised the development of the dominant '90s sitcom *Seinfeld* for NBC, pointed to "The Contest," the classic *Seinfeld* episode about masturbation. "The 'M' word wasn't used in that script," said Ludwin. "Nothing like that had ever been done on television. We read the script, and it was so funny and so clever. And Jerry told me later that he liked the challenge of doing these touchy subjects but with a delicacy that made them acceptable. That, to him, was more interesting than using bad language or doing things that would just shock but not amuse the audience."

According to Bob Costas, "I think that while I completely admire Steve for not being vulgar, and a guy like Jerry Seinfeld never uses profanity, I do not have a problem with off-color material or profanity per se. I think it works for some people. But it's the cheap and easy and obvious and repetitive stuff that's dispiriting. Most of the stuff you see out there now is a far cry from what Richard Pryor's about or what Chris Rock is about. It's just gratuitous and obvious. And on top of it, the mean-spiritedness. You could make a commentary about something in society, or maybe take a well-crafted shot at a prominent person who might deserve it. There's a big difference between that and the rampant mean-spiritedness that's everywhere today, where you say mocking and dismissive and contemptuous things about almost everybody. It's loaded with hostility and it's directed very often toward people that are just out there. The person who's saying it doesn't even know the person about whom he's saying it."

Sargent: "Using foul language doesn't necessarily make the performance or the presentation or the material any less good. Richard

Pryor—brilliant—used terrible language. But he used it well because he made points with it. Chris Rock is terrific. Uses the worst language. But his material is good, still funny, quality is high. Then I've seen the other comics on Comedy Central, and the language is rotten, and the material is rotten."

As for intelligent comedians who pushed the envelope on the Allen-era *Tonight* and prime-time shows, Sargent pointed to Mort Sahl, whom Allen had on several times. "He never used profanity ever. But he would attack people in government." Sargent also cited Lenny Bruce, who "just did a straight monologue on our show, funny, did parodies. He was a good mimic."

Ludwin found Allen's booking of Bruce a major push of the envelope. "A lot of people don't realize how controversial it was for Steve Allen—this mainstream, Sunday night variety show—to have Lenny Bruce as a guest in 1958. Lenny is doing jokes about glue-sniffing, which at the time was as controversial as talking about crack cocaine now. I would assume that NBC or his sponsors must have come to Steve and said, 'Do we *have* to have Lenny Bruce on the show? Why can't we have Myron Cohen? He's a nice comedian and he won't get us in trouble.' And Steve recognized Lenny Bruce's talent and made him come as close as he ever came to being mainstream. I can't imagine the kind of pressures that must have been exerted on Steve at the time to either tone that down or get rid of him. But I bet it was there."

In an interview with the *Los Angeles Times* the year before he died, Allen contrasted Bruce's use of vulgarity to that of lesser contemporary comedians:

> What Lenny Bruce did for a living is not at all what today's foul-mouthed comics do. Lenny was a true social philosopher. Today's comedians just take a pretty good joke and stick a four letter word in it. Very often when I address young audiences, or audiences consisting entirely of comedians who want my advice as an older guy

who's done it, I've often said, 'You want to do hip comedy? Get every Lenny Bruce album that he ever made and spend about six months listening to it. Don't steal his stuff, you can't do that. But listen to his mind-set. Listen to his attitude. Listen to his voice as a social critic. And then, if you're half that hip when you end up, then you'll have what you want.' His satire hasn't been surpassed by anybody now. A lot of comedians just say something dirty and expect the audience to laugh at the word.

Today, said Ludwin, "you can take anything too far. You can get too sensitive on any issue. But that's the world we live in now." He noted that Jay Leno gets letters about jokes in his *Tonight* monologues that begin, "Dear Mr. Leno, How dare you. . . ."

"There's nothing you can do that isn't going to offend someone," Ludwin continued. "As a matter of fact, I've told people many times, 'If we ever stop hearing complaints about *Saturday Night Live* from viewers who are incensed about one thing or another we've done, if we don't offend somebody in some way, I will know that the show has gotten too tame.' We have got to push that envelope, particularly on *Saturday Night Live*, if we intend to be in the vanguard and at the forefront of television satire. If we bland the show out, then we're dead."

Yet, even forty-three years before Ludwin's remarks, Allen, too, was noticing that "almost every comedy routine you do today will offend somebody or other." He recalled a seemingly innocuous sketch on the *Tonight* show about a housewife having difficulty opening a bottle of ketchup. A few days later, he received a letter contained in an envelope that should appropriately have been stamped "fragile," for more reasons than one:

Dear Mr. Allen:

Though I personally did not see your broadcast of Monday, October twelfth, and did not catch up with a kinescope of it until today, a good many of our people did see the live show. To get right to the point, the opinion is general that you were unnecessarily rough on the subject of jars and bottles. GCMI is a trade association made up of companies which turn out over twenty billion new glass containers every year. It is business—like broadcasting or any other. Details of the glass container business are outlined in the attached industry fact book.

It is our belief that glass containers have many advantages over other forms of packaging, and we spend a good deal of time, thought, and money trying to promote these advantages. Your broadcast did the opposite, and we feel that it may well have hurt us seriously in the highly competitive packaging industry. We recognize, of course, that a jar or bottle subjected to the violence they were on your show will break. We also recognize that closures sometimes resist opening. However, when you consider the almost countless number of products which are glass-packed—foods, beverages, drugs and cosmetics and chemicals of all sorts—we believe that the effectiveness and efficiency of glass containers is remarkable. To see them disparaged as they were on your program is accordingly hard to take.

The harm, and we think it considerable, has been done. We did think, however, that you would want this reaction to your broadcast of October twelfth, and any comment you may have would be appreciated.

Sincerely,
Bush Barnum
Glass Container Manufacturers Institute, Inc.

* * * * * * *

Echoes of Burns and Sargent brainstorming ideas for a sketch still resonate, as captured by the *New York World Telegram and Sun* fifty years ago:

> "How about a gorilla on the show?"
>
> "Costs too much. Eighty dollars for the costume."
>
> "Get a live one. Then you won't need a costume."
>
> "How about planting a guy in the audience with a knife sticking out of his back?"
>
> "Too tame. Let's have everybody in the audience have knives sticking out of their backs."
>
> "Goldfish in the water cooler?"
>
> "Nah, the crazy chicken plucker is funnier."

Chapter 5

BANANA U.

Doing the early Tonight *show was like learning to fly.*
—Skitch Henderson

Since the dawn of late night, the house band has been an integral part of the show. It sets the tone, energizes the audience before air time, and sustains the momentum during the commercial breaks. Though largely underrated, it is arguably as important as the host in defining the show's character. According to Steve Allen, the house band tradition dates back to the 1930s, when nearly all the major radio programs had their own live bands, and carried into the television shows of the '50s.

Born in England in 1918, Skitch Henderson is a classically trained musician, having studied conducting with Fritz Reiner and Albert Coates and theory with Arnold Schoenberg and Ernest Toch. In the 1940s, he joined the music department at MGM, conducted for Frank Sinatra on NBC radio's Lucky Strike Show, *and conducted* The Philco Hour *with Bing Crosby. Henderson then served as NBC's music director and was invited by Arturo Toscanini to conduct the NBC Symphony. He conducted the* Tonight *show orchestra under Steve Allen (1954–57) and Johnny Carson during his early years (1962–66). Henderson became an award-*

177

winning composer and arranger of film and television scores. In 1983, he founded the New York Pops, the largest independent symphonic pops orchestra in the United States.

In recent years, Henderson continued to lead the New York Pops and host An Evening at Pops, *a nationally syndicated radio music series. He also continued to guest-conduct symphony orchestras worldwide. On a humid June afternoon in 1997, sitting in his modest Carnegie Hall office, a window air conditioner humming and an unframed '60s snapshot of him and Sinatra taped to a bookshelf behind him, he reflected on how his early* Tonight *experience—a painful one, at first—became the stint for which he wants to be remembered most.*

Born in Arlington, Oregon, in 1927, Carl H. Severinsen was originally nicknamed "Little Doc" after his father, a local dentist. He took up the trumpet at age seven and by age twelve had won the Music Educators' National Contest. After serving in the Army during World War II, he traveled with various big bands and eventually settled in New York City as a staff musician for NBC. Doc's late-night career began in 1954 on Steve Allen's local show under bandleader Bobby Byrne and continued into the Allen Tonight *show under Henderson. When Henderson returned to become bandleader for Johnny Carson in 1962, he recruited Doc as assistant director and first trumpet. Henderson left in 1966, and Doc ascended the following year to the title of Music Director of* The Tonight Show, *which he held until Carson retired in 1992. Seen nightly during those twenty-five years, he became the most consistently visible trumpet player in America, renown for his high musical range and technical proficiency, flamboyant wardrobe, and reputation as an affable, folksy, on-camera cut-up.*

After leaving Tonight, *Doc continued to record and perform, often with prominent members of* The Tonight Show *Orchestra, doing jazz and symphony dates across the country. When he answered the phone at his California home for his interview in April 2005, it seemed fitting that the musical legend's trumpet was not far away. In fact, he was practicing for an upcoming gig. He politely excused himself and put down the receiver momentarily in order to blow out and drain his trumpet.*

*I*t was 1949, and after working on the road with the big bands of Charlie Barnet, Tommy Dorsey, and Benny Goodman, twenty-two-year-old Carl "Doc" Severinsen decided to move to New York City. That's what aspiring musicians did in those days, explained Severinsen. "They'd go out and play with the big bands for a while and then settle in the Apple or L.A., and I chose New York. I just started doing club dates and anything I could get. And I was studying regularly."

Eager to build his career, Severinsen eyed an opening with Skitch Henderson's band, which would be performing for an event at a local race track. "Skitch hired me, and we hit it off really well. I had a solo that came up, and I knew that Skitch worked for NBC. I thought, 'This is my shot right here. I'm gonna give it all I got.' And I did, and he kinda snapped his head around, and so I was workin' regularly for him." Doc became a staff musician for NBC, playing on shows for Kate Smith, Perry Como, and other headliners of the day.

It was a promising start, although not always smooth sailing: "I had assigned Doc to *The Perry Como Show*, but he didn't laugh at Como's jokes, so they got rid of him in a hurry," remembered Henderson with a chuckle.

By 1954, Steve Allen had already established himself as the hot late-night host on WNBT-TV in New York, which had a house band led by trombonist Bobby Byrne. Yank Lawson, who played trumpet in the band, alerted Severinsen to an opening. Severinsen landed the spot but discovered that it would not be just another gig. "I didn't know anything [about Steve Allen]," recalled Severinsen, but "I enjoyed it a lot, because Steve liked the band. He liked the music. If he'd had his way, we'd have done just that and nothing else. And he had really good vocalists. It was a funny show, but what the hell, I was so glad to have anything to do!"

The budget for local shows, however, was austere. "We didn't even have arrangements at all. No arrangements," repeated Severinsen. "[Byrne would] hand us out a piece of paper each night and a pencil, and say [*affecting a strict schoolmaster's manner*], 'All right, now, gentlemen, write down the date!' You had to write it down. 'Here's what we're gonna do. Now write it down!' He was a military guy. He was really a square peg in a round hole."

Byrne would dictate a list of tunes and keys for that night's broadcast. "If we were going to do a back-up to a certain tune, and if we faked on it a little bit, he'd say, 'That's good right there. Write that down.' And we wrote out what we just played. So he was getting arrangements for free—although he was capable of writing them himself. But he wouldn't have known what to write anyway because he didn't know what was happenin'," referring to the show's free-wheeling, spontaneous format that resisted structured, advance planning. In order to fit in, "You had to be like a club date player or a jazz player."

SIBERIA

At thirty-six, Skitch Henderson was riding high in his powerful post as music director for the NBC network. He was responsible for several shows, oversaw a staff of 180, and conducted the prestigious NBC Symphony Orchestra. That year, NBC handed him a new assignment: He was to conduct the network's new *Tonight* show, replacing Bobby Byrne. Although Skitch had played organ for *Smile Time*, a 1940s Allen radio program, he knew nothing about Allen's late-night television show because his daytime duties as NBC music director kept him from staying up late.

The *Tonight* assignment, shuddered Henderson, was "Siberia. I wasn't given a choice. I felt very badly for Bobby Byrne. But that's the cruelty of this business. Nobody asks you. At NBC, the corporate ship was very tight. We sweated blood because it was make or break.

Most of the local stations didn't want us. They ran their movies, which made much more money. They had to pay for us."

Indeed, when *Tonight* opened for business, *Newsweek* reported that the NBC network consisted of only thirty-three stations reaching as far west as Omaha, Nebraska. (Today, there are over two hundred.) "It wasn't like we joined a network that was already up and running and had a whole bunch of stations," recalled Severinsen. Allen would welcome new stations to the network, one by one. "Every few nights," Severinsen continued, "there'd be another announcement: 'Hartford, Connecticut, came on.'"

Arturo Toscanini's retirement forced Henderson to dismiss the NBC Symphony. But he tried to make the most out of the two jarring developments, scrounging to get some of the symphony players jobs that could sustain them until they found work elsewhere. He even put three of them into the original *Tonight* show orchestra.

As for the other *Tonight* musicians, Skitch felt stuck with what he considered to be all the rejects of the NBC music department because the show was live and on late at night and thus was beyond the union spread of his musicians who worked on commercial shows. *Tonight* started without sponsors, so these musicians were on a "sustaining basis," according to Henderson, meaning they got $70 less a week—so, for the players, *Tonight* was Siberia, too. In another edict, NBC advised Henderson that budgetary constraints would be limiting his "orchestra" to ten players.

Already part of the band when Skitch took over, Severinsen, too, initially viewed late night as a hardship post. "But the difference was that I didn't care," he explained. At twenty-seven, he was the youngest member of the band. "I was so damn glad to get a job. It was a fun show. It was really fun. You never knew what was going to happen next. And you got to do things. That's how I got the job. Yank Lawson, the trumpet player, he didn't want to be bothered with that. He had too many record dates and other television shows. So those guys that they might like to have had were not available, so they got me."

Henderson admitted never feeling particularly comfortable outside his classical cocoon: "I came from a classical world. I had a dance band after World War II for about a year, but it was a disaster because I didn't know anything about that world." Then, Frank Sinatra called him to conduct *The Lucky Strike Show*. When that fell off the air, and NBC hired him to be its music director, he was glad to be back in his niche.

The *Tonight* assignment yanked Henderson out of that niche and created new problems. First, admitted Henderson, neither he nor anyone else in the band knew what they were doing. "We didn't know anything about television. All my friends were movie stars who wouldn't be caught dead on television at that time" because given the new medium's harsh, primitive lighting techniques, "they'd look like ghouls. The only person who really had the skill was Steve Allen because he was an absolute genius, thinking on his feet all the time."

But while Skitch may have respected Allen's television expertise, he had serious reservations about Allen's musical integrity. In the beginning, Allen never gave him instructions because Allen wanted to play piano himself. This bothered Henderson: "Steve in those days was in a learning period—now we're longtime friends—but at that time I looked at him with a jaundiced eye and ear. My square musical integrity got in the way. But I had no experience."

A trained pro jazzman at the time, Doc offered a thoughtful assessment of Allen's skills: "He wasn't a *great* musician. He did a lot of things. I don't think he even read music. But, still, he had a knack for knowing the right thing to play and doing a pretty darn good job of it. Most piano players who'd have been better to have around as piano players wouldn't have been any use at all as far as talking and being on television."

Severinsen also acknowledged Allen as an accomplished songwriter, noting that he wrote the show's closing theme, a smoky ballad titled "Tonight," which began with an unaccompanied trumpet solo played by Doc. "It wasn't easy," he sighed.

Henderson did feel somewhat relieved that Allen didn't tamper with what he was: "a square musician. And he pretty much left me alone. That's why he could sit down and play jazz, which is something I could never do, still can't do." In addition, Henderson found Allen very open to music ideas. "I could come in with a tuba player who played with his nose and Steve would say, 'Sure! Try him out.'"

As best as Henderson could recall, in addition to Severinsen and Lawson, the original *Tonight* show band included Bobby Rosengarden (later conductor for Dick Cavett) on drums and Harold Dawson on all woodwind instruments. On bass was Eddie Safranski (who had been a big star with the Stan Kenton band) and sometimes Bob Haggart (formerly with Bob Crosby's Bobcats and who would later join Skitch in the Carson *Tonight* band). On guitars were Tony Mattola and Tony Gottuso. Then there were two French horn players known as the Burr Brothers, and the bass trombone player, Abe Perlstein—the disbanded symphony players Skitch had placed. Also in the trumpet section were Harry "Sweets" Edison, Buck Clayton, and Lou McGarrity, as well as Frank Rosolino on trombone. Some of these musicians played on a rotating basis.

The *Tonight* house band during the Allen era played a broad role on the show—much broader than in later decades. The musicians would occasionally do numbers of their own, back Allen at the piano, and play for the regular singers or behind guest vocalists like Peggy Lee, Mel Tormé, Ella Fitzgerald, and Joe Williams. "We had to be ready at any minute," explained Doc. Steve might just decide on the spur of the moment, 'I'll play a little piano,' and then come over and sit with the band and start playin'—and it was our job to find something to play with him. Or they might say, 'Hey, have so-and-so play a solo.' This happened fairly often.

Allen observed that by 1992, the band had become limited to

playing the opening and closing themes and musical flourishes coming out of commercials. The band would seldom perform a full number unless it was accompanying a guest singer.

Still, the *Tonight* assignment left Skitch feeling "not out of place, but ill prepared. There were four of us that were such horrible squares—the two French horn players and the bass trombonist. Doc and Bobby and the other guys were the hellraisers. But I learned from my experience in vaudeville. You had to figure out what went with what. But that's how we started," Henderson remembered, "like peasants."

BECOMING A BANANA

Henderson's "square musician" label was not necessarily a handicap, for it actually balanced the *Tonight* show cast with a necessary, no-nonsense element that the network, Allen, and Henderson did not fully appreciate at the time. Decades later, Henderson still might not appreciate the unique level of humor he contributed, just by being himself.

To begin with, Henderson naturally projected an extremely dignified persona. This may have been the product of his English roots and European classical musical upbringing. He was softspoken and erudite. There was the neatly trimmed, trademark goatee. Visually, Skitch might be described as the Sebastian Cabot of conductors, certainly closer to the late Boston Pops conductor Arthur Fiedler than, say, the wild Paul Shaffer (conductor for David Letterman) or the flamboyant Doc Severinsen during his Carson days. Henderson's *Tonight* show assignment in 1954 might be like assigning venerated film score composer John Williams today to *Saturday Night Live*. Thus, dropping Henderson into the loose, zany surroundings of *Tonight* offered many opportunities for visual incongruity and humor. In short, Henderson got to become, as he described drily, "a banana."

Obviously, Henderson had no on-camera experience as a banana, nor did he receive banana training. He wasn't even a straight man and had never done stand-up lines. His television hosting experience had consisted of reading a piece of paper or saying, "Here they are, folks." Skitch always felt very uncomfortable in sketches, "partially because I didn't have the confidence. I was working with such skilled people like Louis Nye, Don Knotts, and Tom Poston. All of those people to me were such geniuses. I'd watch them, how they deliver, their timing. The only thing that saved me was my old vaudeville training, working with acts, where you have one line to say."

"Skitch had to learn," said Doc. "There was no script. He had to be able to talk and do whatever, provide a little timing. Like if Steve didn't want to tell the whole story, then Skitch would chime in, and give him a chance to collect himself and then get on with it. He developed a personality. He wore a derby hat and played a character." According to Doc, Henderson took being drawn into the comedy of the show well. "He was a proper Englishman, so he played it kinda straight. That was the way he worked it."

"Stan Burns wrote me a character named Sidney Ferguson," recalled Skitch. "He gave me a derby because I was British-born, and I was married to a German lady [Faye Emerson], which gave great humor to Stan. He invented Sidney Ferguson."

Henderson's willingness to interact with Steve was a departure from the style of his predecessor on the local show, observed Doc. Under Bobby Byrne, the band "was just there. I don't think he [interacted with Steve] at all. That was one of the reasons he didn't stay there," Doc speculated.

While "dignified" and "uncomfortable" may have described Henderson, so did "genial" and "cooperative." He soon found himself trapped in crazy stunts, like one during a road show in Miami where everybody had to ride a bicycle down the length of a narrow wooden plank laid across the width of a hotel swimming pool. The goal was to reach the other side of the pool dry, and only one highly coordinated and lucky fellow did. Others, outfitted in sweats or shorts, hammed their way into the pool, splashing with characteristic abandon. Skitch—primly attired in coat and tie—pedaled cautiously and sensibly until he was just a foot away from the other side, whereupon he and his bicycle tipped over with the kind of dignity one would never think achievable in a swimming pool. The water didn't even splash over the edge of the pool, or so it seemed.

Then there was the basketball skirmish with the New York Knicks. "One of the Knicks treated me like a real basketball player, and he broke my little toe," Skitch recalled. "It was a great trauma with the NBC legal department because they saw a lawsuit, which I would never do, but I was off the show for about two weeks. I felt like a fob with a broken toe, broken in a basketball game."

In contrast, Doc was less inhibited, a self-described smart aleck. He had a mischievous grin that many of his high school teachers must have spotted emanating from the back row of their classrooms. "I was there playing, and whatever they wanted me to do, I was glad to do it. One of the great things for me on that show was Skitch always found room for me to do something, to act up. He promoted me a lot."

One night on the show, Doc played a solo lying down on a bed: "An old iron bed with a sagging mattress," he described. "I remembered when they wheeled one of those beds out and said, 'Doc, lay on that bed and play a tune.' It looked like a whorehouse," he exclaimed—immediately adding with an emphatic but impish tone, "That's what everybody told me."

TRAIN WRECKS

Bombing is a risk inherent to live TV. Henderson estimates that *Tonight* regularly detonated its share of bombs: "Out of the five shows a week, we generally had two bombs—if Steve were being honest, he'd tell you that. That was about the formula with Carson, too—maybe three out of five would swing, and the rest would be hurry-up-and-get-off-the-air 'cause it wasn't worth it. But it was creativity every night." And to Skitch and the rest of the show's staff, the creativity was addicting.

There were, as Henderson affectionately called them, "train wrecks." One involved a circus snake act. A trainer brought a bunch of snakes in a carrier, assuring everybody that the snakes posed absolutely no danger. But in those days of black and white, the studio was inundated with almost blinding light. "We all lost our eyesight on the shows," Skitch quipped, not to mention the resulting high level of heat generated by the lights. When the trainer opened his case, the snakes—apparently jolted by the light and heat—bolted straight up and scattered all over the stage. Everybody, including the musicians, sought the highest rung to get out of there. People ran out of the theater. "But that was the show," said a beaming Skitch, "every night."

Skitch remembered that when Andy Williams joined the company, they thought it would be great to do remotes with singers performing in crazy places. So they sent the gentlemanly Williams to a New York bathhouse. Unfortunately, Andy's audio line from the orchestra went out, so he couldn't hear what was being piped to him from the studio. As Skitch remembered, "his pitch began to vary a little. I could hear him, but he couldn't hear me. I could see that something was wrong, but Andy just kept going and finished the number as though nothing was wrong. He might have been a minor third higher or lower."

Then, Skitch chuckled, there was "the lady whose dress fell down and her boobs fell out in the middle of her number. And it wasn't a big trauma. There were jokes on it, she picked up her dress, and everything was fine."

While the sketches, stunts, train wrecks, and overall zaniness might have turned the *Tonight* show into a circus, Skitch credited Allen for remaining "very much the ringmaster. If anything made it easy, it was Steve 'cause he was absolutely a genius ringmaster." Henderson admired how Allen allowed *Tonight* staffers to purposely keep him in the dark about certain bits or guests planned for the show, just to ensure that his ad-libbed reaction was fresh. "And I respect Carson's ability in the saddle 'cause he took care of that house for so long. But Steve is the only host I saw that never came apart or was thrown in any way."

The loose atmosphere of the show was not lost on Skitch, who selectively absorbed certain elements of it. He began to feel less awkward and more at ease with the spontaneity of Doc and Bobby Rosengarden, and he allowed the band to improvise more. Doc, too, began to emerge as a banana. The band began to play bumps and grinds if a woman of pulchritude came on stage, "until the NBC legal department started screaming at us."

SINGERS IN THE FAMILY

Only during the Allen era did *Tonight* employ a "family" of house singers: Steve Lawrence, Eydie Gorme, Pat Kirby (who joined the show after her predecessor, Pat Marshall, left after six months), and Andy Williams. Each would appear roughly five times every two weeks. Henderson recalled them from his conductor's perspective:

> Steve was straight ahead. Eydie was very temperamental and could drop a few tears at a moment's notice. But she was the most improved singer in the period on the show. She started as a careful singer, singing carefully and politely. She became, as she is today, one of the great esoterically emotional singers, but not over the brim.
>
> Andy was very serious. There was something different about him. From the very beginning, he was the only one amongst us

188

who had a solid idea of the direction he wanted to go. He had the first hit record ["Canadian Sunset" in 1956]. He emerged first, which drove Steve and Eydie crazy, naturally.

"Andy was real showbiz-wise, as a member of the Williams Brothers," recalled Doc, who remembered Andy approaching him to ask if he could write some arrangements for some of Andy's early solo gigs. "I said, 'No, Andy, I don't write arrangements.' Fifty years later, looking back on Andy's monumentally successful post-*Tonight* career, he wondered, "Wow . . . if I did, what a great break that would have been."

Because of the show's fluid nature, all Skitch could go by was not a script, but a rundown. "That kind of gave us an idea of what was next," he explained. But the success of a comedy bit or other segment might prompt producer Bill Harbach to instruct Skitch to cancel a musical number, sometimes only moments before it was scheduled to air. "I used to have to be the curmudgeon to say, 'I'm sorry, you won't get on tonight.' Andy, Steve, and Eydie were very heavy if they were there and didn't sing. It was a growing pain, but a wonderful growing pain."

Pat Kirby, however, "couldn't have cared less," marveled Skitch. "She didn't care if I canceled her song. She'd say, 'Thank you, good night,' and then leave." In fact, Skitch felt that Pat—the least known of the four singers—was actually the best. "Andy was the Cadillac. Steve and Eydie were the Chevrolets. Pat Kirby, to me, was the Rolls Royce, because of her wonderful look at life. How this, too, shall pass, and I'm not going to live or die. She had no illusion about stardom."

Skitch and his singing family developed a camaraderie, complete with secret hand signals. "With Steve and Eydie, when somebody was a jerk, we'd look at each other and say, 'Wrong!' [*fingers in the 'OK' position*], so they wouldn't know what we were talking about. If it worked, then we'd do this [*fingers opening and closing, chatting*]. We were a very tight-knit family. I couldn't wait to get to work, and that was really rare for me."

Steve and Eydie also couldn't wait to get to work for other reasons. "That was the start of their romance," recalled Doc. "They were both single kids. And boy, Eydie had her eye out for him. She just saw him and went for it! It was like watching high school kids fall in love."

Because of so-called budgetary constraints, the singers would lightheartedly accuse Skitch of recycling the same intros and endings on different songs—"borrowing," they'd say. "I said, 'No, I changed it!' But I didn't. We had certain vamps on rhythm songs that we always used. I tried to write something on most ballads."

When Henderson returned in 1962 to conduct *The Tonight Show* band for Johnny Carson, he tried unsuccessfully to revive the "family-of-singers" concept. Carson was right, he admitted, because with what Carson ended up with, he didn't need a family. The Steve Allen approach "gave us a family identity, and we didn't have to have too many guests. And it really saved us. Music guests are a pain in the ass. They don't like the orchestra, or they don't like me, or they want their father to come in and conduct, it never stops. With Carson, it was a nightmare. Something was always wrong. That was the wonderful thing about the *Tonight* show with Steve: When we went to work, that was it. That was kind of a luxury."

MUSICAL COP

Henderson was quick to note that the looseness of the show hardly meant that the music was sloppy. He recognized that great fakers like Doc and Rosengarden would tend to follow Allen's spontaneous lead. Henderson, however, would generally try to corral things and impose a musical discipline: "I was a musical cop. I just cared that if

190

you were paid to come and do a job, you did that job properly. I'm still that way. Dammit, if you're there to play, play!"

Severinsen was comfortable with this approach: "Skitch let the guys be themselves. But he made damn sure that you did what you were supposed to."

In a way, having a disciplined band with a couple of free-wheeling jazz players gave an appealing edge to the total sound, which was fine for both Allen and Henderson. Musically, said Skitch, "there was looseness—with a knot just behind it."

Ironically, Skitch's disciplined approach did not mandate excessive rehearsals. "We didn't rehearse. We never rehearsed. We'd show up. The union call was an hour, which meant you could play fifty minutes out of that hour. And maybe we'd run through a vocal arrangement. But rehearse, per se, was unknown. Most programs rehearsed themselves to death. Underrehearsing is something that I established because I feel that keeps everybody on the edge much more. I still underrehearse. It's always my psychology. Toscanini taught me that: just leave a little bit *not* prepared. Keeps everybody focused in attention."

The vocal numbers were the one thing Skitch did rehearse in order for director Dwight Hemion to prepare his shots. This was mutually beneficial, as Hemion's slow directorial style actually gave Skitch the great luxury of having time to fix things musically.

Henderson suggested that the show's loose image belied a great deal of self-discipline on the part of the nonmusical cast members as well:

There was a time when people showed up in television who were prepared to do what they did. Steve was a monologist. Louis Nye, Tom Poston, Don Knotts were actors, comedic actors. I think there was a time when people came to the medium before anybody knew what the medium was, and they were well prepared as professionals. And their professional ability put a stamp that has never gone away. Stan Burns and Herb Sargent were a part of that, too, because of their diabolical sense of humor.

No one ever said, "We'll do this, it'll work perfect." Because any-time we did do that, it never did work perfect. Being on live was the healthiest thing there ever was. It makes you a better-prepared per-former. You have to think about what you're doing, be prepared for what you're doing, be prepared for your mistakes. Be prepared to say, "I was wrong," when you were wrong and not "I'll do it again and everything will be wonderful." But that had to do with our spirit because the spirit was so incredible.

Skitch emphasized that *Tonight*, happily, was a "we" effort: "There wasn't an 'I' on that show. It wasn't 'I did it,' it was 'we did it.' Makes a helluva difference. I learned a lot doing that show which I've used the rest of my life. We all contributed. I think I brought a certain kind of musical integrity to the performance factor. If you play, you play right."

LEARNING TO FLY

Throughout his more than fifty years in the business, Henderson admitted to feeling governed by a constant professional insecurity. "I felt tomorrow was Armageddon. Always. I've been in this business too long. I worked in the studios, and I watched that go. I came back after World War II, went to Hollywood, no job. I came to New York, became music director of NBC—it's a radio network, then all of a sudden one day I'm on the air with Sinatra, we're doing *The Lucky Strike Show*. We're canceled. It's the end of radio. Then, an NBC vice president came to me and said, 'We're starting a television opera-tion. Why don't you stay here?' I always feel this way. We're in that kind of a business. If you serve the public, you serve a demon."

Doc's approach was less philosophical and more pragmatic: "All I wanted to do was practice my horn and play and try to earn enough money to feed my family," he reflected. "And I didn't know how fortunate I was. I didn't know what was goin' on. I would just go to the theater and do whatever came up."

Henderson also confessed that the period of his distinguished career that he would want to be remembered by most is, surprisingly, the early *Tonight* show. Gazing out of his Carnegie Hall office window, he was oblivious to the series of Disney characters and floats parading on the street nine stories below:

> When I started, I was so unhappy to be sent there 'cause I thought, what in God's name am I doing here? We still had the symphony then, and I was living this strange life of doing Sibaleus on Sunday afternoon and doing the *Tonight* show the rest of the week. Doing *Tonight* was like learning to fly. That was one of the few times ever in my life in television that I couldn't wait to get to work. And remember, I'd worked here all day as an office curmudgeon. We had organ players here doing soap operas, and they were all temperamental stars. All [of my] conductors were unhappy with the musicians they had.
>
> [But on *Tonight*,] I was in a creative unit, and it was creative every night, till the last second we were on the air. I'd leave the theater at maybe 1:30, and I'd get home by three. I was back here at the network by 9:30 or ten the next morning. I've never forgotten that period. One of the eight-by-tens that I absolutely revere was a picture a photographer took on the last night of the show and gave to me for some reason—it's myself and two or three members of the orchestra, all with long faces, and there's Steve smiling, holding up a glass of champagne. I personally was very disturbed. What started off so inconsequential . . . became quite meaningful.

★ ★ ★ ★ ★ ★

Henderson's efforts to promote Doc did not end with the Allen *Tonight* show. When he returned to conduct for Carson in 1962, he asked Doc to return, too. At first, Doc declined: "I was getting pretty busy doin' other things. 'No, I don't think I want to do that,'" Doc told Skitch. "'I don't want to be that tied down, especially late at night.' And he says, 'Now, Carl'—he always called me Carl—'you have to come and play in the band, and you won't be sorry.' And he knew good and well that if he didn't have someone like me to take over, he wouldn't be able to take off and do his symphony things. He didn't want to come out and promise that and say that."

Henderson left the show in 1966. Milton DeLugg took over for a year until Severinsen picked up the baton in 1967. He led *The Tonight Show* Band for the remaining twenty-five years of the Johnny Carson era, transforming it into one of the premiere jazz bands in America, with its brassy, big band sound. From his years with Allen, Doc brought to the Carson show "the general feeling, realizing what the show was supposed to be. As far as my part of it, I just had to feel that I was supposed to be like a character, a wise guy—not a wise guy, but a cut-up, and I always was anyway. I'm glad I was there.

"Steve was great to work for because he loved music and musicians. Up until then, musicians were merely part of the backdrop, and he really made the band a real part of the show."

Carson, to his credit, resisted NBC's continual attempts to downsize the band from sixteen regular members to just six. The network, however, won the battle after Carson retired, and the current *Tonight* band under guitarist Kevin Eubanks numbers just eight players who deliver a lighter brand of jazz than classic big band.

But the loose, lively, spontaneous buzz with which late-night house bands must charge the air endures. *Chicago Tribune* arts critic Howard Reich marveled at the ability of Max Weinberg (leader of Conan O'Brien's house band) to "fire a glance at his sidemen, call out a title, snap a tempo and hear a virtually complete version of a tune the band hadn't intended on playing 10 seconds earlier. In a well-worn TV genre such as the talk show, which easily can descend into a screenful of talking heads, that kind of hair-trigger response can make the difference between a static show and an exuberant one." When the Max Weinberg 7 spontaneously breaks into "Disco Inferno"—just because actor Michael Rappaport suddenly demanded that O'Brien and fellow guest Rosie Perez disco dance to it—one can hear echoes of Skitch Henderson and his men honoring a request for an obscure song from someone in the audience or breaking into bumps and grinds when a female bombshell struts onto the stage.

Such turn-on-a-dime talent remains underappreciated. "I stand up," O'Brien told the *Chicago Tribune*. "Rosie Perez stands up, and Max and the band immediately kick into 'Disco Inferno,' complete with all the horn parts, the guitar parts, the bass line, everything, and it's a pretty complicated song. I dance with Rosie, the whole audience goes crazy, and then we both nonchalantly sit down and continue the interview."

Chapter 6

NIGHT SCHOOL
FOR GIFTED SINGERS

When they were hired to sing on the local Steve Allen Show *in 1953, Steve Lawrence was eighteen, and Eydie Gorme was twenty-one. Initially hired to perform separately, the two were eventually paired in musical numbers and continued into the network* Tonight *show until Allen left in 1957. "Steve and Eydie," as they were popularly known, became a pair in real life when they married later that year. They went on to become one of America's most successful singing duos, garnering several Emmys for their tributes to Irving Berlin (1979) and George Gershwin (1976), as well as Grammys for their single "We've Got Us" (1960) and Eydie's solo recording of "If He Walked into My Life" (1966). Other hits include Eydie's "Blame It on the Bossa Nova" (1963) and Steve's chart-topping "Go Away Little Girl" (1960). In the '70s, Steve's comic talent won him a recurring role on* The Carol Burnett Show. *The duo toured the world for several years with Frank Sinatra, who declared, "Steve and Eydie represent all that is good about performers and the interpretation of a song . . . they're the best."*

Andy Williams was added in time for the Tonight *network debut in September 1954. He, too, remained for the duration of Allen's tenure. From 1962 to 1971, he hosted* The Andy Williams Show *on NBC, a three-time Emmy Award–winning musical-variety series, where he sang alongside guests like Ella Fitzgerald, Tony Bennett, Judy Garland, Bobby Darin, and Bing Crosby and later with Elton John, Ray Charles, Linda Ronstadt, Simon and Garfunkel, and Aretha Franklin. His annual family holiday specials established him as America's musical ambassador of Christmas. Columbia Records once billed him as its number-one best-selling male vocalist, racking up twenty gold and four platinum albums and introducing standards like "Moon River" (1962), "The Days of Wine and Roses" (1963), "Can't Get Used to Losing You" (1963), and "Love Story (Where Do I Begin?)" (1971). Williams hosted the Grammy Awards telecasts from 1971 to 1977, helping establish them as a must-see worldwide event. In 1992, he built and opened his two thousand-seat Moon River Theatre in Branson, Missouri, where he continued to perform nightly to live audiences six months a year, solo and with guest performers like Glen Campbell, Ann-Margret, and Petula Clark.*

Fifty years after their stint on Tonight, *despite their own formidable successes, these show business icons have never forgotten when they were just kids in a cast of accomplished and often legendary grown-ups. Steve and Eydie, as warm and chummy as they were elegantly dressed, sat in their finely appointed suite at Chicago's Drake Hotel on a rainy afternoon in October 1998. Andy, ever relaxed and genial, shared his recollections in September 2002 from his sunny dressing room between shows at his Moon River Theatre.*

*B*ecause Steve Allen revered the great standards by the likes of Cole Porter, George Gershwin, Harold Arlen, and Richard Rodgers and Lorenz Hart, *The Steve Allen Show* would feature two resident vocalists performing musical numbers in between the comedy and other portions of the show. At eighteen, Steve Lawrence, a student at Thomas Jefferson High School in Brooklyn, had already won an Arthur Godfrey competition, cut a hit record, and appeared twice on Steve Allen's popular radio show. His less glamorous but steadier gig was hanging out at the Brill Building on Broadway, the center of the music industry in the 1950s, earning money by singing songs for demo records. In July 1953, he successfully auditioned for Allen's local late-night television show with his rendition of "April in Paris."

A female singer was needed, and a beautiful young blonde by the name of Helene Dixon tried out. Recalled Allen in a 1997 interview,

> Of all the fourteen women who came in and auditioned, we chose her. She was the best. She sang two big rhythmic standards of those days, something like "Life Is Just a Bowl of Cherries" novelties. And she did them well, so she got the job.
>
> At this point, it sounds like a story that, if you saw it in a movie, you'd find it kind of unbelievable. On a Tuesday night she sang one of the songs she had auditioned with, and then on Thursday she sang her other song. And then Billy Harbach said to her, "Great, Helene. What would you like to do next week?"
>
> She said, "What?" And he said, "You know, what songs do you wanna sing next Tuesday and Thursday?" She said, "I don't know any other songs." So he did a four-second blank take and said, "Well, that's okay. You've got a few days to learn." It's not that tough to learn a song if you're a professional singer. Unfortunately, it turned out to be for the poor young lady. And she said, "Oh, gosh, Billy, it takes me a long time to learn a song. And I learned those two, and I've been singing those around town. I don't think I could do this."
>
> So we had to let her go. Isn't that sad? Here she had a job on a show that became the biggest. Maybe she had not much experience at that point, and maybe somebody had heard her sing at a party and said, "You have a nice voice, Helene. Why don't you learn a couple of numbers and hire a piano player?" She had probably gotten that far. Of course, she had to be replaced.

Eydie Gorme had sung with the Tex Beneke Band. She had recorded the hit "Frenesi"—a half-English, half-Spanish jazz number, described Eydie—and performed it on TV with Freddy Martin's band. Her performance caught Allen's attention, and he sent his manager, Jules Green, to invite her to audition. "Who's Steve Allen?" Eydie asked. A United Nations interpreter by day and New York City College student at night, she had been living with her parents in the Bronx at the time, and they didn't own a TV set. Bob Thiele, the head of her record label, Coral, encouraged her to audition, but Eydie was reluctant: "I hated auditions because I never made an audition in my life. I auditioned five times [unsuccessfully] for the Godfrey show. The last time they saw me coming up the stairs, they locked the doors—God forbid, I should come in for one more audition!"

When she arrived at the audition for the Allen show, the brunette Eydie didn't have her hopes up. "They were looking for a blonde, someone who looked like Marilyn Monroe. And I was, well, me. With my bangs. They asked me how many songs I knew, and I said two thousand. I was a walking fake book. There was nothing I didn't know. All of us working singers would go to the Brill Building and get all the new sheet music, which they gave you free in those days. And so everybody knew all the songs. And that's how I got the job."

Although not paired at the beginning, Steve and Eydie eventually began singing together. "It turned out that we always liked the same songs from the same movie musicals," said Eydie. "And we would do [*singing*], 'How could you believe me when I said I love you, when you know I've been a liar all my life?' Or [*singing*] 'We're a couple of swells.' We would be re-creating this for audiences, and they really fell in love with us doing all this stuff."

At eighteen and twenty-one, the two were easily the youngest in the cast. "I think it was a plus," said Steve, "because when you hang around people that are experienced, it's like playing baseball or tennis with better players. You become better. You learn more. They forced you to be on your toes around them. I think that was a great, great education for us. So we would stand or sit around even when we weren't on, and we would just watch everything and listen and just absorb it."

The young singers would often arrive at the studio early, just to hang out with writer Stan Burns and whomever else happened to be around. Their eager attitude inspired other cast members to take them under their wings. "They knew we were in the same vein behind them," Steve said, "very anxious and willing to learn. They were a profound influence. Every great comic, every great singer, every great actor was a guest on that show. And we as kids would sit there and just watch. Sometimes we were thrown into sketches with them. It was great basic training for us."

It was also a place to learn and hone their individual skills. Eydie acknowledged Skitch Henderson's observation that she had blossomed from a "careful" singer to a more emotive one:

It's true. But I wasn't a careful singer before I went on Tex Beneke's band. He would always put me down that I was too show biz: '*You're* not the star of the show, *I'm* the star of this show. Don't do this, don't raise your hands, and don't do that.'

And so when I came on Steve Allen's show, I was still very careful 'cause I was trying to keep my voice modulated and not do all the stuff I was doing on records. I did grow a lot on the show. I became a lot looser also as a performer. You almost had to be, and I loved doing it.

That was school. The greatest school.

That training was not without its awkward moments. Jayne Meadows remembered that on television in those days, "you couldn't wear white or a lot of busy stuff. They said to Steve

Lawrence, 'Bring a pastel shirt. You cannot wear white.' So Steve, still a young boy in school—instead of asking, 'What is a pastel shirt?' so they could tell him—got on the subway, went home, and called all his friends to ask, 'What is a pastel shirt?' Nobody in Brooklyn had ever heard, much less owned, a pastel shirt."

"The biggest thing on the show was the experience we had just watching Steve Allen every night," continued Lawrence. "There's so much of him that's rubbed off on me, I think. In his comedy, he would take things and just turn them around. And I used to find myself incorporating some of that into my thinking. And when you live with a guy and admire him that much, you start appropriating some of his personality or abilities, and then you add your own to that."

STANDING UP TO THE NETWORK

To most of the personnel associated with Allen's local late-night show, the conversion to the network *Tonight* show represented a huge leap forward. As a reward for their talent and loyalty, Allen lobbied successfully to bring as many of them as possible with him into the network. "So we became NBC people," said director Dwight Hemion. "This meant more money, a lot of things."

The network, however, had reservations about Steve and Eydie. Recalled Steve: "The network guys came in and said, 'We love the show. We want to put it on the network. But we want to make a couple of changes.' Steve Allen said, 'Really? What?' And they said, 'We want to get rid of Steve Lawrence and Eydie Gorme.' And Steve said, 'Why?' And they *said* we were too ethnic looking. And the meaning behind that was—"

"Jews," Eydie chimed in, finishing her husband's sentence. Lawrence, born Sidney Liebowitz, was the son of a cantor. Eydie, born Edith Gormezano, was the daughter of Spanish-speaking Sephardic Jews.

According to Eydie, Allen responded, "'[Steve Lawrence] looks like a Nazi. He's got blond hair, blue eyes. What do you mean, *ethnic*? Well, everybody knows he's Jewish.'"

Lawrence recalled Allen proposing his own solution: "I will agree to replace Steve Lawrence and Eydie Gorme if you will get me—for the same money we're paying the kids—Frank Sinatra and Peggy Lee. Now get out of my office. If you want the show, then put the show on the way it is."

"So the network said the only way they would do it is that if they kept us, they would get two other singers," said Eydie, "so that three times a week they would have Gentiles, and two times a week they would have us."

In the end, Steve and Eydie agreed that adding two singers and then alternating the two teams was a good way to broaden the appeal of a nationally telecast show. "Otherwise, it'd be too much of the same," said Bill Harbach. Ultimately, each team appeared three times one week and two times the next. Occasionally, when needed, all four singers would appear on the same show.

Adding Andy Williams

In 1954, twenty-six-year-old Andy Williams was already a show-biz veteran. During the preceding eighteen years, the clean-cut Midwesterner from Wall Lake, Iowa, had sung church, country, folk, and modern tunes with his three older brothers on radio and in patriotic war films for MGM. In 1947, Kay Thompson, MGM's choral director and vocal coach for Judy Garland and Lena Horne, recruited the Williams Brothers for a cutting-edge nightclub act that she was putting together. Kay Thompson and the Williams Brothers introduced an element of Broadway-style theater previously unheard of in nightclub acts. The material, written by Thompson, was sophisticated and witty. It wasn't just songs but stories reflecting Thompson's wry sense of humor. The pacing was frenetic. The arrangements and choreography were complicated, highly rhythmic, and vocally demanding. And for five years, Kay and the boys became the hottest ticket in America and Europe.

The act broke up in 1952, and Williams decided to pursue a solo career. Bouncing around from club to club, he discovered the irony of having made it big as a group singer: It didn't translate into immediate success in a solo career. "I went to New York and opened at the Blue Angel," he recalled. "And I did some of the hotels where Kay Thompson and the Williams Brothers had played—but nobody knew who I was."

Williams persevered. Because of his success with Kay Thompson, he continued to set his sights high. "I thought I was going to be Noel Coward," he said. "So I spent about two years in supper clubs singing 'Mad Dogs and Englishmen' and doing George Gershwin medleys and that kind of thing."

In 1954, Williams was still searching for a break. He had appeared once on Ed Sullivan's show but was not asked to return. Things were looking bleak. To survive, he sometimes ate dog food. Then, one day, he ran into Bill Harbach, who had once briefly managed Kay Thompson and the Williams Brothers. "I'm getting a haircut, I'm leaving the Plaza Hotel," recalled Harbach, "heading for a meeting with Skitch Henderson for the first time to audition about five or six kids that agents had sent over to us. Andy was walking across Fifth Avenue and yells at me, 'Billy!' I said, 'Andy, how are ya doin'?' He said, 'Well, you know, I may be trying to get a record done here.' I said, 'Andy, you've gotta come down, we're doing auditions here at NBC. Come down at two o'clock and, goddammit, audition for us. I mean it!"

"I gave him the big, big push," continued Harbach excitedly. "Steve had never heard of him. I told Skitch, 'This kid is awesome. This, of all of them, is the one that's gonna be right.' He came down that afternoon and sang 'Spring Is Here.' And boom—he did it! Skitch says, 'Wow! That's the kid.' That afternoon—I had forgotten about Andy—I was just coming out from a haircut, and he yells at me. Jesus, Andy, of course!"

Williams never forgot the chance nature of his meeting with Harbach: "Otherwise, I never would have known. I said to him, 'Who's Steve Allen?' because I didn't know. Bill Harbach is the reason I'm on the *Tonight* show."

Allen had heard of Andy's work with Kay Thompson but did not meet him until he came on the show. "But right away," said Allen, "I became a big fan. He was gentlemanly and personable. He wasn't—already, that day, the kids with the leather jackets, or the falsetto 'I'm sixteen years old'-voices, [*singing*] 'OOOH-HOOOO!'—all that teenage stuff, some of which was good, but most of which was garbage. He was not in that category, even though he was young. Andy always had an intelligence to his singing."

Williams was paired with a talented, young female singer, Pat Marshall, who left the show after five months to pursue a Broadway career. Marshall was replaced by Pat Kirby, who stayed with the show for the remaining two years of Allen's tenure.

The combination of Lawrence, Gorme, Williams, Marshall, and Kirby gelled because they all shared Allen and Harbach's musical taste. "We were all freaks of melodic music," said Allen. "We all loved Gershwin and Berlin and Porter and Noel Coward and all the great writers." Because of Harbach's show-business connections, "There were a lot of new shows coming up where he had gotten first dibs on the songs," Eydie explained. "Nobody had heard them." They would introduce songs on television from, say, the new Cole Porter or Harold Arlen show. On some nights, the entire program would be devoted to the music of a single composer, where "we'd have a pile of music, and [the singers] passed it around and took turns running through the catalogue," said Steve Lawrence.

Andy sheepishly remembered the night they did a tribute to Richard Rodgers. He sang Rodgers's classic "Spring Is Here," a song he frequently performed in his nightclub act, but he didn't realize that the opening verse he had been doing was something extra that had been written especially for him by Kay Thompson and incorporated into his arrangement of the song. When he sang Thompson's verse in front of Rodgers, "Richard Rodgers was looking at me like, 'What the hell is this?'" chuckled Andy. "And then he told me later, 'I didn't write that first part!'"

Williams's exposure on *Tonight* led to a record contract with Cadence Records, an independent label run by Arthur Godfrey's conductor, Archie Bleyer, which released Williams's first album, *Andy Williams Sings Steve Allen*.

THE KIDS IN THE CAST

The four young singers were quickly immersed in big-time show biz. "A lot of people we met on the show are people you never dreamed of in your whole life," said Eydie. "In your *whole life*! Gene Kelly. Richard Rodgers. Johnny Mercer and Sammy Cahn. And we all became good friends. Oscar Peterson. Lena Horne. If you talk about being in awe—these were icons. I mean, it was like, we were so astounded just to be in the presence of so many of these people."

"You would never otherwise have had that opportunity to say hello to so many famous people," recalled Marshall in a 2002 interview. "There were many aspects of being that program that were so unexpected and so unique."

The live, spontaneous nature of the show required the singers to be patient. "The very last thing they'd do before the show went on—the very *last* thing—was run through whatever songs we were gonna do," said Eydie. It was, "'Okay, don't worry, it'll be fine,' or they would cut it. It worked!"

"We didn't rehearse for days like you did when you had a role in a play or a musical," said Marshall, who came from a theater background. "You'd rehearse it in the afternoon, then you'd do it in the evening."

The singers also had to be flexible with last-minute changes or cuts to their numbers. "It varied," explained Steve. "Sometimes we didn't do any. Sometimes they were all cut, depending on how hot the show was—how the comedy was going, how the guests were with Steve [Allen], how we were relating to each other." Changes were being made not only until air time but *through* air time. "I would be getting ready to go into a set," said Steve, "and Billy Harbach would yell, 'Cut!' They were rollin'. Steve was on a thing that was much funnier, and they were right."

Sometimes, one singer didn't mind his number getting cut. Williams, arguably the most experienced performer of the four, was discovering that television required a different skill set from the one he had developed for radio and clubs. "I was always kind of nervous being on the *Tonight* show. I was not very secure with myself," he admitted. "I was new to television. I had done a little bit of it, but I didn't really understand it very much." He and Eydie recalled rehearsing an elaborately choreographed duet of "Cherry Pies Ought to Be You." On the night of the show, "they cut it," remembered Eydie. "Then the next week, we're gonna do it. Cut it. For about six months we rehearsed. I'm learning all this choreography. They never did the thing."

"It was canceled four times," recalled Andy, "because Steve Allen kept running out of time. Eydie would be upset, but I was always happy because I was nervous about doing it anyway."

As the youngest in the cast, Steve and Eydie took Allen's penchant for issuing memos seriously. Eydie recalled, "With me it was, 'Wear your lipstick. I want redder lipstick.' TV is black and white: what's the difference? [Allen] said, 'No, I want your lipstick redder. And I don't want black hair. You go get your hair red.'" Because she couldn't afford to spend much money, she "went to this dumb place to get my hair dyed red, and they burnt all my hair off. I ended up with, like, tiny little short, stubby hair." Eydie remembered having to appear for a photo shoot the next day, "And I used to have this real beautiful, black hair with the bangs. And now I come with this little short, red, ugly head, and I didn't even look like myself."

Writer Herb Sargent chuckled in agreement. "Steve had trouble with Eydie's hair every week. He'd see her in rehearsal and say, 'What the hell's wrong with her hair?' She had it up, down. He'd say, 'What have they done to her this week?'"

"Everyday, it was another memo," Eydie continued in mock annoyance. "'Why do you wear this dress? That dress?' There was no budget, so you had to come up and think of what you had in your house. I would sit home, and I would bead cotton skirts, just so they would have a flash. Even after the local show went network, there were no clothes. And every night, you'd figure out a blouse. I would sew beads or sequins on a blouse to give it a look. I actually was doing all these things myself!"

"FUNNY WAS BETTER THAN SINGING GOOD"

In addition to performing great music, the four singers got pulled into other parts of the show. "They threw us into comedy sketches, used us as foils, or we did live remotes, which was unheard of at that time," said Steve. "We were singing on top of the Chrysler Building, the Empire State Building, or hanging over Niagara Falls." Sometimes, he added, it seemed that "the last thing we were called upon to do on that show was sing."

Andy agreed: "They would pan up to a building across the street, and if I was on the show that night, they would put me in a gorilla outfit and have me strangling some lady outside the window. Or if Steve Allen was going to do a sketch and they needed a Russian bartender, I was it."

Sometimes, "even singing wasn't like singing," contended Eydie. "Like Stevie would get to do a great song—let's say it was 'A Foggy Day'—and he would have to walk through this cockamamie set. Well, [director] Dwight [Hemion] thought that this was pretty boring, so he would have, like, fake buildings, and ladies would throw buckets of water on him, and somebody would throw garbage at him, and he just kept singing."

There was the June 6, 1955, show featuring Andy in a mobile unit remote singing from the Luxor Baths, just down the street from the Hudson Theatre. Just as he was about to sing, the audio line feeding the band from the theater into his earpiece went out. "It was a disaster," recalled Andy. "I didn't know how to handle it. I was singing, and suddenly there was no sound. I knew I had to start singing. Maybe the band will find out what key I was in. At least the rhythm section would go along with it. But it had a whole arrangement—'Between the Devil and the Deep Blue Sea.' I think I'm doing fine. And I'm smilin', doin' all my stuff. I just belted my heart out. And nobody's playing or anything. Back at the theater, they were just laughing.

"They told me, 'When you get through with that, get dressed right away and run back' because [the theater] was two blocks away. So I ran back and got there in about two minutes. And they're still laughing. When I came into the theater, they applauded. I didn't know what they were applauding about. I wasn't on camera then, but then they put the camera on me and they were all laughing."

209

The young singers' wide-eyed, youthful exuberance often made them the targets of friendly but risky pranks. When the local show went network, Steve recalled, they had to do more songs, and so cue cards were used for the singers to keep track of lyrics. According to Steve, the writers liked to tamper with the cards: "If I was doing a new Cole Porter song, I would read about four or five cue cards. They'd flip the first one, the second one. Then, the third one would be in Spanish, the fourth one would be in Greek. They're lookin' to see what the hell I'm gonna do. Of course, I'm in the middle of the song."

"They wanted him to go crazy," said Eydie.

"So," continued Steve, "I was writing in my head, making up lines. Cole Porter doesn't know how many songs I wrote with him to this date. That all contributed to the live and the craziness that went on that show."

"Or they would write terrible things on the cue cards. And you knew you were dead," said Eydie. "Then they would get ticked off because then it started not to phase us. So they tried to be more diabolical. Of course, it *did* phase us."

But they never showed it. "What are you gonna do, freeze?" Steve said.

"Andy was a freezer," sighed Eydie affectionately, even though "he was older and more experienced than us." On the one hand, Williams's work with his brothers and Kay Thompson was all choreographed so that with his customarily thorough preparation, he knew, at any given moment, which moves went with which notes. "I was scared, especially at the beginning," said Andy. "My experience with Kay Thompson did not prepare me for television. I could sing—I knew I could do that, but I was not too confident in myself as a solo singer. I didn't know what to do with my hands."

On the other hand, "Eydie and I operated instinctively," said Steve. "So one time Andy came over to me, and he said, 'Hey, Steve, how do you know how to use your hands when you sing?' I thought he was putting me on, so I was putting him on back. So I said, 'Well, the lyrics tell you what to do. If you're singing, "Are the stars out tonight," you point to the stars. "I [*points to himself*] only have eyes [*points to his eyes*] for you [*points to the audience*]."' And the schmuck gets up, and he's singing, 'Are the stars out tonight,' and he's starting to point. I said, 'Oh, my God, he was serious!' I grabbed the man—'Andy! What are you, crazy?'

"He was so choreographed up until that point. But then he found himself."

In fact, it is hard to imagine a time when Williams—who later became legendary for his polished, laid-back manner—ever felt awkward. "The *Tonight* show is where I really learned how to be a television performer, how to be more comfortable with the camera," said Andy.

Besides sabotaging the cue cards, the writers "would do things on the set," said Steve. "You'd lean against a pole, and it fell down. If you were walking, and you sat on a chair, they'd make the chair loose—like a leg would break when you'd sit—just to see how you'd react."

"But you didn't know that until you sat in the chair," Eydie pointed out. "And now you're on live TV."

Having to deal with the unexpected every day on live TV enabled Steve and Eydie and Andy to develop an unflappable poise, both on stage and on camera. "A lightbulb breaks, or somebody goes crazy in the audience," said Eydie. "We would *use* that, so much to our advantage, that people would always think that it was part of the show. We *prayed* for things to go wrong." She remembered how other performers would be rattled by mishaps: "They would get in a huff and walk off the stage. We don't say, 'Hmmph! We're leaving!'" Instead, said Eydie, a mishap "becomes part of the evening. And we learned that funny was better than singing good."

Even when "funny" was accompanied by severe pain, as Eydie learned when she was stung by a bee while singing. "I was very allergic to the bite. And my face is growing bigger and bigger on live television. And they wouldn't stop for nothin'. They just thought it was hysterical."

Sometimes the prankster was the one you'd least expect. One afternoon in Miami Beach, there was little time to rehearse director Dwight Hemion's idea for opening that night's show. Pointing to a little diving board by the hotel swimming pool, Hemion simply instructed Steve and Eydie, "When we open the show, you guys will be up there. You'll go off the board, I'll have a picture of you in the air, and the announcer will say, 'Live from Miami Beach, it's the *Tonight* show.'"

"No problem," they said.

At show time, Steve and Eydie started to step up to the little diving board, getting ready for the opening. Hemion said, "No-no-no-no-no. Not *this* board. You go up to the *top*." What they didn't realize was that there was a high-dive platform thirty feet above—so high, they hadn't noticed it earlier that afternoon. And so they scaled the ladder to the high dive. "It looked like we were going to jump off of a roof," Steve said. "I didn't want to go."

Eydie, now standing behind Steve on the platform, said, "'Come on, don't be chicken!' And he said, 'I'd rather be chicken than chicken salad.' And I said, 'It's the beginning of the show, and you ain't jumping?'"

So she pushed him.

"He did not talk to me, literally—even though we kept doing the show—for a year," said Eydie.

"Six months," corrected Steve.

Allen's colleagues had no problem pushing him into the fray. Steve Lawrence: "Steve had a slant board backstage that he would occasionally relax on to let the blood go the other way. And, literally, he fell asleep. Eleven-thirty came. Billy [Harbach] told the band, 'Don't play any music.' They lifted the curtain, and they had a shot of Steve sleeping. And we just waited for him to wake up. Everybody's watching this man sleep."

"Everybody thought it was a bit," added Eydie.

"And after a while, with the man sleeping," continued Lawrence, "a couple of people started to laugh. A couple more people started to laugh. And then Steve woke up, and it dawned on him—"

"What they did to him," finished Eydie.

"They opened the show with a man sleeping for no reason," said Lawrence with a smile.

"So much of the spontaneity on television is almost nonexistent because of tape," Steve lamented. "If there's a mistake, you do it over again. But the mistakes people really talk about for years. Today, you watch a show, you expect it to be okay. They don't expect anything to go wrong unless it's planned. To this day, there are people who come up to us and say, 'I saw the show the night that this happened.' Accidents, sets falling down, people blanking out, saying things that you can't edit out, bleep out, because it was live."

"And we don't have copies of any of this stuff," sighed Eydie. "There was no tape. If you wanted to buy a kinescope, it was $160— that was our salary! How could you buy one for one night?"

"We were getting $285 one week, $320 the other week," said Andy. "I was staying in the Algonquin Hotel. The hotel cost more than I was making, so I soon got out of there and went to a three-dollar-a-night room at the King Edward Hotel across the street."

Not only did the Allen *Tonight* era predate videotape, it was at the dawn of instant still photography. Andy remembered Allen using him in a live demonstration of the newfangled Polaroid Land camera. In contrast to today's credit card–sized digital cameras, the klunky Polaroid was about the size of a toaster. Allen showed the audience the picture he had just taken of Andy a couple of minutes earlier, "and they'd gasp . . . take a picture in a minute," said Andy.

"One day, [Allen] was passing me in the hall and he whispered, 'Andy, buy Polaroid.' I whispered back, 'What with?' I didn't have any money. None of us did. 'Buy Polaroid—what a great tip!' For a while, it was the fastest-rising stock of all."

"I'll Do It! I'll Do It!"

As frightened as Williams may have been to work on television, it was a paradox that he often volunteered for the riskier stunts that Allen and his team dreamed up. For one of the Miami Beach shows, director Dwight Hemion wanted to have Steve Lawrence perched on the thirty-foot high-dive platform, singing Noel Coward's "A Room with a View." "Steve, we'd like for you to go up on that diving board," requested Hemion. "We'll put a sofa up there and a chair and a lamp."

"No way," said Steve.

"And I'll always remember Andy [*in a polite voice*], 'Could I do it, please? I'd like to do that,'" chuckled Hemion.

"I'd do all the things that Steve Lawrence wouldn't do," laughed Andy, who remembered the time when Hemion needed someone to sing from the bottom of a swimming pool—surrounded by a squid, an eel, a baby shark, and a giant turtle. The singer would have to wear a diving helmet with a little microphone and earpiece in it. The risk of electrocution was, well, a real possibility.

"So long," said Steve.

"I'll do it! I'll do it!" chirped Andy.

At rehearsal, Hemion set up his shots, and Andy practiced coordinating his underwater crooning with the diving helmet on his head and the band track wired into his ear. "So I'm down in the bottom of this swimming pool, and I see this eel come by, and a little baby shark," said Andy, reliving the moment with gusto.

"Skitch Henderson is starting the music, and you could just barely hear it. I'm gonna sing, 'Between the Devil and the Deep Blue Sea'—again. And I'm down there, and I've got an arrangement of it [*clapping his hands*]: "Deep-deep-deep is the deeeeep sea // How ever deep is the deep sea? Deep sea // Oh, my goodness, how deep is the deeeeeep sea—' How *ridiculous* to be doing this down there!

"You can't hear the band. It was so awful. Then the guys took a ten-minute break—all the crew, everybody took a break. And they forgot I was down there. So they stopped pushing this thing that gives me air. Suddenly, I can't breathe. I thought, 'My God, I'm going to die down here.' Then I remembered they told me I had to turn over and turn your head a certain way to get out of this thing, or you'd break your neck turning."

Andy eventually made it back to the surface. But the weather in Miami Beach that January was unseasonably chilly—so chilly, that city officials had expressed their concern when Allen sensibly wore an overcoat and muffler on the show one night. "It took a long time to get out," said Andy. "I got the chills, and they kept on piling blankets on me. I was so frozen. I couldn't stop shivering. I got pneumonia, and I was in bed for two weeks."

More reserved in nature than the outgoing Eydie and comical Lawrence, Andy felt more "in awe of [Allen], and I found it difficult to talk to him because I didn't have anything that I thought was important enough to talk to him about. Because he was always either writing something down or playing the piano or thinking. So unless you were a comic, it was hard."

But it still could be downright terrifying for Lawrence, who recalled a rehearsal for a live musical number to be staged at Niagara Falls. "Dwight was blocking the shot during the day, and I was at the bottom of the falls. I took the elevator down and got out to do this thing in the mist. I practiced it in the daytime. At night, we were going on live, and the guy taking me down in the elevator said, 'You

215

sure are a brave young man!' I said, 'It's not that bad.' And he said, "I mean, at night, when them *rats* come out.'"

Eydie chimed in, whispering loudly for dramatic effect: "The biggest rats you ever saw!"

"Well, now, I'm singin' down there," continued Lawrence, "and I'm frightened to death. And I guess the fear showed in my face. I was doing some happy song like 'Put on a Happy Face.' It was absolute fear. I was vibrating till I got back upstairs."

I Only Have Eyes for You?

The songs for a given evening's show would be selected typically a week in advance by Steve Allen or Bill Harbach, and in later years also by the singers. One night, Lawrence was scheduled to sing "I Only Have Eyes for You." What was not apparent was that the show would be devoted to a charity, as Allen's social conscience often dictated. The charity in question was the Lighthouse for the Blind, an organization dedicated to the visually impaired. Guests included successful blind writers, composers, and artists. A phone number was flashed on the screen for viewers to call to pledge donations. Later in the show, Allen was beginning to introduce Lawrence: "Right now, time for a song from little Steve."

At that moment, according to Lawrence, "Billy [Harbach] turned white"—it dawned on him that a song about having "eyes" might be a politically incorrect choice on a show dedicated to the blind. Immediately, from alongside the camera, Harbach signaled frantically to Allen, "Stretch it! Stretch it!" Allen began doing something to kill time. Lawrence recalled, "Billy came over to me and whispered hysterically, 'You f---in' moron!' I said, 'Me?' He said, 'I Only Have *Eyes* for You'? I said, '*You're* the one who picked it!' He said, 'Give me another song!'"

With not a second to spare, Lawrence blurted the first title that came into his mind: "I'm in the Mood for Love." Because there was no money for arrangements, the band played simple, four-bar introductions that could be used for any number of songs. Harbach said, "Skitch, play the same intro," in time for Allen to say, "Yeah, here's little Steve doin' 'I'm in the Mood for Love.'"

The intro for "I Only Have Eyes for You" was in the key of B flat. Lawrence, however, ordinarily did "I'm in the Mood for Love" in E flat—five keys higher. By using the B-flat intro for "Eyes," Lawrence was forced to do "Mood" a full five keys lower—at a foghorn pitch. "I out-Crosby'd Bing Crosby," Lawrence said in his velvet baritone. "Crosby would say, 'Dip down because that's where the money is!' I did it with a straight face, knowing what the night was all about. Steve Allen is looking at me like he's waiting for me to do a shtick or a somersault or for an artichoke to pop out of my head."

Did the audience find humor in Lawrence's predicament? "Oh, no!" said Eydie. "The audience didn't know anything. They just thought the guy was weird." Recalled Lawrence, "The audience looked at me like I was a little peculiar that night, or maybe I had a cold."

"But the *band* was, like, on the floor," Eydie chuckled. Lawrence agreed: "The band was swallowing their instruments. Everybody backstage was hysterical."

"Everything was ready to collapse because nobody could hold even the camera," said Eydie. Harbach started cackling. "Everybody's cackling. And Steve's going [*herself singing at foghorn pitch*], 'IIII'mmmm in the mood for love.'"

Lawrence added, "Once we got into it, and Billy told Steve what was going on, I heard them cackling, and I'm trying to fight for my life trying to be straight."

In recent years, Harbach questioned the wisdom of his decision to abruptly change songs: "I was probably overreacting. Probably would have gone right by, and nothing would have happened. But I stopped the show!"

THE ONE WHO MIGHT HAVE BEEN . . .

Pat Marshall left *Tonight* in February 1955 to accept an offer to replace Janis Paige and co-star with John Raitt in the Broadway musical *The Pajama Game*. "I was a little uncomfortable when I was asked to take over Janis Paige's role when she was leaving," said Marshall. "[*Tonight*] had been a delightful experience for me, so there was a little reluctance. You feel a little tentative: 'Should I do this or shouldn't I?'" After *Pajama Game*, Marshall landed a role in another Broadway musical, *Mr. Wonderful*, which starred Sammy Davis Jr. She went on to marry Larry Gelbart, a writer for Sid Caesar who would later win acclaim for his work in the television series *M*A*S*H* and the film *O God!*

Despite her immersion in the theater, Marshall still found time for *Tonight*. She recalled that, after the exhilaration of working on the Broadway stage each night, "you aren't ready to go to sleep. You go home, read something, and watch . . . Steve!"

Marshall was replaced on *Tonight* by Pat Kirby, who appeared as a semiregular guest in the ensuing months and eventually joined the cast in October 1955. "It's interesting," mused Allen. "There's no reason to make competition, but sometimes there's a tendency to force that competitive competition. Somebody's a better fighter, somebody has better sneakers. And if anybody ever put the abilities of the four *Tonight* singers into a competitive situation, and the question was, "Guess who you think will be a star?"—if any of them make it at all—I think a lot of people would have voted for Pat Kirby. First of all, she was gorgeous. She was very beautiful—half-Spanish and half-Irish, I think. She has a lovely face and a lovely voice. A very

218

well-trained musician—she could play the piano, read music. Very versatile in every sense. So, you figure, she's gotta make it."

Kirby lived in the most unlikely residence for a singer on a late-night network show—or, for that matter, for any television show: a convent with nuns in Philadelphia. "The nuns would drive her to the theater and take her home. She never socialized with any of us," recalled Jayne Meadows.

"She was terrific," said Williams. "She went on to *The George Gobel Show* as a soloist. She wasn't really interested in her career as much as some guy and getting married and having babies."

Bill Harbach witnessed a golden opportunity slip through Kirby's fingers. After the Richard Rodgers tribute program in January 1956, the celebrated composer approached Harbach and exclaimed, "Bill, that was marvelous! Thank you so much. Steve's fun. By the way, I'd like to see Pat Kirby. Oscar and I are doing another show, and I'd love to talk to her for a second. Would you let me see her?"

Harbach went backstage and found Kirby. "Pat, Mr. Rodgers wants to see you for second."

"Oh, Bill, I've got a date, and I'm awfully late, and he's going to be awfully mad if I don't see him. Would you tell him—"

"Pat," implored Harbach, quietly but emphatically, "R-R-R-R-ichard R-R-R-R-odgers wants to see you for *one minute* back there!"

"Please tell him you didn't see me," said Kirby apologetically as she left the theater.

"She got married to that guy, and they divorced after about four or five kids," said Harbach with a sigh. "Years later, I would see her doing little gigs down in the Village. And she'd look at me, and she'd go like this and smile." Harbach pointed a finger to his head, pulling back his thumb like a trigger. "Could've been."

* * * * * * *

"The whole success of the *Tonight* show was started by Steve Allen," reflected Williams. "He was the prototype for all the other people who have followed him."

Marshall: "There was nothing to do after ten o'clock at night before Steve started the *Tonight* show. It was the beginning. They used to be the dead hours. Steve gave them a life!"

Steve Lawrence: "He really touched successfully in so many different areas of show business. I can't think very readily offhand of too many other people who have done and accomplished what he has in all these different areas."

Did Allen's multifaceted talents dilute the recognition accorded him in any individual area? Lawrence: "Not only dilute it, but I don't think people can relate to one person being that specific in so many different areas, and being that creative and that talented."

Steve and Eydie have mixed feelings about their hero's decision to leave the show after such a brief tenure. "Well, to him, after four years, he thought the time was up for it," said Eydie. "But he was wrong, and he never should have given it up. Look how far Johnny Carson went. He's a genius, there's no question about it. But if Steve Allen hadn't given up so soon . . ."

"But I think that's what Steve Allen is," said Lawrence in 1998. "He had more to do, more to say, and he wanted to go on. He didn't want to be locked into that, and I understood that. But I didn't agree with the decision at the time."

When Allen died in 2000, Lawrence reflected: "I feel particularly sad about this because he was almost like a father in a sense. He just taught me so much and I just couldn't wait to hang around him and watch him and listen to him. I loved him dearly, and I will miss him dearly."

Chapter 7

PIONEERING CREATIVITY
BEHIND THE CAMERA

Dwight Hemion directed the local Steve Allen Show *in New York and continued throughout Allen's two-and-a-half-year tenure on* Tonight, *where he introduced production innovations that have since become commonplace. For Hemion, directing the early* Tonight *show was experimental, thrilling, sometimes catastrophic, but always gratifying.*

Sitting in the airy dining room of his Beverly Hills high-rise condo in 2002, balcony doors slid open to let in the mild December air and the traffic din below, the husky, silver-haired Hemion—whom one might guess to be a judge or a football coach before a director—seemed frustrated with the occasional blurriness of his memories, as if they had emanated from an out-of-focus camera lens. Perhaps this is understandable, for after Tonight, *he went on to become the preeminent director of musical variety shows, holding the record for the most Emmys (eighteen) and most Emmy nominations (forty-seven) won by an individual. The roster of artists for whom he crafted brilliant specials is staggering, including Frank Sinatra, Barbra Streisand, Elvis Presley, Paul McCartney, Neil Diamond, Burt Bacharach, Andy Williams, Bette Midler, Luciano Pavarotti, Shirley MacLaine, Steve Lawrence and Eydie Gorme, and Mikhail Baryshnikov.*

Yet, for a director without peer, Hemion remained remarkably unas-

suming, still in awe of the many stars with whom he worked. Innocent and childlike, he was eager to show the visitor to his condo some artwork Sinatra had given him after he directed the Chairman in his classic 1965 special, A Man and His Music. *("Do you want to see what Frank Sinatra gave me?")* He was just waiting for the visitor to ask to use the powder room, so he could proudly point out the original paintings by Tony Bennett and Peggy Lee gracing its walls. Hemion's awe was so contagious that the bathroom's guest occupant—surrounded by such greatness—suddenly felt embarrassed to flush the toilet.

*I*n the early 1950s, NBC established a new local station in New York, WNBT. According to Richard Pack, director of programming and operations, local stations like WNBT needed to fill more than fifty-five hours a week with locally produced programming, most of it live. To meet this demand, the station assembled a young, workaholic production team that included directors Dwight Hemion, Bill Harbach, and Enid Roth, as well as staff producer Barbara Walters.

Cooking shows were the rage in the early 1950s, raking in big bucks for local stations across the country, the way reality shows do for the networks five decades later. Bill Harbach recalled, "I can hear myself now: 'Pan left on the ketchup. Okay, pull back on the schnitzel. Dolly in on the cream puffs, but not too tight.'"

Hemion previously had directed a morning show for Morey Amsterdam at ABC, *Broadway Open House* at NBC, as well as sports at ABC. At WNBT, he directed his share of cooking shows "and anything with musical stuff, funky kinds of things you'd do early on in the business." One day in 1953, Steve Krantz, the program director, came into Hemion's office and announced, "We just got a new guy who's going to join the staff, a fellow who had been heading up a show at CBS by the name of Steve Allen. We're bringing him here, gonna give him an hour every night." Along with producer Johnny Sterns, Hemion was assigned in 1953 to Allen's new show.

Allen's spontaneous, ad-lib nature impacted Hemion's directing style. "You never knew what Steve was thinking about, or Billy Harbach," Hemion recalled. "It was like doing a football game, an unscripted event, and trying to stay with what was going on. I had done football at ABC with Red Grange. You had to try to be as fast as you could, ready for anything—film clips, reactions from the audience—and get that quickly."

When it came to capturing audience reactions, the director had to be in sync with the host's comedy sensibilities, said Hal Gurnee, who directed both Jack Paar's *Tonight* show and David Letterman's daytime and late-night shows. "Every once in a while, when you take a shot on your own that makes people laugh—I can't tell you how exhilarating that is."

"The wonderful thing about Dwight was, when you had a show that was totally ad-lib and you didn't know what the star's going to do, he could get it on camera," said Jayne Meadows. "When you're doing a show like Milton Berle or Sid Caesar, you rehearsed for a whole week because it was on only once a week. You knew which camera. On *I've Got a Secret*, we never left the desk. We sat there. The director would go from person to person. Not on the *Tonight* show. You never knew what Steve was going to do. Dwight never missed a shot."

Gurnee understood the expertise that this required: "With variety shows, you work all week to make things more cohesive and exactly the way you plan it. In a talk show or comedy show without a script, you try to avoid making it look like the same thing is happening every night."

Hemion's approach to directing *Tonight* was similar to his approach to decorating the gallery white walls of his condo: to try to give the audience "as antiseptic a picture as possible—that is, try to get rid of all of the drudge, clutter of any nature." Hemion attempted to do this while delving into the then-cutting-edge techniques of live remotes and split screen, which the show frequently employed. *Tonight* did mobile unit remotes from Hollywood premieres of such films as *A Star Is Born*, *White Christmas*, and *The Country Girl*, which included brief interviews of the stars of the films. Other remotes included the Birdland jazz club in New York, the Eighth Street Theater in Chicago, and the L.A. Coliseum. One broadcast in November 1954 showed Eydie Gorme and composer Harold Arlen appearing to be seated together. In reality, it was a split screen, and for the first time on live television, Eydie debuted "A Sleeping Bee" singing from a studio in New York, while Arlen accompanied her in Philadelphia.

The technological limitations of the era, however, made "antiseptic" pictures a challenge. Four cameras were used, but there were no zooms. Mounted on each camera was a turret of four fixed lenses that were cranked by the cameraman. "You'd see on the air the camera going from one lens into another, which meant that a big black hole would happen between lenses," laughed Hemion, amused by how primitive this was.

The behemoth studio cameras were not only cumbersome and very heavy, they were also unreliable. "Dwight and I both came from those early days with no tape and big, bulky cameras that constantly broke down," chuckled Gurnee. "You never did a show where a camera didn't conk out. Sometimes two cameras. Your early training was live, and you had to get around the fact that two of your cameras weren't working, and you had to make things go with one camera."

For a show that pioneered the roaming camera, the enormous cameras at the time were not of the handheld variety routinely used on the Letterman and Leno programs. This meant that they had to be wheeled backstage, down the hall, or outside. Elaborate production numbers like Steve and Eydie's "Say Hey Willie Mays" on the premiere *Tonight* broadcast likely required "telephone lines, probably from a remote truck—a sports unit with a telephone line—video and audio, back to the studio," said Gurnee. "This was long before they had handheld cameras. I would say that it was not only complicated, but very expensive as well. You wouldn't do it very often."

Despite these limitations, Hemion blossomed into a progressive technician and artist. "One of the reasons Hemion is such a polished comedy-variety show director," Allen wrote in *Hi-Ho Steverino!* "is that he has a sharply defined sense of his expertise. He is master in the use of camera, lights, studio or remote facilities. He has sensitive taste and impeccable judgment." It also helped that Hemion loved jazz because he would have "the musicians go through their numbers once in rehearsal and make note of the order of choruses. Then on the program, as soon as a guy starts his chorus, there's a closeup!" remarked Allen to *Downbeat* magazine. "Not since the Norman Granz *Jammin' the Blues* film, has jazz received the brilliant pictorial care it gets on the *Steve Allen Show*," wrote jazz critic Nat Hentoff at the time. Moreover, added Allen admiringly, Hemion, unlike other comedy show directors, resisted the temptation to meddle in issues regarding comedy, leaving those decisions where they belonged: with the comedy writers.

The feeling was mutual. "Steve didn't interfere in what we did production-wise on the show," said Hemion. Allen would simply be told that a certain singer was going to do a certain song, leaving it to Hemion to decide how to present the singer. Hemion would typically work with the singer and conductor Skitch Henderson. In musical numbers, the standard staging of the era had the singer standing motionless in front of the orchestra, arms raised at the end of the song. Hemion developed creative stagings for television, beginning with taking the orchestra out of the shot so that the camera could focus on the singer. Andy Williams sang the first verse of the inspirational ballad "Walk Hand in Hand" strolling through a tranquil grove. When he arrived downstage, a glittering gold curtain dropped behind him for a different, more formal look for the final, climactic verse.

These creative stagings helped establish Hemion as a hot director and foreshadowed the "lush look on television," as Gurnee described it, that would become the trademark of Hemion and his future directing partner, Gary Smith. "I think they were very, very influential on almost every director that came after them," said Gurnee. "The two of them made some beautiful television."

"Nobody stood up at a microphone and sang," *Tonight* singer Pat Marshall noted. "That was very infrequent. It was always a production. In a bathtub with bubbles. Lying on the floor by a fireplace. It was a very unusual experience."

Other musical numbers employed a dual-imaging technique. "We used to just light a person on one side of the face and then on the other side, put another angle of that face and superimpose it on the black area of your face. Probably a little bit wider shot, so it was different, not the same close-up."

The use of close-ups in a comedy program was novel at the time. "Wide shots back then were like watching a bunch of ants marching around," said Gurnee. "The soap operas all learned eventually that the extreme close-up was the telling shot, but it wasn't used much back then, and it certainly wasn't used much in comedy that way. I think that was the first time that people realized that a really tight shot of Don Knotts—with perspiration running down his face, being very nervous and stuttering—wouldn't have been as effective if it had been a medium-type shot."

Lighting was always important to Hemion. "I worked a lot with the lighting director," he explained, lighting his second cigarette. "I always had ideas about how I'd like to see certain people look. Do you light 'em from the side? From the front? You'd be surprised how different they are. One is very dramatic, bringing out the high cheekbones if they had them. Female Hollywood stars all felt that they knew how they looked best, lighting-wise. Joan Crawford said, 'I don't want that light up there, I want it over here.' She didn't want a light straight into her because you don't see any features. When you light somebody from the front, their features go away. No shading. The dramatic look is what people like Joan Crawford liked. A follow-spot is not her idea of lighting. A key light—she would play to it. She's like Streisand—I did all of Streisand's stuff, and she's the best one in the world to light. She just has that kind of a face and skin texture."

PIONEERING CHROMA-KEY
AND OTHER AMBITIOUS TECHNIQUES

Hemion was always interested in trying new things. A technical director showed him a technique that could "make a little building large or squeeze automobiles down." Hemion took it from there and pioneered the innovation that became known as "chroma-key," wherein a figure in the foreground of one shot could be juxtaposed against a background comprising another shot. Almost every TV newscast today uses it to enable weathercasters to interact with assorted maps and graphics. Chroma-key is the forerunner to the digital-imaging magic employed by modern-day motion picture directors like George Lucas, James Cameron, and Steven Spielberg.

Before *Tonight*, explained Hemion, "chroma-key had never been done in a variety show form with singers." What made the technique even more attractive was that it was electronic, which meant it didn't cost much. "We would take great liberty because we didn't have a lot of money to work with," Hemion said. "At the beginning, we didn't have scenery for these singers to work in front of. So we had to create these little things that were electronic and consequently less expensive. But we would shrink them—anything for a 'look.'"

That "look"—a word Hemion likes to use—often got bizarre. A thimble-sized Steve Lawrence would stand against a TV screen–sized ashtray and cigarette crooning "Smoke Gets in Your Eyes." Andy Williams remembered how he was made to appear "the same size as a little pitcher of cream and a bowl of sugar. And they'd have me sing 'You're the Cream in My Coffee,' and they thought that was real cute. My mother would always say, 'Why weren't you on tonight?' and I'd say, 'I was! I was the little guy right next to the cream!'"

Eydie Gorme: "Steve Allen was going to do a scene with himself. They would record him doing one part at five o'clock in the afternoon. Then, later, live, with chroma-key, he would be doing this scene with himself." It might end with one Allen bowing toward the other and "bumping" heads.

"And the height was perfectly matched," added Steve Lawrence.

Experimenting with the new technology might have been fun, but it was also complicated and sometimes not that cheap. "What you save in scenery," said Gurnee, "you'd use up in camera time. It was a very tedious process in the early days. The lighting had to be just perfect; otherwise, the images would tear out. You'd get the blue screen, and that was fine, but if there were any shadows or dark areas, the picture would tear out where there wasn't a flat light."

Another "look" pioneered by Hemion employed the theatrical staple known as the cyclorama: a large, white cloth, usually lit with patterns, hung upstage. This provided a background more subtle and artistic than other backgrounds of the day, which often consisted of cartoonish drawings on a board or the standard theater drapes. "The *Tonight* show was the first show to use [the cyclorama] at my urging," said Hemion. "It made for great silhouettes. You could put people in front of it. You could light it with a light blue for a sunset kind of a look."

In an ambitious nod to the 1951 film classic *Royal Wedding*, in which Fred Astaire appeared to be defying gravity by dancing on the walls and ceiling (and as a precursor to Lionel Richie's ground-breaking 1986 video, "Dancing on the Ceiling"), Hemion attempted similar upside-down and sideways effects for Andy Williams and Pat Marshall to do "Dancing on the Ceiling." The number ended with a "whirlwind" camera effect reminiscent of the tornado in *The Wizard of Oz*, dissolving into a shot of Williams and Marshall appearing as though they had been dropped onto the floor, presumably after having "fallen" from the ceiling. The audience, still ooohing and aah-hing at the clever stunt, was unprepared for the literally off-the-wall tag, which had Allen, seemingly perched sideways on a wall, noncha-lantly "pouring" a bottle of Knickerbocker Beer into a glass—sideways.

Ultimately, it was Hemion's imagination, not necessarily the technology, that shaped his artistry and reputation. "Dwight was very creative," recalled Doc Severinsen. "And he had nothing to work with. He could make something out of nothing. He'd use a naked stairwell as a set."

"DON'T BOW"

Steve Lawrence recalled Hemion always lecturing, "Television is dif-ferent from performing in a theater or a stage, where at the end of a song, you take your bows and your applause." Because songs often ended with four-bar instrumental tags lasting up to twenty seconds, "it was difficult to come up with a look for the singers at the end of songs because they were no longer performing," said Hemion. Thus, he would instruct them not to take bows: "When you finish singing, look into the camera, turn around and walk upstage, disappear, and I'll fade the camera."

For example, Pat Kirby performed "The Boy Next Door" from *Meet Me in St. Louis* standing on a set consisting of a gazebo sur-rounded by a meadow. At the end of the number, she remained standing, looking off to the side across the meadow, seemingly lost in thought, not acknowledging the applause, while the camera faded.

"It was a mood kind of thing," Hemion explained. "I found it incongruous to take bows in front of sets. You walk through the trees. You were trying to create a feeling or a look of being in the woods or wherever. Then, all of a sudden, you're bowing?"

To-bow-or-not-to-bow became the subject of good-natured ribbing between Hemion and Lawrence for decades to follow. Said Lawrence: "I always used to fight with Dwight. I'd say, 'Let me at least take a bow.' And he said, 'This is television. I'm interested in pictures.' So he always made me turn around and walk into a mist or behind a tree or something. And I said, 'Because of you, when I walk on the street, nobody would recognize me . . . till I passed 'em!'"

Mused Hemion proudly: "I heard Steve Lawrence talking about it in an interview, 'That f---in' Dwight Hemion!' Even his mother was pissed off."

THE LEARNING CURVE

There was a learning curve for everybody in the new era of television, and because there was no videotape, the technical mistakes of talented directors like Hemion were exposed live to millions of viewers. In one *Tonight* road show from Miami, Steve and Eydie were to sing a number on the beach, half a mile away from the band, which was back at the hotel where the main action was. Fitted with headphones and throat mikes, they could sing while being fed the live band track. "We rehearsed it during the day, and it worked perfect," Hemion said. "But on the air, unbeknownst to us, for some reason the orchestra feed went to a transmitter in Miami, all around the country, and then came back to a monitor. Because Steve and Eydie were taking the feed from the monitor, there was a delay."

Clueless, they were actually singing—and smiling—"four bars behind the band. We didn't know it was going to happen. We should have known. When we heard it and looked at it, we cried," Hemion recalled, grinning. "It was tragic. I was in the control room going, 'Holy shit!'"

There was another road show in which Steve and Eydie were to sing "Let's Get Away from It All"—perched precariously from a tree limb overlooking Niagara Falls. In a forerunner to *Fear Factor* and similar contemporary stunt shows, Hemion recalled that five guys had to help Eydie inch her way across the limb. "And then I asked her on the public address system, 'Eydie, would you mind moving about five more feet to your right?' She started crying."

Steve Lawrence added, "The guy from the police department or chamber of commerce said to Billy Harbach, 'You get them back. That's too far. They could get in an accident!' And Billy goes [*casually*], 'Naaah, don't worry.'" And because they did it, and the limb didn't crack, "We came home heroes," said Hemion, beaming. "A great-looking shot—little Eydie out there over the falls. We'd do anything if it was new or different. We'd do it just for shock."

"CRAZY SHOTS" AND OTHER CLASSIC VISUAL ROUTINES

Occasionally, Allen would come up with an idea for Hemion. "Crazy Shots" consisted of a series of non sequitur comedy blackouts following Allen's introduction at his piano: "One of the things I do regularly on television is play the piano, but I know that many viewers get bored watching a man playing piano on TV because you see the same pictures each time—close-ups of fingers on the keyboards, profile shots, etc. Well, we're going to do something about that tonight. I'm going to be at the piano, but we've arranged for you to have something more interesting to look at while I'm playing."

Cut to actor Dane Clark, who is shown sipping soup, but as the camera pans down to the bowl, the viewer discovers a pair of chattering false teeth slopping soup on the tablecloth. Cut to the next shot. Vincent Price is seated in a dining room, napkin under his chin, ready to eat. The waiter removes the cover from the silver entree platter to reveal bandleader Skitch Henderson's head, his eyes darting fearfully about. Cut to the next shot. A head-on crash on 45th Street (behind the Hudson Theatre) between two cars driven by stuntmen. The camera pans from the collision scene to a hotel across the street where a man is seen slapping a life-size human dummy around. Cut to the final shot, which starts with a close-up of Jerry Lewis eating a large slice of watermelon and spitting several seeds off-camera and ends with a close-up of Allen, watermelon seeds pasted onto his face and glasses.

In another "Crazy Shot" involving soup, Don Knotts is seated at a diner counter and drops his spoon into the bowl. He reaches deep into the bowl—past his elbow—before he finally retrieves his spoon.

Abbott and Costello, as Siamese twins joined at the shoulder, illustrate how, if one of them sips water from a glass, the other can spit it out like a fountain.

Writer Herb Sargent is smoking a cigarette between his toes. "Somebody held his feet up," explained writer Stan Burns. "Then we pulled back, and we showed he's smoking with his feet. Somebody wrote and says, 'How could you show such crippled fingers?'"

An Egyptian mummy's tomb, resting vertically, is opened to reveal Steve Lawrence making a call from a pay telephone.

Louis Nye, dressed in a trench coat and fedora, deposits a letter into a mailbox and lights a cigarette. A hand comes out of the mailbox door, waving the envelope Louis had just deposited, startling him and causing the cigarette, match, and matchbook to fly out of his hands.

"It was Steve's idea to go away from the piano," said Hemion.

"The reality is, even if we had thought about going away as he was playing the piano, we would have been a little afraid to leave the star performer" out of the shot.

Camera on the Street

Another popular routine originated one night, recalled Harbach, when the elephant doors to the studio's loading dock were opened during a broadcast to move a big set out. Quite by accident, Allen, who was seated at his desk, saw the elephant doors open on 45th Street, as well as the camera looking out the doors. At that moment, Harbach remembered, "Steve said over the air, 'Take that shot, Dwight.' And we looked out these doors and saw people walking down the street and gawking at the camera."

A camera and a light were mounted, recalled Hemion. "And people who would walk by the back of the theater would look up because they'd see the light. And the camera would focus in on them. Steve would then talk about what these people either did or were thinking about, ad-lib commentary." Added Harbach, "Steve could find something funny, right out there. The audience would be looking at the monitors, and Steve is describing somebody. But you don't write for that. That's Steve's brain."

There was a Friday night in May 1956 in which Allen noticed one gawker with four toothpicks sticking ridiculously out of his mouth and drily observed, "That man just kissed a porcupine good-bye."

"A policeman would come down on a horse," recalled Ed McMahon. "And [Allen would] start talking to the policeman, and he'd get five or six minutes of comedy, never written, never planned. He just saw this guy—'What's it like out there? What's your name? Charlie? Well, Charlie, tell me'—and he'd have a whole five minutes out of it!"

Decades later, David Letterman did a similar bit that tickled

Allen, describing unsuspecting passersby as though they were models in a fashion show. Today, Jay Leno does "Sidewalking," in which he mines found comedy by leaving a camera and mike on a sidewalk, letting people come up and show off their talent.

A dazzling, one-time stunt originated with the aid of professional magician Bob McCarthy and involved taking a real baby grand piano at center stage and levitating it. "When Steve started playing, we had the piano rise upward and turn upside down," Hemion said, smiling proudly. "A real baby grand—Steve was really playing it!" The piano slowly rose ten feet above the floor and then turned over completely three times while he continued playing. Allen was belted onto the bench, but a flower vase resting on top of the piano wasn't secured, so it came crashing to the ground as the instrument turned over. To further bolster the credibility of the stunt, Allen recalled, "we filled the stage with singers and dancing girls, to one of whom I threw a flower as I whirled about."

* * * * * * *

"God, I'd love to live those days over again," Hemion reflected dreamily, as he reminisced about his *Tonight* years during the two-hour interview. "I remember night after night, going to bed and not being able to sleep, just thinking about things that happened on the show—mostly good. Your days were full of reactions to the show. It was a happy, happy group."

Chapter 8

THE READY-FOR-
PRIME-TIME PLAYERS

MULTITASK KING

*A*s Steve Allen's star began rising across the late-night sky, there seemed no limit to the projects he could capably undertake. While doing the local late-night show in New York, he was also writing an episode of the prime-time drama anthology series for CBS *Danger*—a precursor to *Playhouse 90* and an early television project of emerging film director Sidney Lumet (*Dog Day Afternoon, The Verdict*). Allen wrote an episode in which he co-starred with Jayne Meadows. "While we took a break from rehearsal," recalled Meadows, "Steve was in the corner writing what he was going to do on his own show that night."

When the local show went network, Allen continued his multitask routine. Newspapers of the day assigned reporters to write day-in-the-life features that offered glimpses into his workday. On a typical afternoon, after getting his usual nine-plus hours of sleep, he arises at around one o'clock and eats breakfast. At three o'clock he arrives at the Hudson Theatre to begin working on that night's

Tonight show. Cast and crew are running back and forth or milling about. Stan Burns is laughing at how well a punch line he had written was delivered by one of the previous night's guest stars. In the midst of the commotion, in strolls Allen, calm and serene. Several people immediately pounce on him with instructions or questions about the show. Unruffled, he answers every question and heads into his office.

Sitting at his desk, he checks the setup for the show. His first appointment arrives, a guy from an advertising agency asking Allen to write a new jingle for Knickerbocker Beer and inquiring with great deference, knowing what a busy man Allen must be, whether this task might be possibly accomplished in, say, a couple of weeks. "I'll have it for you in a day or two," replies Allen, startling the man. "Music writing requires the least expenditure of time," Allen told *Redbook* magazine at the time. "It's like wiggling your ears. Ninety-five percent of the stuff today is easy to write."

Now it is time to go through the day's batch of mail and gifts piled atop Allen's desk. Telephone installers arrive to hook up a direct line from Allen's office to NBC president Pat Weaver. An old friend from Phoenix calls and wants to come and see the show. At three forty-five, an arranger comes in to work out a musical number with Allen for that night.

At four o'clock, producer Bill Harbach drops by to suggest a skit depicting two television newscasters eating and conversing in a restaurant in stilted newscaster-speak. "Using an unimpeachable sauce?" puns Allen, catching on quickly.

"Yeah," replies Harbach. "And things like, 'A check has just been handed to me by a waiter.'" Allen calls in writers Stan Burns and Herb Sargent, who kick around the idea and turn it into an eight-minute sketch.

It's now four thirty, and a production assistant walks in with more mail and gifts as Allen dictates letters to his secretary. At four forty-five, he goes into a meeting with "someone important at NBC," which lasts until five fifty. He next goes downstairs into the theater to shoot a kinescope commercial. In the meantime, Eydie Gorme and Andy Williams are rehearsing a song-and-dance number to be performed on the show that night.

At about seven o'clock, Allen returns to his office to sign letters and orders a late lunch, which he consumes while checking notes and going over the show with Bill Harbach. At eight forty-five, he takes a nap on his slant board—legs raised, head lowered. "All the talent rushes to your head," he is fond of explaining. By ten o'clock, a newspaper reporter arrives to do an interview, and Allen invites him to sit next to him at his desk on the set, while he casually runs through that night's commercials by reading from a teleprompter; Allen sandwiches the interview in between readings.

Although other cast members and guest stars might rehearse their sketches and songs, Allen—unlike Groucho, Godfrey, and Fred Allen—rehearses very little, if at all. Why? "No one remembers any joke for twenty years," he explains. "What people remember are the little experiences they live through, like the time Joe dropped the beer on the floor. That's what I try to get them to do—live with me through the little adventures I have on the show every night. If I've succeeded at all, that's the reason."

At ten forty-five, Allen relaxes yet again by going to his piano and jamming with the band for fifteen minutes. Next comes makeup, and then at 11:05, he is back onstage warming up the audience. ("If you're not laughing by eleven thirty," he warns, "an engineer pushes a button and ice picks come up through the cushions of your chairs.") He keeps talking right up until the curtain goes up on the local *Steve Allen Show* at eleven fifteen, followed by the network *Tonight* show at eleven thirty. The show wraps up at one, and he is back home by one thirty. He doesn't wind down for at least another hour or two.

Allen tells an interviewer that *Tonight* is the kind of show he has always wanted to do: "It's been so important to me that I've had to turn down several movie and Broadway offers," including *Brigadoon*, *Seven Year Itch*, and *The Pajama Game*. He even dropped his acclaimed participation on the CBS game show *What's My Line?*

This still, however, leaves Allen with a very full plate. How does he do it? "Jayne always wonders why I don't fall to pieces with my schedule," he tells the interviewer, " but she's beginning to realize I have no problem relaxing. My composure is actual and not pretended—which may mean that something is wrong with me."

* * * * * * * *

In 1955, well into the *Tonight* show's first season, Allen was tapped to star as one of his boyhood heroes—clarinetist and big band leader Benny Goodman—in *The Benny Goodman Story*, a motion picture co-starring Donna Reed and featuring jazz greats such as Gene Krupa, Lionel Hampton, Harry James, and Stan Getz. Throughout the entire film shoot, *Tonight* originated from the NBC studios in Burbank, California (where it would originate under Johnny Carson seventeen years later). But whereas Carson became notorious for frequently taking nights off, Allen juggled both his movie and late-night roles—without missing a single *Tonight* broadcast.

For eight weeks, Allen would rise at 4:30 a.m. at his Ambassador Hotel suite and get whisked by limo an hour later to Universal Studios, where he would spend the day shooting. Come 6 p.m., he would be whisked back to the Ambassador for a quick dinner and then off to NBC to begin the live *Tonight* show telecast at eight thirty (eleven thirty on the East Coast). "At the time I saw nothing unusual about this," mused Allen. "But if God had wanted man to be able to do a ninety-minute telecast at night and keep a busy motion picture filming schedule by day, he would've made him a sleepless creature.

I was so young and naive, it never occurred to me to ask NBC if I might have a few weeks off while making the film. I suppose they figured that if I was too stupid to make such a reasonable request, they would take advantage of my inexperience."

Before long, Allen began to feel the strain: "I was in a somewhat vegetative state disguised to the public because I'm a rather low-key creature anyway. The last few weeks on the film, understandably enough, I had trouble remembering lines and took to pasting little scraps of dialogue on the upstage side of walls, pianos, between the shoulder blades of other actors, wherever."

In 1956, during Allen's second season on *Tonight*, NBC approached him with an ambitious idea: a prime-time show of his own. The network was looking to provide some real competition for a long-standing nemesis—*The Ed Sullivan Show* on CBS—that since 1948 virtually owned eight o'clock on Sunday nights. According to *Tonight* producer Bill Harbach, NBC programming director Pat Weaver said, "I think that the *Tonight* show, if we give 'em some money and dress 'em up a little more, could go against Ed Sullivan. Let's see if we can knock Sullivan off, or at least come up alongside of him."

NBC and Allen struck a deal whereby Allen would star in a live Sunday night comedy hour and continue hosting *Tonight* five nights a week, ninety minutes a show. Later that year, Allen would write the words and music for *The Bachelor*, an NBC musical comedy special, which yielded two songs that became standards: "Impossible" (which became a hit for Nat King Cole and was revived decades later by Diane Schuur) and "This Could Be the Start of Something Big" (which became Allen's theme song). The latter song actually came to Allen in a dream: "I dreamed the first main theme, up to the bridge, and dreamed the first seven or eight lines of the lyric and, thank goodness, remembered them when I woke up, and wrote them down." It was one of over nine thousand songs that he would compose during his lifetime, landing him a place in the *Guinness Book of World Records*.

"This has been a pattern all through his life," observed Meadows. Allen was doing other things during the day, "but he also had to figure out what he was going to do each night on his live late-night talk show," said Bill Allen. "Filling ninety minutes of television time was a more daunting task when there were far fewer commercials in those days. Most late-night shows today are only an hour long, with commercials, and a large writing staff can develop several routines for each episode. The star may go through those routines and say, 'I don't like this one. Let's flesh this one out.' They'll have some creative input. They'll go through the jokes and eliminate some. Then they have the cue cards right on stage. You can see them looking for the next joke. But Steve didn't enjoy that level of protection in those days."

The Sunday night *Steve Allen Show* premiered live from the Hudson Theatre on June 24, 1956. Allen and his *Tonight* show team of Bill Harbach, Dwight Hemion, Stan Burns, and Herb Sargent took on both shows. Another integral member of the production team was Nick Vanoff, whom Harbach initially hired in 1956 as associate producer on *Tonight*; he would go on with Harbach to produce the celebrated ABC variety series *The Hollywood Palace* (1964–70) and become a founding producer of *The Kennedy Center Honors: A Celebration of the Performing Arts* (for which he won three Emmys) before his death in 1991. Additional writers included Arne Sultan, Marvin Worth, and Leonard Stern (who also directed the comedy segments of the Sunday show and became executive producer of the classic spy spoof *Get Smart*, for which he won an Emmy in 1967 for outstanding writing in comedy). It didn't take long for them to discover that the sixty minutes of comedy they were presenting in prime time required exponentially more work than the looser, ninety-minute, late-night format, five nights a week. Whereas *Tonight* had been 5 percent scripted and 95 percent ad-lib, the Sunday show reversed these proportions. The Allen team had to create a solid hour of comedy and music in six days.

"Of course," noted Allen, "if I'd elected to do a show in the Sullivan formula—hiring several acts and presenting them one of after another—there would've been no such problem. But we created fresh sketches for our guest stars and the members of our regular company, and this required hard work—morning, noon, and night, with no days off."

Writer/producer David Pollock, who would work for Allen a decade later, was an Army private who used to sneak into the Hudson Theatre during weekend leaves from Fort Slocum to watch dress rehearsals of the show. "Witnessing all the elements of a live 60-minute variety show coming together was magical," he wrote in a 2001 tribute to Allen in *Television Quarterly*. "Invariably the sketches and musical numbers would be in such tatters only an hour before airtime that I'd be convinced the thing could never get off the ground. Yet, somehow it always did."

Several weeks into the Sunday night show, Allen reached his limit. He was spending his daytime hours writing, booking, and rehearsing the Sunday show, in addition to preparing the *Tonight* show, and he was continuing to do *Tonight* from eleven thirty until one the next morning. Harbach: "The Sunday night show was so much pressure. Prime time, baby—now you've gotta be hot. Plus, we had to keep [*Tonight*] the way it had been and not let it go down." Allen informed NBC that he had to give up *Tonight*. NBC, however, urged him to reconsider, and they reached a compromise whereby Allen would continue with *Tonight* for three nights a week.

Throughout the summer of 1956, a number of guest hosts took over on Mondays and Tuesdays, including Ernie Kovacs, Jack Paar, Gene Rayburn, cartoonist Al Capp, game show host Bill Cullen, Morey Amsterdam, comedian Henry Morgan, '20s crooner Rudy Vallee, actor Tony Randall, and even a ghost from the past, Jerry Lester (*Broadway Open House*). In October, Kovacs became the designated Monday-Tuesday host/producer. Allen, still burned out from this breakneck schedule, asked to be relieved of his Wednesday-Thursday-Friday *Tonight* duties as soon as possible, and on January 25, 1957, he hosted his last *Tonight* telecast.

* * * * * * *

The Sunday show was comedy sketch oriented, somewhat more formal and structured than *Tonight.* "But we were still crazy," writer Stan Burns emphasized. Herb Sargent: "The main difference between the *Tonight* show and the Sunday show was the budget. So there was more scenery, more sets, more rehearsal, and bigger-name guest stars."

Elvis Presley appeared on June 1, 1956, predating his appearances on Ed Sullivan's program. Because the Sunday show format, like *Tonight,* emphasized guest star involvement in comedy, Allen had Elvis sing "Hound Dog" (which he had just recorded for RCA the previous day)—to a sad-faced bassett hound dressed in a top hat. Allen said that for added effect, he dressed the King "in a classy Fred Astaire wardrobe—white tie and tails—and surrounded him with graceful Greek columns and hanging draperies that would have been suitable for Sir Laurence Olivier reciting Shakespeare." Some rock critics and Elvis fans were not amused by this comical approach, as well as the fact that Elvis was not allowed to wiggle his pelvis. Later in the show, Presley appeared in a sketch with Andy Griffith, Imogene Coca, and Steve, in which the four were supposed to be a country and western group, singing and telling jokes. "That was the only sketch he ever did in his life," claimed writer Stan Burns. "He did something with Sinatra, but it was just a little musical thing. But we did a comedy sketch with him."

As Jerry Lee Lewis rocked and rolled in a July 1957 guest spot on "Whole Lotta Shakin'," he stood up from his piano stool and kicked it out of his way. Allen playfully threw the stool back at Lewis, along with a hail of other objects after it, whereupon Lewis began playing the piano with his foot. (Allen reenacted this scene for the 1988 Lewis biopic *Great Balls of Fire*.) Lewis so appreciated his network television break that he named his baby boy, born shortly thereafter, Steve Allen Lewis.

In a rare noncomedy segment, beat novelist Jack Kerouac read passages from *On the Road* over Allen's unobtrusive jazz piano background. The two, in fact, recorded an album in which Kerouac recited his manuscripts, randomly pulled from his suitcase, while Allen spontaneously laced jazz chords in and around his words. Recalled Kerouac: "We finished the session in an hour. The engineers came out and said, 'Great, that was a great first take.' I said, 'It's the only take.' Steve said, 'That's right,' and we all packed up and went home."

As a telling sign of the thirty-four-year-old Allen's stature in the industry, his guests included Groucho Marx, Milton Berle, Bob Hope, Liberace, Abbott and Costello, Orson Welles, Esther Williams, Errol Flynn, and Rosemary Clooney. There was also a rising star, Johnny Carson, who wowed the audience with his seldom-recognized ability to do impressions. In a one-man routine, he played three different characters—Ed Sullivan, James Garner as Bret Maverick, and Allen himself—sitting around a table, playing poker. Carson would jump from seat to seat and hurriedly switch character. In another routine, he impersonated Edward R. Murrow and Jack Benny.

Even the musical numbers reflected the Allen team's imagination. With Allen at the keyboard, Sammy Davis Jr. energetically tapped and sang his way through a jazzy rendition of Alan Jay Lerner and Frederick Loewe's "I Could Have Danced All Night"—atop Allen's grand piano. While Ginger Rogers and her troupe sang and danced their way through "Life Is Just a Bowl of Cherries," the set was filled with balloons that they popped in time with the music. One of the more hilarious numbers occurred the night Frank Sinatra appeared in August 1956; his voice had gone out, so he lip-synched his recording of Cole Porter's "Night and Day," deliberately off-tempo.

In addition, the Sunday show booked serious actors like Claudette Colbert, Kirk Douglas, William Holden, Jack Lemmon, and Gloria Swanson in rare comedy routines written especially for them. "It was always obvious that both the writing of the series and our regular cast were terrific," reflected Allen in 1990, "but what is remarkable to me, now, seeing this material again after so many years, is how we were able to build strong and funny sketches around major stars who had never had the opportunity to test their comedic wings before. I think audiences today will get a kick out of the real laughs generated by some of their favorite *dramatic* film stars."

One example was Henry Fonda, who found himself "jamming" with Allen and a cool jazz sextet. With authority, Fonda raised his horn and blew the first three notes of the melody (coincidentally, "Night and Day"). The band came in and picked up the song from there, while Fonda just stood there grooving, snapping his fingers, and wiping his brow with a handkerchief. Several measures later, he raised his horn again, in time to play the same three-note riff, and it became apparent that his musical training consisted of learning how to play that one note three times. "My chops are beat!" Fonda exclaimed in mock exhaustion at the end of the number.

After Orson Welles finished a funny routine with Allen, he put on a robe and sat at a small, mirrored dressing table. It was a dead stage, recalled Bill Harbach, "no scenery, just a dynabeam on him." As Welles donned makeup and costume—while the audience watched—he offered his insights into some of the great Shakespearean characters. And then he performed a soliloquy. Harbach summed up Welles's impact on the audience in two words: "*Othello*. Lethal."

Because the Sunday show, like the *Tonight* show, was live, even additional rehearsals didn't guarantee a polished product—but that really didn't matter. On the first show, the glamorous Kim Novak appeared to repeat a sketch that had scored high on *Tonight* several months before. The sketch offered a tongue-in-cheek solution to the growing problem of schoolchildren watching excessive amounts of television: incorporate more educational value into TV programming. Allen played a fugitive on the run, and Novak played his wife. When Allen pulled out a revolver from his pocket, a shocked Novak cried, "A revolver!" Then, turning to the camera, she lifted Allen's arm—with the gun still in it—and deadpanned, "Revolver. R-E-V-O-L-V-E-R. Noun. A firearm, commonly a pistol, with a cylinder of several chambers so arranged as to revolve on an axis and be discharged in succession by the same lock."

So far, so good, until later in the sketch when the script called for Novak to say: "Well, you're going to leave without me. Why should I get involved in this mess? You started out like a big shot, but you're just like all the rest of them. And I thought you had a brain," whereupon she would turn to the camera and say, "Brain. B-R-A-I-N. Noun. The large central mass of nerve tissue enclosed in the skull." Recalled Allen: "Unfortunately, she forgot her lines at that point and had to make several attempts before she could say, 'And I thought you had a brain.' I made the best of the awkward situation by ad-libbing to her, 'and I thought *you* had a brain.'"

The bloopers weren't limited to the guests. Allen himself committed a blooper that became the most requested clip from the Sunday series. As Big Bill Allen, the over-the-top sportscaster, he fell victim to a fit of uncontrollable laughter that lasted over two minutes. According to Allen,

Before the show, I had put some greasy tonic on my hair to make it stay down; the reverse occurred. Having no time to fix it, I grabbed the fedora I always wore for the routine and hurried onstage. When I glanced at myself in the monitor as I started the bit, the way I looked—like Mark Twain's Injun Joe in *Tom Sawyer*—struck me so funny that I began to laugh. The fact that it was striking me funny struck me funny. It was the old laughing-in-church syndrome.

"Oh, if only the script were this good," I said, falling back in my chair in hysterics.

Another reason I kept laughing was that the always funny rotund comedian Jack E. Leonard, the next guest scheduled to appear, was yelling lines at me from the wings. I was eating into his time by laughing for so long. "Come on, goddammit," he bellowed. "I've got only five minutes, and you've blown three of them already!" He had a point, since live shows had to be strictly timed and controlled, so that at the end of the hour you didn't find yourself with either three minutes to fill with absolutely nothing planned, or else go off the air before you had completed the scheduled entertainment.

But I laughed anyway.

So did Steve Martin. In a 2001 posthumous tribute to Allen in *Entertainment Weekly*, he wrote: "There is nothing, nowhere, not anything funnier than the black-and-white two-minute kinescope of Steve Allen on his evening show, sitting at his desk, out of control, laughing, unable to speak his next line, squealing, dying, trying to get through his bit. You can see him gather himself, get ready to speak, and then suddenly giggle and shriek with a high-pitched inhuman noise that evoked in us our own form of uncontrollable, responsive laughter. This unplanned moment defines so simply Steve's early sense of joy, of comedy, of pure cut loose, laugh-riot silliness, and embodies the soul of a kind of comedy that inspired many of us to become comedians."

The bigger prime-time budget made it possible to attempt more ambitious stunts, such as having Allen play a concert grand piano from atop the roof of the Capitol Records Building on Vine Street in

Hollywood. This required the heavy piano to be hoisted fourteen stories up the outside of the building. The result was breathtaking: Allen performing against a panorama of mountains and toy-sized automobiles zipping along the winding freeway. Some people assumed this was all a camera trick, said Allen, a tad annoyed by the irony of the stunt's success.

A WEALTH OF COMIC ACTORS

One of the hallmarks of the Sunday show was its strong sketch comedy. But the effective execution of the sketches required a team of brilliant comic actors. Although they played an endless assortment of Mafia gangsters, German soldiers, obtuse scientists, screen idols, members of Senate investigating committees, and quiz-show contestants, these actors garnered their greatest fame from "Man on the Street," one of the best-known running sketches on the Allen-era *Tonight* and the Sunday prime-time show.

"Man on the Street" satirized the newspaper practice of asking randomly selected persons questions on topical issues, and then printing the answers along with close-up head shots of the respondents. Allen adapted the practice for television by playing the straight, questioning reporter in the studio. Comic actors Tom Poston, Don Knotts, and Louis Nye would play basically the same wacky characters, purportedly found at random out on the street. There was little ad-libbing, said Allen, as "all the bits were written—mostly by Herb Sargent and Stan Burns—and rehearsed."

Knotts was the trembling and nervous little guy who would invariably identify himself as a brain surgeon, a carnival knife-thrower, or a member of some other unlikely occupation:

> KNOTTS (*trembling*): My name is D. D. Morrison, and I'm a body-guard for Vice President Nixon.

STEVE: Well, it's nice to have you here, Mr. D. D.—but by the way, what's the D. D. for?

KNOTTS: Duck, Dick!

STEVE: My goodness. Nixon's bodyguard. That's a very responsible job. Tell me, sir, does that make you nervous?

KNOTTS (*startled and wide-eyed*): Noop! [*The audience roars.*] Makes *him* kinda nervous. . . .

Nye played a flamboyant advertising man: "My name is Gordon Hathaway and I'm from Manhattan. Move over, Big Ben, I'm clanging tonight!" Nye popularized the salutation "Hi-ho, Steverino!" into a 1950s catchphrase. Poston played a befuddled, Stan Laurel–type character who could never remember his name. There was another comic actor, Dayton Allen (no relation to Steve), whose sole response to Steve Allen's questions—such as "Do you plan to vote in the coming election?"—also became a national catchphrase: "Whyyyy not!!!"

As the routine expanded, other participants included Bill Dana, Pat Harrington Jr., Gabe Dell, conductor Skitch Henderson, and assorted guest stars like Jonathan Winters, who frequently appeared as any of an assortment of odd characters, including Hawaiian Princess Leilani-nani, the world's oldest hula dancer. ("They call me 'Old Happy Hips.' If you'll lower your camera, I'll give you a little demonstration.")

Allen's secretary, Marilyn Jacobs, proved hysterical on-camera. Even Allen's mother, Belle Montrose, occasionally got into the act as "Mag Haggerty"—a name she used to call herself when Allen was a child. "I would write lines for her in hip language, jazz musicians' language, and she had no idea what she was talking about," Allen told USA *Today* in 1997. "I would say, 'What is your name, madam?' And she'd say, 'It's cool. What's yours, pops?' And stuff like that. You don't even need jokes. Just hearing that old woman talking like that was hysterical."

Here are some of the talented comic actors who emerged from *Man on the Street* and other comedy sketches on the Sunday show.

Louis Nye

When the Sunday show premiered, Louis Nye was already a Steve Allen veteran, having done several routines on Allen's local late-night show and later on *Tonight*. Allen literally plucked Nye during a chance meeting in an NBC elevator, as Nye explained in a 1998 interview, sitting in the den of the Pacific Palisades home where he has lived since the early '60s. Allen had seen Nye's ad-lib routines on a local program. "So now I see him in an elevator," said Nye. "I don't know who he is, never seen him before, and he says, 'I like your work, and I'll be doing a show soon, and I'd sure like to have you.'" Nye, knowing that his own show was about to fold, was delighted to accept the offer, although he wasn't sure if the polite stranger in the elevator who made him a job offer was for real.

"And I'll be darned," Nye said. "In three weeks, I got a telephone call to go on the show. No audition."

Nye's performing experience had been more practical than formal. As a member of the Hartford Players in Connecticut, he was coached by a director who "never gave you anything psychological. He said [*affecting a theatrically booming, authoritative voice*—Nye was fond of illustrating his points by going into character]: 'You're not talking loud enough. We can't hear you.' That kind of direction. 'A play is nothing unless the audience hears what you're saying. Scream that out! Turn your head to the audience when you say that line, or they'll never understand you.' And it was practical, wonderful direction. The other kind of direction came later in life. They had directors and people in drama in New York who got into the bowels of everything."

Nye felt that his training helped him on the *Tonight* show: "I was very much aware of it. That kind of acting is instinctive. And then by watching others, that has an effect on you, too. I mimic the English so much in comedy because they're so wonderful. I do a Cockney, where you don't understand a word but you know what I'm doing." With that, Nye broke into a sample of outrageously unintelligible Cockney-speak.

One of Nye's most well-known characters was flamboyant Gordon Hathaway, one of the legendary Men on the Street. "When I was in the Army, we had a lieutenant who spoke this way," explained Nye, going into character: "'Okay, guys, we're out for an eight-miler, so get a good night's sleep. I'll see you in the morning. *Hip-hop!*'" As Hathaway, Nye would open with something like: "My name is Gordon Hathaway, and I'm America's party doll!" Here's one of his exchanges with Allen:

> LOUIS [*smilingly broadly*]: I'm Gordon Hathaway from Manhattan, and I'm the original Boy on a Dolphin!
> STEVE: All right, Gordon, here it is. Just what is it that makes *you* laugh?
> LOUIS: Well, naturally, my sense of humor is different from other people's. I've found that I just don't laugh at the same things that everybody else laughs at.
> STEVE: Oh? And what *does* everybody else laugh at?
> LOUIS [*no longer smiling*]: At me.

"We knew Louis could play this guy," said writer Herb Sargent. "The first name we tried was 'Harvey Trimble,' but 'Gordon Hathaway' had a lilt to it."

In another sketch, Nye played a highbrow book critic being interviewed by Allen. Nye grew increasingly outraged over a book detailing lurid scandals in the entertainment industry. His volume, pitch, and intensity rose with all the drama of a Richard Burton soliloquy, and he even began to rise from his seat. When he reached a fever pitch, Allen asked for the book's title. Nye suddenly broke into an ear-to-ear grin, girlishly giggling, "Hooray for Hollywood!"

Nye was famous for his death scenes because "I'd never die right away. They'd keep shooting me, but I don't go down. Then, finally, I'd lay down, do a balletic thing," a kind of dance of death. This tickled Jackie Gleason so much that he brought Nye on his show to do the same routine—four times.

Nye was struck by the instant chemistry between himself and fellow comics Tom Poston and Don Knotts. Until the Sunday show, the three had never worked together. But at a reading of their first sketch, "My God, it just felt like we knew each other," said Nye warmly. "It was a good contrast. Tom Poston's sort of sleepy kind of thing that he did [*affecting Poston's sleepy, slow cadence*]: 'Well, what happened after that . . . I wasn't told about it, so I don't know.' And Don Knotts was small and thin with that [*exaggerating Knotts's nasal tone*] crackly little voice up here like that. He was [*relishing the mimicry*] crackly.

"And then there's me, who's very expansive and played all kinds of nationalities—Frenchmen, loved makeup and hats and jackets. And the acting that we did was a remarkable blend because when you do a show and they cast it, there's a hope that everybody will get along, that the leading man will look good with the ingenue, and the juvenile will play the scene well with his mother, and everything is cast right. We just blended together."

Nye's ability to ad-lib—broadly—sometimes came at a price. "The writers would not complete my part too much," Nye said, cracking a smile. "It used to drive me crazy." In a famous Sunday show sketch, Charlton Heston starred as a handsome but hilariously inept western actor muddling his way through a film shoot set in a bar. Each piece of physical business he is asked to do proves too much for him. He is simply too clumsy to perform any of the western movie bar scene cliches, such as throwing his leg over a chair as he sits or catching a beer slid down the bar by the bartender. Nye was simply expected to play the director's assistant, snapping the clapboard and making perfunctory announcements like, "Scene twelve, take six!"

"They didn't give me many lines," explained Nye, "but I wanna be important, too. So here's what I would ad-lib." He illustrated by diving into character, affecting an excessive cheerfulness that belied his exasperation with Heston: "'Cut! Let's try this again, please. They're becoming very fond of you! You're doing a splendid job!' That wasn't in the script," continued Nye. Then, out of Heston's view, he would roll his eyes. "It would go on that way. I'm building up my part. They're allowing it, they're expecting me, if I find some little area. At the end of it, I'd be considered the most creative, because I'd always find something."

Yet, for as much as Nye was challenged by the open spaces left for him by the writers, he greatly admired Allen's "great power over the language. He knows words, phrases. So if you're doing a sketch with him, he would say, 'Let me see your script,' and he'd pick up a pencil and do the best editing of anybody. He'd say, 'Change this word; it has better rhythm. Who the hell talks like that in television? Make up something right here. Too awkward, too many words. This will tighten it up.'"

Don Knotts

Before his immortal characterizations of Barney Fife on *The Andy Griffith Show* (1960–64) and Ralph Furley on *Three's Company* (1979–84), Don Knotts was struggling to establish himself as an actor. The Morgantown, West Virginia, native did Army shows during World War II, played an old-timer in a radio western, and did a television soap opera, *Search for Tomorrow*, in the early 1950s. Then the job offers dried up. "It was at that time I was afraid I was going to have to get a job somewhere else because I had a family to support, and I thought I had to get out of the business," said Knotts. But director Perry Lafferty kept encouraging him and did what he could to help. "[Lafferty] told me I was a good actor," recalled Knotts in a 2003 interview. "He wanted to keep me, so he threw me these bit parts just to keep me in the business. He put me on *The Imogene Coca Show* [starring Sid Caesar's comedy partner]."

In 1955, Knotts finally landed steady work with a supporting role in a Broadway play, *No Time for Sergeants*, starring his future television partner, Andy Griffith. By then, Knotts had accumulated substantial experience, but still, "I wasn't known at all," he said. While still doing the play in 1956, he showed up for an audition for the *Tonight* show. "I was kind of surprised that [*Tonight* writer] Bill Dana was the guy doing it because I happened to know him. I auditioned with a monologue I had written about a nervous guy. I'd never done [a nervous character] before. That gave me a whole new thing to go with. I saw an actual speaker who was almost that nervous once, and it struck me as funny. And I had a little dream about it and almost dreamed part of a routine. That's when I sat down and wrote it. That opened a lot for me. This was an after-dinner speaker. And Bill liked it so much, and he said, 'Why don't you go on tonight?' I said, 'My suit's in the cleaners. You better wait until another time.'"

Knotts made his *Tonight* debut the following night, November 8, 1956. His nervous speaker monologue killed. Dana told him to write another one and come back. Knotts recalled that his second *Tonight* appearance consisted of a bit he had written about a nervous tranquilizer salesman filling in for a doctor who was supposed to address a medical convention: "Dr. Harry Hillary couldn't make it, and believe you me, taking his place is having to fill a couple of awfully big shoes. Oh, I don't mean to imply that Dr. Hillary has big feet [*laughter*]. Just big shoes [*bigger laughter*]." Knotts read a letter from a prison warden explaining how a prison guard, after taking three of the pills, had allowed inmates in solitary confinement to throw a party, and the guard attended the party unarmed: "He will be buried on Wednesday [*laughter*]. Of course, the important thing is that he [*awkward pause*] enjoyed the party."

"It was the *Tonight* show that really got me going," acknowledged Knotts. But even though his monologues on *Tonight* were a smash, he did not aspire to become a stand-up comic. "I had worked as a stand-up before back in Pittsburgh and Morgantown, where I was from," he explained. "Being on stage alone didn't appeal to me that much. I wanted to be an actor or a sketch comic, working with other people."

"All this time, I was still on *No Time for Sergeants*," recalled Knotts. Allen invited him, fresh on the heels of his *Tonight* show appearances, onto his Sunday show to do "Man on the Street" segments. There, he expanded his repertory of hilariously nervous, twitchy characters. "The most fun was doing the 'Man on the Street,'" said Knotts. "I enjoyed the fact not only that I was doing the nervous character, but Tom [Poston] and Louis [Nye] and I were the first three of the Men on the Street. We did that almost every week. Then Pat Harrington and Dayton Allen came on. It was overall such a wonderful group to work with. We had the best of the best there for a long time. Everybody was totally different from everybody else. There were no two guys who were very similar at all."

The audience's initial response to Knotts's nervous character was "unbelievable. They wrote this thing where I was supposed to go, 'Noop!' when they asked, 'Are you nervous?' When I did that, the house caved in—I mean, it was the biggest laugh I'd heard in my life." Knotts hadn't done that type of comedy before. "I almost jumped. It was really a shock. I thought, 'Wow!' So they decided to make that a permanent part of my character—the line 'Are you nervous?' 'Noop!' became something we did every week."

After a while, however, the nervous persona—which had little in common with Knotts's true nature—began to wear thin. "I used to get a little upset that people used to think I was really nervous," Knotts admitted. "Everywhere I'd go, people would say, 'Are you nervous? Are you nervous?' I got so tired of hearing that."

Fortunately, Knotts's roles on the Sunday show were not limited to nervous characters. "We did everything," he said. "We got a chance to appear in all kinds of sketches doing all kinds of characters, where we didn't do just the nervous guy or the guy who couldn't remember his name [Poston's 'Man on the Street' character] and so forth."

On one show, a sketch had been written for Knotts in which he, playing a lion tamer, was supposed to step into a cage containing a real lion. During rehearsal, "I said to the trainer, 'I don't think that's a safe thing to do to go in there with that lion.' He said [*affecting a reassuring tone*], 'Aw, this lion's an old lion. He wouldn't hurt a flea.' When I started to open the door to go in, I saw the guy start to pull out a gun and aim it at the lion. I said, 'Hey, if he's so safe, why are you aiming a gun at him?' And he said, 'Well, you never know.' So I refused to go in."

Knotts appreciated that "Steve's always giving you all kinds of freedom to do whatever you thought was going to be funny. He was just an easy, easy guy to work for. We had such good people around us."

Tom Poston

In 1954–55, Tom Poston hosted his own daytime show that ran two-and-a-half hours a day, five days a week, live, on the local ABC station in New York. It was a musical/comedy/variety show called *Entertainment*—"an unassuming little title," Poston quipped drily in a 2002 interview in Beverly Hills. He was required to ad-lib for thirty-six minutes a day. "You can imagine the quality of that show."

Stan Burns and Herb Sargent were writing for one of the Dead End Kids, Gabe Dell, a comedian who once shared the bill with Poston at a local nightclub, and the four hung out together. Later,

Burns and Sargent would watch Poston on *Entertainment*—and, according to Poston, use "some of the things I was doing on the afternoon show and introduce them on the *Tonight* show. Those dirty rats!" laughed Poston.

In 1956, Burns and Sargent asked Poston if he'd be interested in doing the prime-time *Steve Allen Show*. Poston came to their office and was interviewed by Sargent. It was an awkward meeting, recalled Poston. What he hadn't realized was that Burns and Sargent were taking advantage of their prime-time budget, upgrading "Man on the Street" by recruiting more professional performers. Sargent knew what he wanted, even if Poston didn't. Suddenly, Sargent said, "Look, you're standing there, and the camera comes up on you, extratight close-up." He pushed his hands toward Poston's face, framing it like a director would, and announced urgently, "Here's our next man on the street. What is your name, sir?"

"I was in character as a nebbish for a two-man thing I was thinking of for me and Steve," said Poston. "Herb startled me enough so that I couldn't think of my name. Then he laughed. He was intrigued by the guy who couldn't remember his name. We showed it to Stan, and he laughed." Allen laughed, too, and said, "Fine. Put him on the show."

Elated, Poston asked Bill Harbach when he would begin working on the show. "Tomorrow," Harbach replied.

"I had worn my best clothes to the interview," recalled Poston. "A camel-hair coat and a cashmere scarf and Italian handmade shirt, Countess Mara tie, the French flannel light grey suit, cordovan wing-tip shoes. So I said, 'I see this guy as kind of a nebbish, couldn't think of his own name. He obviously isn't stylish or connected. So what do you think I should wear for a costume?' Billy says, 'Just what you got on. It's perfect.' So I never wore that outfit again."

The exposure Poston got in his first appearance was staggering. Before the Sunday show, he had done burlesque, vaudeville,

Broadway, motion pictures, local television, nightclubs, singing, and dancing. "Eleven years of doing everything there was to do in show business, and nobody outside my immediate family knew who I was," he said. "But the week after I did the man who couldn't think of his own name on *The Steve Allen Show*, I was nationally known. Cab drivers would wave and yell on the street, 'Hey, stupid!'"

Poston's man-who-forgot-his-name was so successful that he was asked to return and do it again. "They're not going to hold still for me not knowing my name twice in a row, that's ridiculous!" he thought. But the character was an even bigger success the second time. "And I thought they'd throw stones at us all for making this dope just as dopey. I did this character for the next three years," said Poston, who went on to win an Emmy in 1959 for Best Supporting Actor in a Comedy Series.

Working with Louis Nye, Don Knotts, and Bill Dana "was just absolute heaven," Poston said with a smile. "They're still very close friends." Poston remembered first seeing Knotts on the *Tonight* show, "doing his pharmaceutical man introducing a tranquilizer pill, if you can imagine that for humor. And Don said, as he's addressing doctors, 'Is there a doctor in the house?' I thought to myself, 'Not a good joke.' Then he said, 'A little humor there.'"

Poston had to adjust to Allen's technique of minimal rehearsal. "Steve won't rehearse, hates to rehearse, doesn't want to hear the jokes before the actual performance. Will not allow us to repeat the punch lines before the performance. For me, coming from the theater, it was 'Rehearse, rehearse, rehearse. Polish, polish, polish.' At first, it was terrifying because you had no idea what the response was going to be to the punch line. But when it was great and wonderful, you get over that worry."

When Poston asked, "Steve, why don't you say the joke before the show?" Allen answered, "I want to get that first hot laugh from the band. Because the band was large, and it was between us and the audience, a lot closer to us than the audience. And the cameras were between us and the audience. The sound people were between us and the audience. The ADs, the stage managers were between us and the audience. So if they all heard those jokes in rehearsal, they wouldn't laugh. Why would they laugh? They just heard 'em four times."

Poston remembered when actress Peggy Cass tried out to be on the show. He encouraged her to do things to surprise Allen, but "she brushed me," said Poston. "By air time, Steve was so bored with what her exchange was about—he had heard it eight times. And Steve had this funny notion that if he heard it, he assumed the rest of the world had heard it. Peggy wanted to practice it because she was coming from the theater. As a result, he saw no reason for her to be on the show anymore. Didn't think she was funny because he knew what she was going to say. And she would have been far better off if she had done things to startle and surprise him, rather than, 'See how well I'm doing this line that you've heard before.' She was a spontaneous human being. But she was from another discipline. And Steve knew nothing about that."

"So we always did 'ring-ding,'" explained Poston about Allen's practice of substituting nonsense syllables for the punch lines during rehearsal. That way, the actors and crew wouldn't hear the punch line or the key words to the setup. Example: "Why did the ring-ding cross the ding-dong?" "To get to the ribbi-tibbid."

The script would call for Allen to ask the nervous Don Knotts, "Are you nervous?" to which Knotts, in character, would respond, "Noop!" "But in rehearsal," remembered Poston, "Steve said, 'Are you ding-dong?' And Don said, 'Zeeep!' We just howled."

The Sunday show, unlike *Tonight*, was largely scripted but only up to a point. Explained Poston,

> What we did was always make sure that you do something to surprise Steve. Don't adhere to the material to the point where he's going to

258

get bored and not want to do it. But if he knew that you always had something up your sleeve, that kept him interested and excited about doing this stuff. Nobody could stop Louis from improvising terribly funny things—just a laugh could set Steve off. It'd just be Louis embellishing his lines. Some of those sketches Steve never saw until we did them on the air. All he had to do was read his straight lines. But in watching what was going on, Steve would get hysterical. He would see it for the first time and just love it like an audience. And then if his straight lines required embellishing, he'd do it with no problem at all. Glib ad-libber and funny and witty and in good taste.

Poston found working on the Sunday show euphoric. "We were in heaven," he said, "and none of it was our responsibility. It was all Steve's responsibility. Everything that happened. We could go our merry way. It just happened that I don't think anything really bombed. First of all, he wouldn't let it. A bomb to Steve was like adrenalin. He would cover it with witty humor and self-deprecating humor. It's live. You can't walk off, there's no place to walk to. So we had to cover. And we used to encourage Steve, and he was so ready to be encouraged."

Bill Dana

In addition to his writing duties on both *Tonight* and the Sunday show, Bill Dana joined the Sunday show's cast of comic actors. One of the Sunday show's departments that he developed with partner Don Hinkley was a spoof of *The Huntley-Brinkley Report*, NBC's nightly news show anchored by Chet Huntley and David Brinkley from 1956 to 1970. The Sunday show's send up was called *The Weekly Nuttley-Hinkley-Buttley-Winkley Report*. A November 1959 sketch was a news feature titled "Pre-Christmas USA," which looked at what people around the country were doing to get ready for the holiday season. "I thought if we had a school for Santa Clauses, and the instructor happened to be Latino, that we could have some fun with the spelling of the famous Santa Claus laugh, 'HO! HO! HO!'" said Dana.

"I did the reading in rehearsal. Everybody knew that I was a dialectitian, and I did a quasi–Puerto Riqueño accent—'I teach Santy-Klows how to es-speak.' It was no surprise to Steve that I could do a dialect, and as it usually was, we were close to air, that Steve said, 'You do it.' So what happened—which changed my life totally in twenty-five seconds—was that Pat Harrington played Chet Nuttley, and he said, 'We're here at a school for Santa Clauses.' In the meantime, I'm standing there—no beard—and behind the cardboard is written in big letters, 'JO! JO! JO!'"

When asked his name, Dana uttered what would become his signature response: "My name—Jose Jimenez." As the character caught on, audiences eagerly anticipated this catchphrase (just like audiences twenty years later would clamor to hear Steve Martin's "Well, ex-*cuuuuuuuse meeeee!*").

"And the rest," Dana added, "is *jistory.*" His obtuse, unassuming, yet earnest character became a national phenomenon. "The public was so used to strange people showing up on the *Steve Allen Show*, they thought Jose was the real thing. It wasn't that this was an actor portraying a character. Instantly, when you get something that scores like that, you figure you own that, so let's use it again," said Dana. "We established just by doing it the fact that this guy, who was obviously Latino, would never ever be presented as he actually was. So he became a senator, a bobsled racer. If there was something in the news, then we were able to do a sketch and be right on top of it. That established the 'Walter Mitty' Jose Jiminez, the guy who was fantasizing in front of everybody being these exotic professions."

Jimenez became the heroic submarine captain being interviewed by Allen. Jimenez (proudly): "I went around the world underwater in eighty-three day." During the course of the interview, he revealed that one day, the sub sprung a leak. Allen: "How long did it take you to fix the leak?" Jimenez: "Eighty-three day."

"It never particularly mattered what his alleged job was," said Allen of Jimenez, "but when he finally claimed to be an astronaut, the timing could not have been better. In the late '50s and early '60s, the nation was fascinated by the space program, and Bill apparently had become the only comedian dealing chiefly with that subject matter." In fact, the Smithsonian Air and Space Museum acknowledged and enshrined Dana as the official eighth Mercury astronaut (out of a possible seven).

In later years, Dana, who became active in Latino causes, was honored by the prestigious National Hispanic Media Coalition with its first Impact Award.

Although Jose Jimenez made Dana a hot TV property, he used to get all of $125 for each appearance on the Sunday show. "So it was not a place you went to get rich," Dana mused.

Pat Harrington Jr.

Named after his Broadway actor father, Pat Harrington Jr. hungered to get into show business but did not have much in the way of formal training or experience. After getting his Bachelor of Arts degree from Fordham in 1950 and his discharge from the Air Force in 1954, he tried to get into the business through the side door, by surrounding himself with people in the business. Harrington found a job in the NBC mailroom. By 1957, he had graduated to time salesman, which was well suited to his jovial, gregarious, dramatic, and very Irish personality. A gifted storyteller and compulsive prank puller, he seemed to befriend everybody, including fellow salesman Lynn Phillips.

Just for kicks, the two decided to put on prospects and friends with an act in which Phillips purported to interview Harrington as

Lt. Guido Panzini, the surviving junior officer of the ill-fated Italian luxury liner the *Andrea Doria*. Harrington affected a convincing Italian accent, which was remarkable, considering that he did not speak Italian, although he grew up on Manhattan's west side. (Phillips: "When did you realize, Guido, that you were on a collision course?" Harrington: "Well, I was-a on-a the breedge with-a Captain Calmai. And-a Captain Calmai ask-a the question. And somebody answer—in-a Swiddish.")

One day in 1958, the two were in Toots Shores, a New York restaurant, when Phillips spotted Jonathan Winters at the bar. Phillips, totally fearless, walked up to Winters, introduced himself, and then introduced Harrington as Lt. Panzini. Winters was thoroughly fooled by Harrington's dead-serious performance—so much so that his face fell when Harrington fessed up. "After twenty minutes," recalled Harrington in a 2003 interview in his West L.A. home, "I told him, 'I have to say something to you. My name is Pat Harrington, I'm a salesman at NBC, and I'm Irish.'" At that moment, Winters grabbed Harrington's coat by the lapels and whispered, "I'm takin' over for Paar Monday night. I want you on the first show!" It was an invitation to appear on *Tonight*, which was by then hosted by Steve Allen's successor, Jack Paar.

"And in that instant, my entire life changed!" marveled Harrington, who made his national TV debut as an Italian golf pro (also named Guido Panzini) and made fifty-eight appearances over two-and-a-half years on the show. "It was a huge hit," recalled the ebullient Harrington. "The Knights of Columbus wanted to make me their Man of the Year. I said, 'You know, I'm Irish,' and there was silence on the phone. The immigration people called NBC and said, 'We don't have any date of entry or port of entry for this guy, Panzini.' I got letters from people who totally believed me that were utterly unanswerable: 'Guido, do you know my son who was killed at Anzio?' This was from an Italian woman in Italy!"

While doing Paar, Harrington was spotted by Jules Green, Steve Allen's manager, who invited him to be on Allen's Sunday night show. Harrington found himself in a room with Don Knotts, Louis Nye, Tom Poston, Allen, and six writers. "So my first line is supposed to be, 'Yes," in response to Steve's question, 'Now you, sir, you're Italian, aren't you?' And I said, '*Jess*-eh!' And he was f---ing gone. On the floor, bring in the gurney, I.V., he was finished. And the rest of the guys—I don't know if they thought it was that funny, but what Steve was doing was contagious. So everybody in the room—it was tumult!" yelled Harrington, reliving the moment with deafening laughter. "I couldn't believe when I got an invitation to be on the Allen show. For me, that was way above my station. It was like matriculating at a graduate school of comedy. So there I was in the middle of this group of incredible performers who were incredibly funny and surrounded by writers who were funnier. I had no experience. These guys had all done radio, theater, stock. I hadn't done any of that! My dad brought home Crosby, Pat O'Brien, and Jimmy Dunn, and I'd have eggs with them in the morning, but that's not getting your bones in order. So I was really a neophyte. I was insecure and nervous because I knew I hadn't done what these guys had done."

Harrington's acceptance of the job on Allen's show alarmed his father, a professional actor who knew just how little professional experience his son had. "My father was scared to death," laughed Harrington. He had leaped into the big leagues, naive and ill prepared. But he was outgoing, and he had guts. "I learned from Louis and Tom and Don and Gabe Dell and Bill Dana and Steve. It was such a break for a guy."

A talented guy. The key to Harrington's talent, wrote Allen, was his versatility. "Oddly enough, his talent at submerging himself in a role was so great that frequently he did not get the credit he deserved simply because, although people would enjoy his characterizations (a famous jockey, a former boxing champ, an Italian busboy, a Scottish laird, etc.), they often didn't realize it was the same man playing all those parts." Harrington's favorite portrayals involved Irish characters, which Allen often had him do as race car drivers, jockeys, bartenders, and other occupations. "My uncles and aunts were all Irish, so I had this wonderfully authentic Irish accent, in addition to the Italian things. He loved the little Irish speaking traits that I brought into the sketches." One sketch he did as a boxer, John L. Great:

> ANNOUNCER: Have you ever thrown a fight?
> HARRINGTON: An' you, sittin' there, and after askin' me that question. You should be *ashemmed* of yerself!
> ANNOUNCER: So how many?
> HARRINGTON [*nonchalantly*]: About thirteen.

Harrington remembered the lion sketch incident related by Don Knotts:

> This poor old lion—no teeth, no claws. So the logical choice for the lion tamer is Don—the sketch was written for him. Don's in the cage [*mimicking Knotts in a meek voice*]: "Hey, buck! Get over here!" The lion turns around and snarls. And Don put the whip down and the chair down: "I'm not doin' this."
>
> One of the guys on the floor—Bill Harbach or Nick Vanoff—was telling Don, "Geez, Don, we've got a seven-minute hole in the show. You can't walk out on a sketch!" So Gabe Dell says, "I'll do the tamer!" Yaaaay, Gabe! So Gabe goes in there and gets the chair and goes *crack* with the whip. And the lion comes over to Gabe and knocks him over with his paw. In a nanosecond, Gabe is nine feet up this temporary cage, which is on cables, and the whole cage is rocking. Gabe is waving back and forth and screaming, waving a prop pistol: "If these weren't blanks, I'd be shoot'n' *you*!" So the trainer came in, they took the lion out, and they scratched the bit.
>
> It was what I have always considered to be one of the funniest afternoons of my life. I looked over at Steve, and he's in the fetal

position on the floor, laughing harder than you have ever seen him laugh before.

Harrington continued laughing heartily as he recalled the lion snarling. "We all know what a snarl can lead to," he said, with a twinkle in his eye.

"A divorce."

Tim Conway

"The first time I saw Milton Berle," recalled Tim Conway, "I was one of those guys who stood in the snow in front of a hardware store because nobody in our town had a television. But when we finally got a set, and when I was in the Army and already in college, Steve Allen was always the show that I'd watch. I decided that if I was ever going to do anything, that would be the thing to do."

Years later, Conway ended up in Cleveland as one of two inept co-hosts of a daily ninety-minute morning movie—a situation that would likely have made for a great Allen sketch. "The movie would run an hour and fifteen minutes, but I couldn't time it [with all the commercials] so that it would end when the show ended. So we didn't have any endings of movies," Conway said. "*Citizen Kane* annoyed people because they wanted to see Rosebud, of course. So then we started showing the ends of the movies on Friday. It got to be kind of an in thing in Cleveland that these two clowns—who shouldn't be in the business—were in the business. And Rose Marie happened to come into town to promote *The Dick Van Dyke Show*, and she thought that was hysterical."

Marie brought a tape of Conway's show back with her, and Carl Reiner, creator of *The Dick Van Dyke Show*, saw it and agreed. "We said, 'This guy's great!' She took him under her wing," said Reiner, "and the first thing she did was call Steve and say, '*You've gotta see this tape!'* She bugged him twice because he was so busy—people around him were saying, 'You oughta see my Uncle Fred.' But as soon as he looked at [Conway's tape], he hired him."

Allen hired Conway for the 1961–62 season of his show, which had moved from NBC to ABC. But first Allen had to change Conway's name. When Conway moved from Cleveland to Hollywood, he discovered that the name by which he had always been known—*Tom* Conway—was also the name of another actor, the brother of actor George Sanders. "You couldn't have two people in the union with the same name," Conway explained. Allen suggested, "Why don't you just dot the 'O'?"

"I remember my first experience on the ABC show," Conway recalled as he sat backstage after a sound check in Aurora, Illinois, where he was performing with Harvey Korman in 1999. "[There were] Bill Dana, Don Knotts, Louis Nye, and Tom Poston—these wonderful, funny people who wouldn't shut up. We were getting close to air time, and Leonard Stern, who was directing us at the time, was in the audience, all by himself. He stood up and said, 'Shut up!' And he went into a long diatribe of, 'We've got to get this done. We've got to get it organized.'

"Everybody was standing there staring at him. And he said, 'All right, now, let's go.' He went to sit down. The seat had come up in the meantime, and he sat on the floor. He did have the presence not to come up. He just crawled down to the end of the aisle and went out the side door."

On one show, Conway, playing a karate expert, was interviewed by Allen. With authoritative reassurance, he instructed Allen to hold a wooden board for a demonstration: "Just hold it. You won't get hurt." Conway delivered a sharp blow that didn't even make a dent. Silently but visibly writhing in pain, violently shaking his hand, he calmly explained, "I must have had the wrong side. I'll be right back, Steve." Conway took the board, exited the room, closed the door behind him, and while Allen kept talking to the audience, sawing noises could be heard off-camera.

During rehearsal for another show, Conway was supposed to fall into a pool containing a porpoise. The porpoise would come and pull Conway on a cable to the other end of the pool. Conway asked Allen if this was dangerous, and Allen tersely replied, "No, it's a porpoise, not a shark." Later, Conway noticed a guy standing next to the pool. He was holding a gun. Conway asked him why, and the guy replied matter-of-factly, "A lot of times, if you excite a porpoise, the way they attack is to go as fast as they can and run into you. If I see that coming, I'll shoot him."

"That's security," Conway deadpanned.

"There was probably never a show that didn't have some minor disaster during the night because it was live. It was a different era: You could do those things, and it made the show much better," Conway reflected. "Some of those old kinescopes—the one where Charlton Heston was in a bar with Don Knotts, and they were sliding beers down the bar—it was live. If you did that today in movies, it would take a day to shoot because you'd have to make sure that the glass came all the way down [the bar]. This was a one-time only. You did it, it worked, it was funny. *That* was the pressure of the show. Steve loved the pressure of live."

Conway remembered the night another animal was on the show—a crocodile:

The trainer was telling Steve the difference between a crocodile and an alligator. He said [*affecting an authoritative tone*], "A crocodile, when he opens his mouth"—and he touched the crocodile's nose and he opened his mouth—"he cannot see me now because his eyes are on top of his head. So the only way he knows something is in his mouth is if you put something in his mouth." And with that, he kind of indicated that if your arm went in there, he would know that.

He must have touched the crocodile's teeth because the crocodile snapped his jaws closed. And the guy, very calmly—Steve was sitting at the piano—very calmly said, "Steve, I suggest you and your audience don't move now. If we excite this crocodile at this point, he will tear my arm off."' So he said [*affecting a casual tone*], "Dave, could you come out here a minute?"

And Dave came out with a two-by-four and hit the crocodile on the head for him to get his hand out.

Conway "absolutely" considered Allen a comedic influence and also a personal influence. He pointed to something he learned from Allen that he carried over to Carol Burnett's show: respect. "Respect for where you were in the business, respect for all the people in the business. Not just the talent you were working with, but the stage hands, pages, the audience, everybody. Steve teaches respect. His result was humor, but whatever he decided to go into, whether it would have been politics or whatever, he would have been extremely successful because Steve never forgot what respect means to people."

The Smothers Brothers

Allen first spotted the Smothers Brothers, a folk-singing comedy duo, on a 1961 *Tonight* show hosted by Jack Paar and decided to add them to his growing collection of prime-time players by signing them for his ABC show. It didn't take long for the wisecracking siblings to catch fire with a national audience, appearing a staggering seventy-two times on various programs over the next two-and-a-half years. This led to more guest spots, record albums, and finally their own CBS network series, *The Smothers Brothers Comedy Hour* (1966–69).

In their early twenties in 1961, the brothers' experience had been limited to clubs, so they had to retool their forty-five-minute set into a series of three- to six-minute sets for television. They also had to adapt to the start-and-stop grind characteristic of television work. Recalled Dick Smothers in 1998, "We felt very uncomfortable with the audience so far away, and with the cameras and distractions. We got our timing from the audience, [and] we thought it was hard on the audience to react and get the full impact of the show because they had all this stuff going around."

Allen's show taught the brothers how "to be really flexible, change our expectations, and change how we presented the show," continued Dick. "And those nuances are really larger than they would appear to the viewer." Doing the same show with the same technique and energy for a nightclub of a hundred or a theater with three thousand will result in overplaying one audience and underplaying the other, he explained. "And when we had to adjust for all these distractions, our reactions were never as good as when we were in a club. We had to learn to accept that. It was a different level of response."

Working with Allen as regulars also taught the brothers how to put together their own comedy-variety show on a weekly basis. In contrast, said Dick, the occasional guest spot required only minimal participation: "You come in on Monday, read your script, and you're out of there. You don't even want to know the other stuff." But as regulars on *The Steve Allen Show*, "we saw arguments, give-and-take, and stuff being written and thrown out, modified. We saw that freedom. And what Steve was looking for was the highest level quality. It's almost an oxymoron: high level of quality, but write it and do it in one week! And the only people you test the material on are the people who wrote it, and they all laugh at their own jokes!

"Steve had an amazing group of creative people. I think our show was the next show after Steve's, which reached as high as Steve's to be unique. No effort was spared for quality. There were changes right up to air."

The Smothers Brothers' staff included Mason Williams, Rob Reiner, Steve Martin, Bob Einstein, and Steve Allen alums Stan Burns and Mike Marmer. "Our writers weren't probably as full as, say, Sid Caesar's, as Steve's. But ours—together—produced just fabulously."

Tom Smothers, in a separate 1998 interview, went a step further. "The biggest thing I brought with me from working with Steve was his open-door policy. He listened. It didn't matter if it came from the janitor, the head writer, or the guest. If an idea was valid, you could talk to him and have a chance. No idea would go without being at least looked at. Steve worked so spontaneously and was willing to change things very quickly. I adopted that open-door policy."

The brothers also learned how to trust Allen and his writers, even when they had misgivings. "Steve was so fearless about sketches," said Tom. "Some were so broad that I was fearful. It'd be Bill Dana or Steve who'd say, 'Now this is good. Just do it. Give it a try.'"

In one sketch, they were supposed to be lighthouse keepers on a foggy night. Dick asks Tom, who is wearing a raincoat and rain hat, to go out and check whether the light is still on. Tom looks out the window and exclaims, "Boy, that fog is as thick as pea soup!" He goes out and checks, and when he returns, he's covered with pea soup. "But it don't taste like Mama used to make."

"I thought it was so stupid," admitted Tom, "but I did it, and it worked, which I never would've guessed."

Allen "had a real sense of blue collar," observed Tom. "He loved his working people. And after every show, there was always a cast [party] where everybody went to dinner, and he picked up the tab—for everyone! Everybody hung around, laughed a lot. Most other hosts are more distant from the cast. I took his lead, and we always had cast parties after shoots.

"The other thing I remember so much about Steve is a sense of loyalty. He loved talent. Even when he had too many comics, he would keep 'em all on. I'm sure the producers said, 'We can't afford all these guys.' But there were so many comics that were so talented on that show."

Not the least of whom, Tom noted, was Steve Allen. "This is one of the brightest men that ever worked in television. The quickest mind. A man who never wasted a moment in accomplishing something, in getting a project finished, a song done, a note written. It's very impressive to know the breadth of him, his incredible love for music, his incredible love for comedy and literature and history. He's a renaissance man probably more than any other entertainer I've ever met. The wit that was so quick on a pun, that was as fast as a jackrabbit. Yet he even appreciated slow comics like me and Don Knotts, where speed was not the essence. He could understand silences, yet he was a man of very quick insight."

Tom marveled at yet another side of Allen that he discovered several years after working on his show: "I didn't realize how passionate he was about fairness, about free speech, about equality. I didn't realize it until when Dickie and I had our own show in the late '60s and had our censorship problems."

Those censorship problems resulted in the Smothers Brothers getting fired by CBS after the network brass had grown squeamish about their irreverent takes on Presidents Johnson and Nixon. "We were in the era of biggest cultural crisis in US history besides the Civil War," recalled Tom. "We were dealing with the Vietnam War. You were either a hawk or a dove. It was a cultural clash of styles. You know how they try to manipulate opinion now on different issues? Well, we were there on Sunday night with twenty million [viewers], saying, 'Let's get out of there! That war is dumb!' And making satire of it, and [the network] just didn't want that. And when Nixon got in, we were fired."

It was at that point that Tom "realized what a profound thinker and passionate man Steve was. I wish we had some conversations then because he is an exceptional man. It takes an exceptional audience to understand his profundity—how good he was at what he did and how talented he was across the board."

ON-AIR HIGH JINKS

The chemistry and camaraderie between Nye, Poston, and Knotts became legendary. On the Monday before one show, Poston showed up to rehearsal drunk and began to exhibit signs of a drinking problem. This was, however, all part of an elaborate gag staged for Nye's benefit. Poston was not drunk at all. "The idea was that nobody could break me up on stage," recalled Nye because, as Poston explained, "Louis never breaks concentration during a sketch."

By Wednesday, Poston had convinced Nye that he was a semi-alcoholic. "He came in one time and soaked his clothes with beer, and you know what a stink that is on wool," said Nye. With the help of Don Knotts—who specialized in acting nervous—there was the added twist that the cast had to "protect" Poston and his "problem" from Allen. According to Allen, Knotts continued his jittery act the entire week, so that by Saturday, Nye himself was on edge as to what might happen on the air the following night.

They were scheduled to do a sketch set in a seedy waterfront saloon. Nye was to play a Mafia gangster and Knotts, one of his flunkies. At the beginning of the broadcast, while Bill Harbach distracted Nye backstage, Allen quietly let the audience in on the stunt.

The sketch began. Nye and Knotts walked into the saloon and stood at the bar. Knotts, in character, walked across the set and into a phone booth. At that point, he pretended to forget his lines and started mumbling gibberish into the telephone. Standing twelve feet away, there was no way Nye could rescue him by ad-libbing. Director Dwight Hemion took close-up reactions shots of Nye as he listened, "with growing consternation," described Allen.

Following the script, Nye said to the bartender, Gabe Dell, "Give me a double." Instead of pouring amber-tinted ginger ale, which Dell had been doing in rehearsal all week, he poured a genuine double scotch. "Naturally," said Allen, "we had set it up in the script that 'he downs the drink in one gulp.' When Louis did that with the actual booze, his eyes practically crossed."

"The lines kept coming in badly," chuckled Nye. Knotts called Nye by the wrong name and garbled his lines. "Now, if you're in a scene and another actor doesn't give you the right cue, you can hardly just go ahead as if nothing had happened because your next line may not make sense," explained Allen. "Consequently, Louis had to keep revising the text, which he did quite well, although still puzzled by all the hysterical laughter."

The scene called for Poston to enter the saloon, confront Nye, and eventually pull a gun and shoot him. But Poston had fired the gun offstage during the sketch, which Nye didn't expect. And then Poston took all the blanks out of the gun.

Enter Poston, acting high as a kite. His speeches were nonsense, and when he told Nye, "Stick 'em up," and reached inside his pocket to pull out a gun, there was no gun. So he pulled out what he did find—a pack of cigarettes—which he pointed, with a goofy grin, at Nye. "Louis looked kind of peculiar," said Poston. "He looked down at the cigarettes, I looked down at the cigarettes—'Oh, wait a minute.' I reached down and got the gun and said, 'I mean, stick 'em up.' He grabbed the gun, pointed it at me, and it went click, click, click when it was supposed to go *bang, bang, bang.* Try to guess what he did. He stabbed me to death with an imaginary knife—still in character! Oh, my God! He doesn't break character! You should've seen Harbach, Billy Dana, the property guys—they were down at the end of stage jumping up and down, screaming with laughter with everything that happened."

Nye: "The whole thing was to break me up. I never squealed to Steve, 'Look, we can't do the sketch. Tom is drunk.' I never did. And that became a big classic thing."

Poston: "Louis protected me. I'll never forget him for that. He said, 'Tom'll be all right.' He was the only one who didn't know."

One year, for Knotts's birthday, Nye and Poston got him a present: "A girl," beamed Poston with an impish smile that momentarily made him look fifty years younger. "We put her in the dressing room we shared, and when he came off from doing a sketch, we all rushed to the dressing room together, making sure Don was in front, so when he got into our dressing room, we slammed the door shut. Well, some guys got wind of this, and the hallway where this was taking place was like, cheeks, noses, faces—everybody was listening, and Don was inside [*in a squirmish voice*]: 'Oh, don't do that! Listen, I have to—oh, don't do that!' We were choking, dying outside."

Knotts had to get ready to go back on and do his next sketch—about a nervous weatherman, continued Poston. "So he said, 'I have to get dressed, I have to change—ooh, don't do that!' So we finally had to open the door and let the girl out, and let him go about his business. And he's giggling, all red faced. [*Singing*] 'Happy birthday to you, happy birthday to you!' So he thought that was pretty funny. Don did his weatherman, and it was a wonderful success. And as he came off all flushed with victory, as he well deserved, we congratulated him, shook his hand, and he brushed by. We said, 'Where are you going?' He said, 'I'm going upstairs and finish.' We said, 'Oh, Don, w-w-we sent the girl home! We didn't know that you—oh, I'm sorry! She's not there. She's going home.' He said, 'That's OK. I'm going upstairs and finish anyway.'"

* * *

"To me, there is nobody more influential or funnier than Steve Allen," said comedian Billy Crystal. "He has meant more to me in my development as a comedian than anyone I can think of. When I was a kid, watching *The Steve Allen Show* was the greatest treat you could have. Not only was he hysterically funny, but he was generous.

He was willing to be a straight man for Tom Poston, Louis Nye, Don Knotts, Bill Dana, and Gabe Dell. Here it is, how many years later, and you can still remember their names. That's because Steve made them great."

On November 12, 2000, a memorial service for Allen was held at the Academy of Television Arts and Sciences. Poston, Knotts, Nye, Dana, Harrington, and Conway sat onstage, along with Bill Harbach, Skitch Henderson, Dwight Hemion, and Stan Burns. Before the hundreds gathered in the auditorium, director Leonard Stern assessed the spontaneity that characterized the Sunday show: "The spontaneity I saw here happened on a regular basis. When we did the Sunday night show and we staged the comedy, the script was vital, but the contributions made by these gifted people during the rehearsals led to something unique. I think the Sunday night show has no precedent. While there have been variations on it since then, it's still unique, and that's a reflection of Steve. He was willing to risk, and he was the one at risk. Whatever we did, he encouraged it to be as different, innovative, and revolutionary as possible."

At the same service, Poston reflected on the long association that he and his fellow comic actors had with Allen: "The thing that stands out today and throughout our relationship is the love that exists between these fellas and each other and the love that existed between Steve and all of us. We were always aware of it. It was like an encompassing blanket of warmth and love. We thrived under it."

Chapter 9

BEYOND *TONIGHT*

CATCHING UP TO ED SULLIVAN

Sunday—traditionally television's most-watched night of the week—has always been crucial for television programmers and sponsors. On that night, a network heavily plugs its lineup of shows for the coming week. Because Sunday night viewership often foreshadows a network's ratings for the rest of the week, a Sunday night ratings victory is highly coveted.

By 1956, CBS had owned that prize for eight years with a variety program hosted by Ed Sullivan. Launched in 1948 as *The Toast of the Town* and later renamed *The Ed Sullivan Show*, the Sunday night eight-to-nine hour was considered indestructible. And the irony was that Sullivan, a New York entertainment columnist, was an unlikely host. With his wooden manner; hunched, Nixonesque shoulders; and nasal speaking voice that were widely mimicked ("We've got a *rrrreeeaallly* big *shew!*"), it was apparent that his expertise was not in performing.

But Sullivan was a shrewd judge of talent, regularly criss-crossing the country in search of acts to present in a vaudeville revue format. His formula consisted of collecting diverse acts that could appeal to each segment of his viewing audience. A typical *Ed Sullivan Show* might open with a pop vocalist, followed by a circus act, a distinguished opera singer, a comedian, a rock act, and then a scene from a Broadway play. With a formula strategically calculated to hook his audience, Sullivan opened his shows with his strongest talent and paraded as many as four acts before the first commercial.

On stage, all Sullivan needed to do was to look into the camera and announce with gusto, "Ladies and gentlemen, the Fabulous Dancing Elephants!" or whatever the name of the next act was. As *Newsweek* put it, "He has no delusions about being a performer, but he has proved beyond doubt his technical value as a consistently effective catalyst for others more gifted than himself."

No doubt, Sullivan's success was a thorn in NBC's side. He consistently clobbered whatever any competitor dared to throw in his path. Over the years, he destroyed numerous spectaculars (the early term for "specials"), two different NBC comedy hours, a quiz show, and several variety shows. NBC managed to edge him on two occasions with spectaculars starring the hot comedy duo of Dean Martin and Jerry Lewis. NBC execs were spooked, for there seemed no end to Sullivan's enduring appeal. By the week of June 17, 1956, its *Comedy Hour* hobbled in the Trendex ratings (a dominant, respected ratings barometer of the time), finishing a laughable 6.2 to Sullivan's 29.1.

When he accepted NBC's offer to star in a prime-time comedy hour against Sullivan, Steve Allen was seen as NBC's last hope for Sunday night. Although the media hype was in a frenzy ("Sunday Slugfest," headlined one newspaper article), Allen took a characteristically low-key approach: "We are not going to try to revolutionize TV. We're just going to try and relax. I definitely don't want to be known as the guy who went in with his sleeves rolled up to knock

off Sullivan. I'm going to do the show as if we had no competition,"
he said in an interview the week before his show's premiere.

CRITICAL SUCCESS PROPELS RATINGS

The Sunday night *Steve Allen Show* premiered on June 24, 1956, with
guests Bob Hope, Jerry Lewis, Sammy Davis Jr., Kim Novak, Vincent
Price, Dane Clark, and Wally Cox. There was an exciting ballet
sequence featuring Bambi Linn and Rod Alexander performing on
the rooftop and fire escape of the building next to the Hudson Theatre. Sullivan staged a self-congratulatory eighth anniversary show
featuring Kate Smith for the over-forty set, Teresa Brewer for the
teenagers, Jack Paar for the urbane, the Klauson Bears for the children, and the universally popular Harry Belafonte, Louis Armstrong,
and Phil Silvers, as well as anniversary tributes from Lucille Ball,
Desi Arnaz, and twenty-five Broadway and Hollywood personalities.

Network execs held their breath. The ratings came in, and Allen's
new show made a respectable dent in the Trendex ratings, clocking
in at 13.3 against Sullivan's 24.6—more than double the rating for
the show Allen replaced.

Equally important were the reactions of the TV reviewers across
the country, who proclaimed *The Steve Allen Show* a resounding
critical success. According to the *Newark* (New Jersey) *Star-Ledger*,
"Production and show-wise, the difference between the two hours
[Sullivan's and Allen's] was marked, with honors going to Allen by
a wide margin and all the way. Steve put together a fast-paced,
musical, youthful, funny program that was expertly written, tightly
produced, and featured unique presentations of [its] guests."

In contrast to Sullivan's appeal-to-every-member-of-the-family
approach, the *San Diego Union* said, "Allen played his card differ-
ently. His show had quality, although it was quality concentrated

more in a single groove—that of sophistication—and directed, I would guess, at a younger audience than Sullivan's."

"'The same old thing' has no place in a Steve Allen format," wrote *Broadcasting-Telecasting*.

"In his customary easy-going manner, he brought on an engaging array of performers within the framework of a show that had style," wrote the *New York Herald Tribune*.

"Steve Allen, who has been called the most promising comedian since the death of Fred Allen, imparts a special seasoning and flavor to everything he undertakes," assessed the *Chicago Daily Tribune*.

According to the *Washington Daily News*, the varied musical and comedy elements "were strung together by a fine performance by Allen, who filled a hefty claim as the sprightliest, most versatile practitioner of the emcee's trade."

"Allen's long suit is his fresh and witty reactions to lines or situations," the *Washington Evening Star* said.

"If the *Steve Allen Show* . . . can maintain the high standards and all-around class which it showed last night, then Ed Sullivan has finally met his match," proclaimed the *Boston Daily Record*.

The Steve Allen Show won the coveted George Foster Peabody Award in 1958 in the category of Television Entertainment with Humor. The award cited the show for bucking the trend "in a television year when genuine humor and frank experiments have been so conspicuously lacking. . . . Allen and his talented associates obviously are willing to try anything on their show, and the percentage of clean hits has been amazingly high." In addition to Tom Poston's Emmy in 1959, the show was recognized with Emmy nominations for Best Musical or Variety Series (1958, 1959), Best Actor (Steve Allen—1958, 1959), Best Supporting Actor (Louis Nye—1958), and Best Writing of a Single Musical or Variety Program (1959).

WITH A LITTLE HELP FROM A FUTURE KING

The critical success of the Allen show's premiere swung the momentum in his favor, intensifying interest in the show and loosening Sullivan's stronghold. The following week (July 1), Allen's guests were Imogene Coca, Milton Berle, and Andy Griffith, as well as America's newest singing sensation, Elvis Presley. Just a few months earlier, Allen had seen the hip-swinging rock'n'roller's nationwide TV debut on what must have been an incongruous setting: a program (*Stage Show*) hosted by two bandleaders of the big band era, Tommy and Jimmy Dorsey. Allen decided to book the rising but controversial star. In the ensuing months leading up to Elvis's guest spot, his records—including "Heartbreak Hotel," "Blue Suede Shoes," and "Don't Be Cruel"—began to explode on the national charts, conveniently propelling the singer to a new peak, just in time for his appearance on Allen's show.

Sullivan countered with a more adult-oriented show, featuring a tribute to director John Huston, along with guests Gregory Peck, Lauren Bacall, Jose Ferrer, Orson Welles, and Edward G. Robinson.

The Trendex ratings for Allen's second week handed him a stunning victory: 20.2 (a 53.3 share) over Sullivan's 14.8 (a 39.7 share). In only its second week on the air, *The Steve Allen Show* cracked the coveted top ten as the number six show in the country, whacking Sullivan out of the top ten altogether. "Steve Allen Knocks Sullivan Off Throne," declared the *Columbus* (Ohio) *Citizen.*

Rubbing salt into CBS's wounds was the revelation that Sullivan had previously turned down Elvis when the William Morris Agency offered him on a one-shot basis for $15,000. "He's not my cup of tea," sniffed Sullivan, adding that he didn't believe Presley would help him sell cars and "didn't care to have people accuse him of having lunatics 'on our show,'" reported the *New York World Telegram.* Sullivan righteously insisted that he wouldn't have Presley on his family hour "at any price."

In an astonishing flip-flop ordinarily reserved for politicians, Sullivan proved that he was, first and foremost, a businessman. Recalled Allen, "Before we even left the studio the night Elvis appeared on our show, Ed telephoned Presley's manager, Colonel Tom Parker, backstage at our own theater. So desperate was he to make the booking, in fact, that he broke what had until that moment been a $7,500 price ceiling on star-guests, offering the Colonel $10,000 per shot. Parker told Sullivan he'd get back to him, walked over to us, shared the news of Sullivan's offer, and said, 'I feel a sense of loyalty to you fellows because you booked Elvis first, when we needed the booking; so if you'll meet Sullivan's terms, we'll be happy to continue to work on your program.'"

In contrast, Allen proved that he was, first and foremost, an artist. He declined the Colonel's offer, telling him that he should accept Sullivan's offer instead. "The reason," explained Allen, "was that I didn't think it was reasonable to continue to have to construct sketches and comic gimmicks in which Presley, a noncomic, could appear. Ed's program, having a vaudeville-variety format, was a more appropriate showcase for Elvis's type of performance."

Ultimately, the deal reached between Sullivan and the Colonel was for Elvis to make three appearances for the then-unprecedented fee of $50,000. Until then, the top fee Sullivan paid to a performer was $13,000 to renown Norwegian Olympic skater Sonja Henie in 1952. "Though I wouldn't have [Presley] on our show, I'd be happy not to have him against me," admitted Sullivan.

Elvis's fee to appear on Allen's show was $5,500.

"Why NBC didn't tie Presley up after [his success on Allen's show], I can't understand," said Sullivan. "I talked it over with one of their guys. He very frankly told me he couldn't understand it either."

Even without Presley, Allen's comedy hour performed impressively in its first year. The show was consistently getting a 30 percent share, according to Trendex, and often between five and ten points higher. Though he remained exceedingly popular, Sullivan no longer owned eight o'clock on Sundays. On January 27, 1957, Allen surpassed Sullivan for the second time, winning a 28.3 rating with guests Pearl Bailey, Don Adams, and Steve Lawrence. Sullivan garnered a 25.0 rating for his show, which featured Louis Armstrong and a scene from the Metropolitan Opera's production of *Madame Butterfly*. Some speculated that the opera caused many viewers to tune away from Sullivan. According to *Newsweek*, when Sullivan "discovered a definite correlation between Metropolitan Opera stars and dipping ratings on his show, he had no compunction about first cutting their appearances to the bone, then amputating them." This was seen as the last straw for Sullivan, who pleaded with and got a jittery CBS to assign several top publicity personnel to his show.

In early March 1957, Allen came within three-tenths of a point of Sullivan, who had pulled out all the stops with a lavish and heavily promoted first anniversary salute to *My Fair Lady*, featuring cast members Rex Harrison and Julie Andrews, lyricist Alan Jay Lerner, and composer Frederick Loewe. Audiences seemed drawn to the Allen team's intelligence, freshness, and good taste. His guest stars performed, and his policy was not to book a star unless the star could be used properly to suit the performance standards of the show. In contrast, a Sullivan guest might merely appear on a film clip, do a quick walk-on to accept an award, or take a bow from the audience. These were appearances strictly for name value, and audiences may have grown leery of such gimmickry.

On April 14, 1957, Allen topped Sullivan for the third time and by his biggest margin ever: 30.9 to Sullivan's 22.2. *Chicago Sun-Times* entertainment columnist Irv Kupcinet wrote, "Allen apparently has fingered the 'panic' button at CBS. . . . All CBS stations and affiliates have been told to plug the Sullivan show as often as possible." By May, Sullivan placed out of the Nielsen Top 10 list for the first time in five years, with the Allen show placing number six among total audiences. By the end of 1957, Allen had beaten Sullivan eleven times.

The Allen-Sullivan ratings battle became a media sensation, the subject of cartoons in the *Saturday Evening Post* and the *New Yorker*. Even the irreverent *Mad* magazine devoted a full-page cartoon strip to Allen and sidekick Gene Rayburn. But perhaps the most telling indicator of the effect Allen's show was having on Sullivan came in June 1957, when automobile manufacturer Lincoln announced that it was going to drop its sponsorship of Sullivan for the upcoming 1957–58 season. This meant a loss of $5 million, or half of the annual tab for *The Ed Sullivan Show*.

A NETWORK-ORDERED SNUB

There had already been behind-the-scenes bitterness between NBC and CBS, and Sullivan's snatching of Presley from NBC only fanned the flames. In October 1956, a memorial to the late rebel actor James Dean was announced, first for the Allen show and later for the Sullivan show. Allen's team arranged with Warner Brothers to televise clips from one of Dean's movies and to interview Dean's aunt and uncle in his hometown of Fairmont, Indiana. At the last minute, Warner Brothers informed Allen's representatives that the Dean clips were going to Sullivan. Charges and countercharges of piracy and lies erupted, until each show did its own Dean memorial. Allen, sans clips, traveled alone to Fairmont and interviewed Dean's family and friends.

Forced to make another moral choice, Sullivan rejected the idea of signing Ingrid Bergman, who had just had a child out of wedlock. According to a *Newsweek* special report on the Allen-Sullivan race ("Television's Biggest Battle"), "Allen stepped in and bolstered his ratings with a special Bergman interview in January [1957]."

But the personal relationship between Sullivan and his rival apparently remained cordial. In fact, Allen told his *Tonight* audience that he had invited Sullivan to make a drop-by appearance on *Tonight*. Confirmed Sullivan to the *New York Post*, "[Allen] wrote to me before he came on the air opposite me on Sunday night. He said, 'I don't think you or I want this to get into the stratum of acrimony or bitterness and, to indicate to the public that it's not going to happen, I'd like to have you come over and sit down with me where we can talk things over in a normal manner.'"

"But CBS turned it down," continued Sullivan, citing two grounds. First, a few years earlier, CBS asked NBC if Martin and Lewis could appear briefly on one of Sullivan's anniversary shows to take a bow. In the meantime, CBS asked NBC to allow Sullivan and pioneer broadcast journalist Edward R. Murrow to receive awards from *Look* magazine on an NBC telecast; NBC said yes. Immediately after the *Look* awards, however, NBC changed its mind on Martin and Lewis. "So when this Allen thing came up, CBS looked at it and said no dice. I can't blame them," said Sullivan.

MOVING TO PRIME TIME: A LOGICAL CHOICE

Given the longevity of the *Tonight* show and its eventual elevation to an American institution, many Allen colleagues and admirers contend that it was a mistake for him to step "down" from his *Tonight* show throne and into prime time. At the time, however, the decision was logical from an entertainment standpoint and sound financially. In 1957, despite Allen's groundbreaking success, late-night television was still new territory, not as prestigious as the playground that Milton Berle, Sid Caesar, Jackie Gleason, and Lucille Ball had established in prime time. On a good night, only six million viewers might be tuning to *Tonight*, whereas the audience for Allen's prime-time show would average over thirty million.

It was also more important to Allen to own his prime-time show. Although he participated in the profits of the *Tonight* shows in which he starred, it was NBC that owned the *Tonight* show itself. In contrast, the arrangement between Allen and NBC for his Sunday show was "the opposite deal—Steve was the owner of the prime-time show," explained Bill Allen. And it didn't hurt that the Sunday show paid Allen many times as much as did *Tonight*, which reportedly paid him $250,000 a year.

One thing was for certain. Allen could not do both shows, although he tried to for about seven months. "I soon realized I'd underestimated the amount of work that doing a once-a-week comedy show takes," Allen once said. "It became obvious to me very early that I'd bitten off more than I could chew. I had to make a choice. One show had to go." Moreover, Allen admitted, "In those days, none of us connected with the *Tonight* show thought it was a big deal at all. It's amazing. It seems a big deal now. It's now part of the national psychological furniture."

NBC kept *The Steve Allen Show* in its Sunday night slot opposite Sullivan during the 1956–57, '57–58, and '58–59 seasons. During the show's second season, ABC launched *Maverick*, its entry into the increasingly popular western genre. (In 1957–58, there were no fewer than twenty westerns in prime time, including *Gunsmoke*, *Rawhide*, and *The Rifleman*; by 1958–59, westerns composed seven out of the top ten shows.) *Maverick* gave both Sullivan and Allen a run for their money. The hour-long western aired at seven thirty, a half hour before the two variety shows, often siphoning audiences from Sullivan's and Allen's first half hour. In their second half hour—without *Maverick*—Allen frequently recovered the most (for example, with a February 4, 1958, Trendex rating of 28.2 against Sullivan's 20.9). By April 1958, Allen's first half hour was beating the competition in the Nielsen ratings, 37 to 32 (Sullivan) to 31.4 (*Maverick*).

But, as Allen recalled, "there were certain Sunday nights when

Ma*verick* had a higher rating than Ed's and mine together." In the fall of 1959, NBC moved Allen to Mondays at 10 p.m., a slot Allen described as "a ratings graveyard, but we were grateful that the network had not simply scrapped our project." The show's title—*The Steve Allen Plymouth Show*—added the name of its new sponsor. There was yet another change: The show moved from New York to the West Coast, which allowed Allen more time with his three sons from his first marriage, who lived with his first wife in California. However, three key members of the Allen gang—Tom Poston, Gene Rayburn, and Skitch Henderson—remained in New York and thus did not make the transition. The show broadcast live in color from NBC's Burbank studios. Les Brown would now conduct the band.

The 1959–60 season would be the last season that NBC carried *The Steve Allen Show*. Even before his pre-*Tonight* days, Allen frequently chose to speak out on controversial issues, from organized crime to nuclear warfare to the death penalty. In the early hours of May 2, 1960, he, along with Marlon Brando and Shirley MacLaine, journeyed to San Quentin State Prison to protest the impending execution of convicted serial rapist Caryl Chessman, in an unsuccessful attempt to get California Governor Pat Brown to halt it. (Chessman was gassed at 10:03 that morning.) Allen's outspokenness contributed to a decline in his ratings, which, although still respectable, probably factored in the sponsor's decision not to renew its contract. When his wife expressed her concern about the effect his positions were having on his ratings, he responded, "Jayne, I care much more about the ratings of mankind than I do about the ratings of my television show."

Allen's willingness to speak out on public issues earned him the respect and admiration of one of his most controversial guests: comedian Lenny Bruce, who wrote in his 1963 autobiography, *How to Talk Dirty and Influence People*: "Of all the comedians I have ever met, Steve Allen is not only the most literate, but also the most moral. He not only talks about society's problems, but he *does* things about them. He's a good person, without being all sugar and showbiz, and I really dig him for that."

After a one-year hiatus, the show moved to ABC in September 1961, where it aired on Wednesdays at 8 p.m. Unfortunately, that pitted it against NBC's *Wagon Train*, the number-one-rated show in the country and one of twenty six popular westerns that dominated prime time. The Allen show debuted to a modest viewership, which was compounded by minimal promotion from the network. Despite its steady climb in the ratings, ABC canceled the show after thirteen weeks.

Nevertheless, the ABC show managed to launch three newcomers who went on to enjoy enormous television successes: Jim Nabors (*The Andy Griffith Show* and *Gomer Pyle, U.S.M.C.*), Tim Conway (*McHale's Navy* and *The Carol Burnett Show*), and the Smothers Brothers (*The Smothers Brothers Comedy Hour*). With head writer Bill Dana and a production team that included Arne Sultan, Marvin Worth, Leonard Stern, and Buck Henry, the show continued Allen's creative comedy tradition. Allen fondly recalled a wicked send-up of the then-popular *Sing Along with Mitch* program—a sort of forerunner of karaoke in which viewers were encouraged to "follow the bouncing ball" and sing along with lyrics flashed on their TV screens. While the goateed Mitch Miller conducted in his identifiably wooden, mechanical manner, a chorus of wholesome-looking singers in straw hats and striped jackets would line the stage in a large horse-shoe pattern, while the camera panned across their freshly scrubbed, smiling faces.

In the Allen version of *Sing Along*, Pat Harrington, the Smothers Brothers, and Tim Conway were in the chorus. As Allen recalled,

> The camera moved in much too quickly toward their smiling faces, converting the smiles to looks of horror as they perceived, at the last possible moment, that the giant camera was going to run right into them and knock them all down. In a moment, a dozen bodies were writhing on the studio floor in apparent pain, having been

With (*left to right*) Tom Poston, Don Knotts, and Louis Nye in the "Allen Bureau of Standards," a popular department on the prime-time *Steve Allen Show*. Poston, Knotts, and Nye became renown for portraying wacky characters in the show's most famous recurring routine, "The Man on the Street."

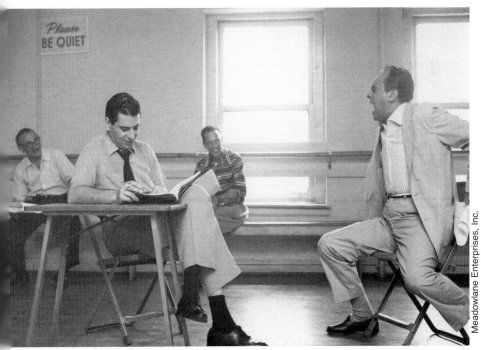

Louis Nye (*right*) emotes during a rehearsal with director Leonard Stern (*seated, foreground*) and Don Knotts (*center*).

"I saw him when he first started," recalled old friend and comic legend Sid Caesar about Allen. "I watched him every right."

Early in Allen's career, Groucho Marx called him "the funniest Allen since Fred."

Allen found Jonathan Winters, his most frequent *Tonight* guest, so funny that he made it a point to book Winters whenever the show went on the road—not only to entertain the studio and TV audiences but also to crack up the cast and crew.

Clowning in the office with his good friend Bob Hope, who was one of the first fans of Allen's late-night Hollywood radio show.

Steve invited his mother, vaudeville comedienne Belle Montrose, to come on his prime-time show in 1960 to reenact a routine that she used to perform with his father, Billy Allen, more than forty years earlier.

Jonathan Winters as a "young" Maude Frickert during one of his many appearances on the Allen *Tonight* show. Years later, Johnny Carson became so associated with his own Aunt Blabby character—whom many claim was appropriated from Frickert—that Winters couldn't perform Frickert as often or as freely.

Johnny Carson in a brilliant one-man sketch on a 1958 Sunday night *Steve Allen Show*. He impersonated Allen and his TV competitors—James Garner (as Bret Maverick) and Ed Sullivan—seated around a table, playing poker. Carson quickly jumped from chair to chair as he changed character. (Note the eyeglasses on the table in front of Allen's chair.)

The iconic Muppets also made their national debut on the Allen *Tonight* show in 1956, followed by an appearance on Allen's prime-time show a few weeks later.

Jack Paar claimed credit for introducing Shelley Berman to a national audience, but Berman (*pictured here*) first appeared on the Allen *Tonight* show and debuted what would become his trademark telephone routine in 1956.

Allen on his prime-time show with regulars (*left to right*) Bill Dana, Louis Nye, Don Knotts, Pat Harrington, and Gabe Dell. Tom Smothers admired Allen's loyalty: "He loved talent. Even when he had too many comics, he would keep 'em all on."

When four tarantulas crawling up the host won't do . . . try five.

Before Jim Fowler and Joan Embery brought exotic animals to visit Johnny Carson, Steve discovered the appeal of inviting tigers (*above*). tarantulas (*right*), kinkajous, llamas, and assorted furry (and not-so-furry) friends to his show.

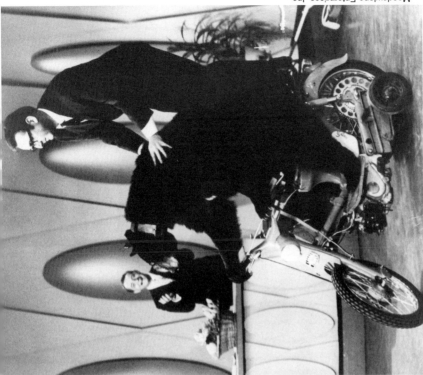

David Letterman, an avid fan of Allen's nightly Westinghouse series (1962–64), found animal stunts like this the inspiration for his own "Stupid Pet Tricks."

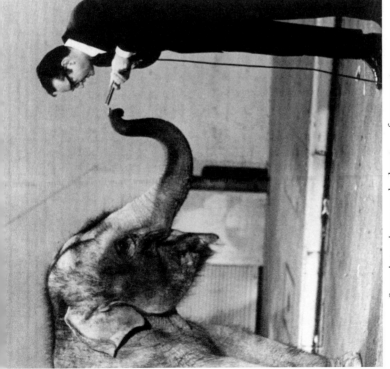

Steve interviews an elephant . . . for peanuts.

Way over the Top. Precariously strapped to the wing of a World War I biplane, Allen flew high above southern California as the plane engaged in a series of dangerous maneuvers. Members of Allen's family watched from the ground, horrified.

Combining the whimsical and the daring: Waking up on a light and airy mattress over Vine Street in Hollywood.

With the aid of magician Bob McCarthy, Allen played a grand piano that ascended, floated over the stage, and then rotated a full 360 degrees in the air—on live TV.

Allen's production team liked to involve the studio audience in stunts, including this classic pie fight in 1963. "To see this white, gooey mess in the audience was an image that I've never forgotten," said NBC vice president Rick Ludwin. "That sort of anarchistic late-night comedy was very influential to me."

After actress Rose Marie brought a tape of Tim Conway's local daily show in Cleveland to Allen's attention, Allen added him to his ABC prime-time series in 1961. Here, Conway plays a karate expert whose demonstration goes awry.

Early in their careers, as *Steve Allen Show* regulars, the young Smothers Brothers observed the complex process of assembling a live, weekly comedy-variety series. Their experiences with Allen prepared them, as they have often publicly acknowledged, to launch their own successful series on CBS five years later.

In his clean-cut, pre–Mothers of Invention days, Frank Zappa demonstrates on a 1963 *Steve Allen Show* how to turn an ordinary bicycle into a musical instrument.

Ed Sullivan once vowed never to invite the hip-swinging Elvis Presley to appear on his variety hour. But Allen's July 1, 1956, booking of Elvis—which aired opposite Sullivan—dealt Sullivan a severe blow in the ratings, forcing Sullivan to reconsider.

Carl Reiner (*left*) and Mel Brooks had performed "The 2,000-Year-Old Man" only for friends at parties because they didn't think its humor would appeal to a mass audience. In 1960, they reluctantly turned their act into a comedy album at the insistence of Allen, who paid for the recording session and debuted their act on his prime-time show.

"Steve on the Street." Going outside to have fun with late-night audiences is a tradition that Jay Leno and David Letterman have continued on their own programs.

knocked off their pins by the rolling juggernaut of the camera and its platform. This somehow led to a combination revolution and mutiny during which I, as the mechanical Miller, was chased up the aisle, out of the studio, and towards the ABC parking lot below, where I was finally trapped and apparently beaten to a pulp by an angry mob of singers, ushers, network executives, studio audience participants, and anybody else who felt like jumping up and joining the melee.

THE 1960S: A RETURN TO VARIETY/TALK

Allen returned to hosting a late-night talk/variety show, this time a syndicated one for Westinghouse Broadcasting in Hollywood, that premiered in June of 1962, a full four months before Johnny Carson would take over the *Tonight* show. This series, which ran for two seasons and more than 450 ninety-minute episodes, was more *Tonight*-like in format, regularly featuring the segments initially established on the Allen-era *Tonight* show: "The Question Man," "Letters to the Editor," "The Late Show Pitchman," audience tight shots, and wild stunts—the very segments regularly airing during the period when Carson and his staff were planning what the elements of their *Tonight* show would consist of.

The Westinghouse series is what David Letterman and his fellow baby boomers used to watch growing up, and it is what he has often credited as forming his comic consciousness and inspiring his television career: "When I was, like, twelve or thirteen, on Friday night my family would let me stay up, and I would watch *The Steve Allen Show* that I remembered later in my life as being just wild and uncontrollable and unpredictable and silly and goofy," Letterman told Charlie Rose in 1995. "Those are the shows that we went over to dig up out of the [television] museum, and we looked at those Steve Allen Westinghouse shows."

It was Letterman director Hal Gurnee who had recommended that Dave go to the Museum of Television and Radio in Manhattan because, as Gurnee recalled in a 2005 interview:

> I think the things that Dave found funny were the same things that Steve Allen found funny. Dave was fond of the way Steve did the shows. He always felt that the show should be like a bunch of high school kids had snuck into a studio and were doing their own show. It was high school humor done in a serious way, which made it even funnier.
>
> That's what Steve brought to late night, and that's what Dave continued to bring. When you think of when Dave did the Velcro suit [in which Letterman, wearing a suit made entirely of Velcro, made a running leap toward a Velcro-lined wall and affixed himself to it], that's strictly Steve Allen.
>
> I remember Dave in the middle of a conversation, and we had a shepherd with a big herd of sheep walk right through the studio. People would say, "Well, this is unusual." But that's exactly the kind of thing that Steve Allen would have done.

"It just used to make me laugh till I had tears in my eyes," recalled Letterman. "This was the period when Steve was yelling, 'Shmock! Shmock!' and going out and raiding the Hollywood Ranch Market across the street."

"You *have* to watch the old Steve Allen shows," said Steve O'Donnell, former head writer for Letterman and former writer for *Seinfeld*. "They're like the comedy equivalent of jazz, almost Salvador Dali–like surreal images. Back then it was far-out, daddy-o. It was really great stuff on TV."

Freed of the structural rigidities of a prime-time comedy hour, Allen and his team returned to zany stunts they did during his *Tonight* era, only wilder. As they began to assemble the new series, writer Stan Burns told Allen, "We did everything possible on the

Tonight show and the Sunday show. We must get crazier, Steve, to get an audience and make us happy."

And so they tried to top their earlier stunts. In one legendary stunt, Allen—in a sensible suit and tie—was ordered by his staff to jump into a vat of Jell-O. "We didn't tell him about it; he didn't know about it," laughed Harbach. "I don't wanna jump!" yelled Allen, upon discovering what was in store for him. Of course, it was standard practice not to tell him what was in store so that he could react genuinely to the stunt in real time. "You never told Steve [in advance] what it was about," explained Bill Harbach, "because the fun with Steve was his reaction, cold, when you threw something at him that he didn't know anything about."

In another stunt, Allen became a human tea bag being lowered into a tank of water; he emerged victoriously and announced, "Ladies and gentlemen, tea is served!" There was Allen, in a wire harness and wearing a Superman suit, flying over the studio audience; Allen actually attempting to fly using a huge kite and a giant fan; Allen enjoying a bath in a tub hung from a crane over Vine Street in Hollywood (later pulling the drain plug and showering the traffic on the street below); and Allen mud wrestling with one very tough woman.

Allen took a wild ride in a wrecking ball that smashed against a wall across the street from the studio. "Steve would get into this ball we built," said Burns, "ten feet in diameter, reinforced steel. Maybe he had a helmet on. He says, 'Hi, I'm talking to you from inside a wrecking ball. And we're going to let you people know how it feels to be inside a wrecking ball.' It didn't knock the wall down, just a lot of banging. He was jarred."

Some of the stunts involved fire and were downright death defying. In one, Allen, wrapped in mummy bandages, was set afire and made to race down La Mirada Avenue and jump into a vat of cold water. "Intellectually," he recalled, "I was perfectly willing to submit to being partially ignited, reasoning that it would take only a few seconds to run down the street and leap into the water, should anything go wrong." Yet, the moment he saw the floor manager sneaking up behind him, smelled the smoke, and felt the intense heat, "My concern was obvious to our studio audience, if not to at-home viewers."

In another stunt, Allen, clad only in swim trunks, had to jump off a diving board into a ring of fire. Although the stunt coordinator had explained that the setup was entirely safe, Allen had second thoughts when he reached the end of the diving board and felt the heat from the flames prickling his skin. "The fact that the audience was watching me made me feel that I had to go through with the routine purely because I was too embarrassed to back out."

Turning up the heat even higher, another stunt had Allen, spread eagle, loosely strapped to the hood of an automobile to be driven through a wooden fence that had been—you guessed it—set afire. As the car barreled down the road, recalled Allen, "I looked up at the wall of fire we were approaching at about sixty miles and hour. I was, frankly, petrified."

Even riskier was the day Allen went to a local airport, climbed onto the wing of a biplane, grabbed a steel brace mounted on the wing with both hands, and let the plane take off, climbing thousands of feet up, as the stunt pilot executed barrel rolls and other dangerous maneuvers. "During the day they taped it, Jayne was there worried," recalled Burns. "The plane wouldn't even start. Finally, it took off, and there he was. Years later, Johnny Carson did things like that. He went up in a plane. He went under a bridge while the train went over."

Bill Allen remembered witnessing the stunt as a young boy. "The strap of Dad's cap and goggles had unsnapped and was flapping against his face, and so he had to let go of the brace with one hand in order to resnap it. I was terrified."

"Steve will do anything, which was amazing," marveled Stan

Burns. "He never questioned. Well, maybe he questioned once." It was when the writers asked, "Steve, we want to catapult you into a pool across the street from the studio." Allen thought it sounded good, "so we got a dummy made up the same way as Steve" in order to visualize the stunt, said Burns. "We cut the rope, and it flew into the pool."

Later, continued Burns, Allen had second thoughts. "This is the only time he says, 'I don't think I'll do it. Something tells me I shouldn't do it.' But we *had* to do it. We were all set to catapult somebody. So a stagehand or somebody stood in for him, and Steve was the narrating voice. They cut the rope and catapulted this guy."

The guy landed on the edge of the pool and broke his leg. "It was a shock," said Burns. "But it was the only time Steve turned something down, which was amazing."

These stunts were so zany and unpredictable that viewers felt compelled to tune in. It was, as Rick Ludwin, an NBC senior vice president, described, "guerilla television." Combining the silly and the substantial, Allen also downed one vodka after another to illustrate the dangers of drunk driving.

Decades later, David Letterman would revive many of Allen's stunts, often adding a clever twist of his own. One stunt had him wearing a suit covered in Alka-Seltzer tablets and jumping into a thousand-gallon water tank. "Our head writer at the time, it was his idea," remembered Hal Gurnee, "so we tested it on him, and he actually passed out because of all the gases coming off the water. So we had to tone it down, so that there wasn't so much Alka-Seltzer."

The stunts didn't involve just Allen. One night, the audience was subjected to an in-studio earthquake. "This is live," recalled Stan Burns. "That day we had the whole studio rigged for fake beams and dust and things to fall. And then we started to shake the camera."

"Steve did these very surreal and messy and complicated comedy bits involving, in one case, the entire audience having a pie fight," recalled Ludwin, "with everyone having rain slickers and throwing the pies at each other. I remember vividly that Steve Binder, the director, had a camera in the ceiling of the theater and was shooting straight down on the audience. To see this white, gooey mess in the audience was an image that I've never forgotten. That sort of anarchistic late night comedy was very influential to me."

It wasn't only the stunts that became elaborate. Burns believed that even the openings had to strive for originality. "As writers and performers, you always try to give audiences new things," Burns reflected in 1997. "A writer always feels good when he thinks of something that's never been done before. That's the way we live. That's why everybody says, 'Oh, we saw that.' You can sing the same song for forty years and everybody applauds. You tell the same joke twice and you're out."

Burns suggested that the first Westinghouse show open with Steve, Jayne, and the guests, decked in formal wear, and with a lavish orchestral fanfare—live—climbing out of a sewer on Vine Street in Hollywood. "Nobody questioned this," laughed Burns. "The sewer cover comes off, Steve comes out, followed by Jayne. They had fumes down there. The audience in the theater was screaming with laughter. That set the tone. After that, you can do anything."

The sewer fumes were overpowering. "Jayne was coughing, almost dying—asphyxiation, who knows?" said Burns with a twinkle in his eye. "*I* wouldn't go down there. I just write!

"Every day we had a crazy opening. For example, we had a Greyhound bus pull up outside, and the door opens, and fifty live greyhounds came out."

There were elaborate stagings of "Funny Fone Calls," the comedy gag Allen had pioneered in the early '50s, with guests Jerry Lewis, Mel Brooks, Louis Nye, Shelley Berman, Carl Reiner, and Bill Dana. Allen made one such call to an unsuspecting Johnny Carson, who at that hour was apparently at home watching *The Tonight Show with Johnny Carson* that he had taped earlier that afternoon:

JOHNNY: Hello?

STEVE [*affecting a foreign accent*]: Hello, this is American Research Bureau calling. May I ask what program you're listening to, please?

JOHNNY: I beg your pardon?

STEVE: I said, this is the American Research Bureau. May I inquire, sir, what program you are watching now on television?

JOHNNY [*chuckling*]: I'm watching *The Tonight Show*.

STEVE: I see. And who are the guests on it at present time, please?

JOHNNY: Well, there are no guests yet.

STEVE: I see. Could you describe who you are seeing at present moment, please?

JOHNNY: Yeah, I'm watching myself.

STEVE: Yourself?

JOHNNY: Mm-hmm.

STEVE: I do not understand, sir.

JOHNNY: Steve! [*The audience roars. Horns, sirens, and whistles go off in the studio*].

STEVE: Listen, Johnny, you're wrong. This is Jack Paar.

JOHNNY: I'm watching *The Steve Allen Show* now. How are ya, Steve?

STEVE: Did you guess it was me right away?

JOHNNY: No. You had me hung.

STEVE: Really?

JOHNNY: You had me the first couple of lines there.

STEVE: Hey, John, I just saw a column the other day that said you're doing a good show, and I'm doing a good show, but there's something missing: a good old-fashioned feud.

JOHNNY: Yeah.

STEVE: What could we feud about?

JOHNNY: I don't know, Steve. Uh, your hair's gettin' kinda long. [*Audience laughter*].

STEVE: Well, you're mouth's gettin' kinda big, Johnny.

JOHNNY: Yeah! You're on the air now?

STEVE: Yeah, we're on the air now.

JOHNNY: Yeah, I was sitting here watching the show. I'm watching you now.

295

STEVE: Really? What am I doing tonight there?

JOHNNY [*referring to a taped broadcast of Steve's show airing at that hour in New York*]: Well, you're not too funny yet, but—[*audience laughter*]—there's always hope, Steve.

Allen didn't need to call celebrities for laughs. One night, he called the mother of a man in the audience, Art Goldstein, and encountered a delightful woman on the East Coast with an Edith Bunker–like accent and innocence in her voice:

STEVE: Art Goldstein. Is he your son?

MRS. G: Who? [*Audience laughter.*] What's so funny?

STEVE: This is the Santa Ana Police calling.

MRS. G: Aw, c'mon, stop being funny.

STEVE: Art Goldstein is here, and he says you're his mama. You don't have a son named Art Goldstein?

MRS. G: Art?

STEVE: Yes!

MRS. G: A son, Ar-thuh Goldstein. [*Audience laughter and applause.*] Where is this call coming from? [*Extended audience laughter and applause.*]

STEVE: Art is here in a saloon—I'll be serious with you, this is Steve Allen calling from Hollywood.

MRS. G: Oh, go on! [*The audience roars.*] You don't sound like him at all!

STEVE: Oh, go on, yourself!

MRS. G: Really, I mean it. Are you calling from California?

STEVE: Sure. Incidentally, you will accept the charges, won't you?

Musical icon Bob Dylan made one of his earliest television appearances on the show, singing "The Lonesome Death of Hattie Carroll." The show introduced other newcomers like the Supremes, the Carpenters, and Lou Rawls. A then-unknown Frank Zappa and a couple of his cohorts came on to perform the bizarre nonmusical feat of decimating an old car on stage with a sledgehammer, breaking its windows, crumpling its fenders, and reducing its other components to a junk pile. He also rigged a bicycle to enable him to "play" it as a musical instrument.

* * * * * *

Following the nightly Westinghouse series, Allen returned to weekly prime time from 1964 to '67 as host of *I've Got a Secret* for CBS (replacing Garry Moore), on which his wife, Jayne, had once served as a regular panelist from 1952 through '59. Following his third season as host, he starred in a weekly summer series for CBS, *The Steve Allen Comedy Hour*, co-starring Jayne and featuring regulars Louis Nye, Dayton Allen, Ruth Buzzi (later of *Laugh-In* fame), and impressionist John Byner, with musical guest stars that included Sonny and Cher, Lou Rawls, and Dionne Warwick and with Richard Dreyfuss and Rob Reiner making their network television debuts. It was on this series that Allen did what became one of the most famous parodies of tacky charity telethons that was rebroadcast decades later on the Showtime cable network. "The Prickly Heat Telethon" featured Byner as an over-the-top Henny Youngman wannabe; Buzzi as the smiling, Vanna White–like tote board girl; Jayne as an overcoiffed but undertalented singer; and Allen as the cantankerous telethon host. One of the highlights was a nine-year-old boy poignantly explaining to Allen how the affliction had scarred his life: "You see, my mother and father had prickly heat, and they were so busy scratching, they didn't have time for me."

Allen found the line so silly and perfectly delivered that he had to bury his head in his hand, but he couldn't suppress his laughter. His reaction threw the young actor's concentration, forcing him to look right at the camera and smile sheepishly to find his next line on the teleprompter. Allen, in turn, reacted by doing the same thing.

Allen returned to variety/talk with nightly series for Filmways (1968–69) and Golden West (1970–71). These shows, like those for Westinghouse, were more like *Tonight* in format, but were now in the hands of a new generation of writers and producers. David Pollock and Elias Davis were both high school–age fans of the Allen *Tonight* shows and were still in their twenties when they were hired as writers for the Filmways series (they went on to produce for Allen and later wrote for *The Carol Burnett Show, Mary Tyler Moore, All in the Family, Cheers, M*A*S*H,* and *Frasier,* winning Emmy nominations and Humanitas awards along the way). "Elias and I were fortunate to slip into shoes that had been well broken in years before on *Tonight* by producer Bill Harbach and writers Stan Burns and Herb Sargent," wrote Pollock in a 2001 tribute to Allen in *Television Quarterly*.

"Our daily working procedure was arrived at quickly and never changed. Elias and I would bring our material directly to [Allen's] dressing room, where Steve, usually lying on his slant board, glasses usually pushed up on his forehead, would read the scripts silently while we sat there idly. Often he would chuckle softly to himself, and I'd furtively try to gauge the angle of his gaze on a particular page in a mostly feeble attempt to determine which joke had amused him."

Of course, there would be more wacky stunts. Allen would find himself in vats of oatmeal and cottage cheese. He became a human hood ornament, strapped onto a car and driven down the street. In another stunt, wearing only bathing trunks, he was instructed to lie down on the floor and slathered with canned dog food, whereupon fifteen hungry dogs backstage were unleashed to feast on the free food. As the stage hands were pasting dog food to Allen's body, his surprise and shock were apparent: "What are you doing? Lie down? Oh, no! Oh, that's cold! Ooooh! That's freezing! Why don't you heat it, at least? That's sickening! This program goes into saloons all over America. Holler what? Gravy train? GRAAVVY TRAIN! Why would I—" [The dogs rush the stage.]

"Through it all, Steve never balked nor complained," wrote Pollock, "though on one occasion he commented, 'You guys must really hate your fathers.'"

It was on the Golden West series in 1971 that Allen introduced several young comedians, including Albert Brooks and Steve Martin, who recalled: "He gave me my first break as a young standup comedian. I remember his first introduction of me. 'Ladies and gentlemen, when you see this comedian, you might not get it at first. But then when you think about it, you still won't get it. So it might be a good idea to go up and talk it over with him.'"

MEETING OF MINDS

By the late 1970s, Allen had hosted more than two thousand episodes of the talk/variety format he had pioneered and had frankly grown weary of it. Now in his mid-fifties, his never-ending thirst for intellectual and creative stimulation led him to develop a much more dramatic innovation with the format. In 1977, he produced what critics hailed as the "ultimate talk show" in which actors portraying prominent historical figures would sit at a table and engage in intellectual, philosophical debates, based on the language and views of their writings. *Meeting of Minds* ran on PBS from 1977 through '81 and grew from Allen's love of literature, history, and the often-conflicting ideas of the great men and women of civilization. One show might feature Marie Antoinette (Jayne Meadows), Sir Thomas More (Bernard Behrens), Karl Marx (Leon Askin), and Ulysses S. Grant (Joe Earley) pondering revolution, communism, and love. Another discussion might bring together Teddy Roosevelt, Thomas Aquinas, Cleopatra, and Thomas Paine. One especially imaginative show, subtitled "Shakespeare on Love," had the celebrated playwright sitting with his own creations: Othello, Romeo, Juliet, and Hamlet.

It was Allen's dream to stimulate viewer thinking by allowing these figures not only to present their ideas but to be subjected to criticism. "How would Lutherans respond to seeing the founder of their church pointedly criticized by Voltaire?" wondered Allen. "How would feminists react at seeing Susan B. Anthony and Florence Nightingale subjected to penetrating questions?" Allen wrote the scripts himself.

Allen originally conceived *Meeting of Minds* as a segment for his Sunday night prime-time series in 1959, a discussion of a contemporary issue like capital punishment with Sigmund Freud, G. W. F. Hegel, Michel de Montaigne, Clarence Darrow, and Aristotle. He had his friend, journalist-critic Nat Hentoff, research the chapter on crime and punishment from the Syntopicon of the Great Books of the Western World Library and draft a script based on the various viewpoints. Allen showed the script to friends, including Norman Cousins of *Saturday Review*, who not only loved it but immediately planned a cover story on the subject.

A few days later, however, NBC asked Allen to scrap the segment. The reason given was that it was not the kind of fare to present on a comedy-variety program. "*Meeting of Minds* is not comedy, but *variety* is a more elastic word," Allen protested. But he would later learn that the network's disapproval "was tied to my connection with the National Committee for a Sane Nuclear Policy, as well as to having permitted the use of my name in an anti–death penalty campaign centered on the Caryl Chessman case." Although Allen vehemently denied any connection between his personal views on such issues and his desire to use his program to explore the great ideas of others, the network feared antagonizing its potential customers and Chrysler-Plymouth, a sponsor.

The cancellation of the segment received more publicity than the broadcast would have, said Allen. "The network, the agency, and the sponsor were subjected to bitter criticism." Allen's office was flooded with mail expressing support and interest, and he gladly honored requests from individuals, schools, churches, and social groups for copies of the script. Five years later, on his nightly Westinghouse show, he and an acting troupe finally got to perform the segment.

Allen attempted to revive the concept while doing another nationally syndicated talk series in 1971. The first episode aired to great acclaim from Hollywood-based critics, but the show's distributor—without notice to Allen—never supplied the show to the other markets across country, only the local Los Angeles area from which Allen was broadcasting. Ironically, now that the program became deemed a local show, it won three local Emmy awards.

Such critical recognition inspired Allen to personally finance the development of six additional one-hour programs and attempt to sell them to syndicators or networks. There were no takers. Not even PBS would bite. But a few years later, Loring d'Usseau, executive producer of the 1971 telecast, became program manager of KCET, the Los Angeles PBS outlet. The remaining question became one of funding. E. F. Hutton listened—one of its executives, William Clayton, saw one of Allen's pilots and pledged his support. The first of six hour-long specials aired nationally on January 10, 1977.

In one episode, St. Thomas Aquinas expressed his belief that women were inferior ("Woman should look on man as her natural master") and that every female birth was a flaw of nature. This did not sit well with Cleopatra (played by Jayne Meadows). Aristotle and Fyodor Dostoevsky argued about capital punishment in the Caryl Chessman case. Darwin reproached Attila the Hun for his military ruthlessness, and Emily Dickinson (played by Katherine Helmond of *Who's the Boss?*) glared in agreement. Attila rejoined, "I wasn't aware, Dr. Darwin, that the British Empire was built by pacifists," and contrasted the indiscriminate murder of civilians in World War II with his own battle, which he contended was limited to soldiers who chose to enter battle.

Meeting of Minds was received with enormous critical acclaim. In 1977, Allen was honored with a Personal Peabody Award for creating and hosting "a truly original show. . . . As historical celebrities come alive in a discussion rich in philosophical fireworks and engaging wit, host Allen keeps proceedings as orderly as possible." The Peabody award also recognized Jayne Meadows for her portrayal of various historical characters. In 1981, the show won an Emmy for Outstanding Informational Series. There were also Emmy nominations for performances by Meadows and Beulah Quo (1978), writing by Allen (1978), and videotape editing by Terry Pickford (1977).

In addition, the show "elicited a kind of mail none of us connected with its production had ever seen," observed Allen. "What appealed to the thousands who wrote, I believe, was that they were actually given the opportunity to hear *ideas* on television, a medium which otherwise presents only people, things, and actions."

A FOILED RETURN TO LATE NIGHT

In April 1980, while Allen and his wife, Jayne, were vacationing in Jamaica, his secretary called him to relay a message from NBC's president, Fred Silverman, asking him to fly back to Los Angeles immediately to discuss an extremely urgent matter. Allen optimistically suspected it involved an offer of employment, but his secretary couldn't cajole Silverman to discuss the issue with Allen over the phone.

Allen cut his vacation short by one day and reported with his agent, Irvin Arthur, to NBC, where Silverman had them brought into the network's executive dining room. According to Allen, Silverman said, "I don't know if you've heard, but Johnny is cutting down from ninety to sixty minutes, so he'll be on from 11:30 to 12:30 at night. Here's my suggestion: *Johnny Carson from 11:30 to 12:30; Steve Allen from 12:30 to 1:30!*" Silverman, beaming broadly, was waiting for an answer. "The reason I was in such a rush to talk to you about this is that on Monday I'm meeting with the affiliates, and I know they'll give me a standing ovation when I announce this. Ordinarily, I wouldn't be rushing you, but in this case we really do need an answer right away. You can see why."

Silverman's offer for Allen to host a revamped *Tomorrow* show should not have been a total surprise. The network brass was elated that Allen had been handing over ratings successes and nearly universal critical acclaim from his several stints hosting NBC's variety extravaganza, *The Big Show*. They were "virtually salivating over the prospect of having Johnny Carson and Steve Allen as a back-to-back tandem on an almost nightly basis," reported *Chicago Sun-Times* TV critic Gary Deeb.

Allen hesitated. "To tell you the truth, Fred, I'd like to cooperate with you and give you a quick yes or no right now, but I'm going to have to give the matter at least a little thought," said Allen. "Having done thirteen years of talk-show duty, I'm not sure I want to make a move back in that direction. I'm always available, as you know, to do prime-time comedy series or specials, but the middle of the night isn't exactly—"

"I understand," replied Silverman, "and I really don't want to rush you into an answer unless you're tremendously enthusiastic about it." Silverman asked if Allen could get back to him the following day because he wanted to make that exciting announcement about the Carson/Allen combination. Given that NBC was in general ratings doldrums at the time, he knew that it would be a great morale booster for the affiliates.

After the meeting, as Allen and Irvin Arthur were walking out of the dining room, Silverman approached Arthur and told him, "I have a good feeling about this thing. It'll work out great for all of us. I'll just run it by Johnny now, but I'm sure there'll be no problem about that."

"Had this scene been acted in a movie," Allen later mused, "the director would have called for a tight close-up of Irvin's face at that moment, perhaps even suggested a tense musical phrase to underscore the importance of what had just been said."

The next day, after much thought, Allen called Irvin to say that he was inclined to accept NBC's offer, but Irvin had to cut him short. "I'm sorry to have to tell you this, but I just heard from NBC. Carson nixed the deal."

The news about what had happened inevitably leaked, causing considerable embarrassment to the network. This also had to be awkward for Tom Snyder, who was at the time still doing the *Tomorrow* show in the slot following Carson's and could not have been pleased to learn that the network had decided to replace him. "At first, there were flat denials," recalled Allen, "assertions that Johnny Carson had no authority to make such a decision, but eventually Brandon Tartikoff, who had taken over as president of NBC Entertainment, conceded that the matter had indeed been discussed with Carson but hastily added that 'Johnny does not, *by contract*, have veto power.'"

But Gary Deeb reported that "Carson did veto NBC's intention to create a new talk-variety format for 'The Tomorrow Show,' but that Johnny's thumbs-down decision referred only to the talk-variety format—not to the possibility of Allen hosting the program." According to Deeb's source, Carson "vetoed the show, regardless of who would be hosting it. Steve Allen's involvement had nothing to do with it."

Or did it? Despite the network's attempts to minimize the controversy by contending that Carson simply didn't want another comedy-variety show following his own, that was exactly the kind of show NBC would slot to follow his. But instead of Steve Allen hosting, it would be David Letterman. Ironically, Letterman, a big fan of Allen, would periodically revive his mentor's old routines.

Late Night with David Letterman premiered in 1982 and went on to win a Peabody Award in 1991 "for television programming which, at its best, is evocative of the greats, from *Your Show of Shows*, to *The Steve Allen Show*, and *The Ernie Kovacs Show. . . ."*

"With the exception of David Letterman, who took over the spot and who was willing to let Carson's production company control his program, all the rest of us involved came out of the experience with a bit of egg on our faces," wrote Allen.

Even if the deal with Allen had gone through, it may not have worked out for long, speculated Bill Allen, who suggested that Carson's arrangement with NBC, formal or otherwise, may have allowed him control over not only his own *Tonight Show* but also any show that followed it. Had Steve Allen taken over at 12:30 a.m., it may have resulted in Allen—the inventor of the late-night format and first *Tonight* host—working as an employee for one of his successors. Such an arrangement may have been awkward, at the very least.

Moreover, the prospect of Allen following Carson may have posed a threat to Carson's production team. Carson was not enthusiastic about the idea, wrote Bill Carter in *The Late Shift*. "He didn't see any reason to allow a show likely to be much like his own to come on the air right after he said good night." Imagine Steve suddenly appearing right after Johnny with updated versions of the comedy bits he pioneered in the 1950s, such as "The Question Man" and "The Late Night Pitchman"—bits that audiences in 1980 may mistakenly have assumed were pioneered by Johnny. Slotting the two shows back-to-back may have invited obvious, awkward comparisons.

* * *

In 1986, Allen was inducted into the Television Academy Hall of Fame for his lifetime contributions to television. Ironically, it was David Letterman who presented him with the award:

My earliest memories of television [were when] I was a small boy in a room in my home and could sit in front of an old black-and-white television. I think it was an RCA or GE. The truth of the matter is, I could sit there hour after hour and just laugh and laugh and laugh. Did you ever laugh till your sides actually ached from laughing so much? Maybe it hasn't happened here tonight . . . but it could!

And I remember this very clearly, as if it were yesterday. One evening, my mom came into the room where I was seated in front of the set and said, "Dave, why don't you turn that thing on?" So I turned the set on, and I began to laugh even harder because the face on the screen was the man who is one of the most creative, original comedic minds of our time. It was also the face of a man who has meant a great deal to me personally and professionally: Steve Allen.

Steve Allen's contributions stood out like an original in a sea of carbon copies. So, for his remarkably facile mind and quick wit, for his outstanding contributions towards the creation and development of new forms of TV programming, for the legacy of laughter and nurturing new talent, and for deep-seated and active interest in matters of social, political, and intellectual consequence, the Television Academy is proud to induct into its Hall of Fame Mr. Steve Allen.

Comedian and talk-show host Bill Maher had this to say about the man who discovered him in 1982 and gave him one of his first jobs: "It's just like that line from *Sunset Boulevard*: 'The pictures got smaller.' He never changed. He was never different. He was funny from the beginning to the end. I never saw any difference in this guy or any diminution in his skills. The country changed, unfortunately. The country could not keep up with this man. The country got dumber and less appreciative of wit."

But before he died, on October 30, 2000, Allen did get to savor a most fitting national tribute. It occurred on September 27, 1994, on the fortieth anniversary broadcast of *The Tonight Show*. Jay Leno introduced Allen as his first guest: "He started this very show forty years ago today, the very first *Tonight Show*, a brand new show—it was called *Tonight*. Nobody had ever done this before. He made it what it is." When Allen came on stage, Jay literally got down on his knee and reverently kissed Allen's ring. Later in the show, it was time for a stunt, and so strongman John Evans, also known as "The Great Balancer," balanced a large object on his head: seventy-two-year-old Steve Allen. Allen also composed his five thousandth song on that episode, based on four random notes that Leno had given him live, on the spot. Leno closed the anniversary show by telling Allen, "I must thank you for all of us that do this in late night, on any network and any syndication, for showing us how it's done. Thank you very much!"

Epilogue

AS SEEN BY HIS PEERS

Sid Caesar, Carl Reiner, and Jonathan Winters were stars on the rise when they first met and befriended Steve Allen in the early 1950s. Caesar was the most established, headlining the groundbreaking comedy classic from television's Golden Age, Your Show of Shows *(1949–54), on which Reiner was a cast member and writer, as well as the Emmy-winning* Caesar's Hour *(1954–57). Winters was just breaking into his television career with original, hysterical stand-up routines. All three guested on* Tonight, *with Winters gaining the most exposure from his frequent appearances, his first on national late-night television.*

For his pioneering contributions to television, Caesar was inducted into the Academy of Television Arts and Sciences Hall of Fame in 1985. In the mid-'90s, he received Emmy nominations for outstanding guest performances in the comedy series Mad about You *and* Love and War. *Caesar also enjoyed a formidable career in films, with prominent roles in* It's a Mad Mad Mad Mad World *(1963),* Mel Brooks's Silent Movie *(1976),* Grease *(1978), and* National Lampoon's Vegas Vacation *(1997). In recent years, he has been actively involved in compiling and producing the DVD releases of his television work.*

On a balmy December afternoon, Caesar, eighty, was sitting for his interview at the breakfast table in his Beverly Hills home, where an assistant in the adjoining kitchen was washing dishes, banging pots and pans, and loudly opening large, brown paper bags, periodically drowning out the conversation. Because Caesar spoke nonchalantly above the clatter, refusing even to acknowledge it, one would be convinced that the whole scene was a Your Show of Shows *sketch in the making.*

Reiner was interviewed later that afternoon. Hale and energetic at eighty-one, Reiner was just returning from a full day working in a recording studio. Watching him stroll with a spring in his step into his Beverly Hills home, one couldn't help but recall the familiar opening of The Dick Van Dyke Show (1961–66), which he created and wrote (and won twelve Emmys for) and on which he regularly guest-starred as Alan Brady. He became a major Hollywood director and writer whose hits include Where's Poppa? (1970), The Jerk (1979), All of Me (1984), and That Old Feeling (1997). In recent years, Reiner has appeared in the popular Ocean's Eleven and Ocean's Twelve films. In 1999, he received the Kennedy Center's Mark Twain Prize for American Humor.

Winters is often regarded as America's premiere improvisational comedian. His television credits include several appearances on the Tonight show under all of its hosts, frequent guest spots on Hollywood Squares, The Andy Williams Show, Mork and Mindy (with Robin Williams), and Bob Hope specials. Winters "is a highly influential performer, probably the most so since Jackie Gleason," wrote Allen in Funny People. In 2000, he received the Kennedy Center's Mark Twain Prize for American Humor. Winters answered the driveway intercom on his estate outside Santa Barbara but at first did not recall the prescheduled interview about Allen. His memory jogged, the electric gates opened. Winters, reputed to be irrepressibly funny both on camera and off, was on this day, at age seventy-seven, serious and at times melancholy.

Also interviewed was renowned writer Larry Gelbart, formerly a writer for Caesar, whose credits include developing and writing the celebrated and very literate comedy series M*A*S*H (1972–83), writing classic films such as Oh, God *(1977, directed by Carl Reiner) and* Tootsie *(1982), and a co-writing the lyrics for the Broadway musical,* A Funny Thing Happened on the Way to the Forum *(1966). It was through Gelbart's wife, Pat Marshall, one of the original* Tonight *house singers, that he first met Allen in the mid-'50s.*

In December 2002, these four legends sat down in separate interviews to analyze their late, dear friend. They discussed their memories of Steve, the early Tonight *years, and how the industry has changed through the decades. Through some of his earlier writings about his dear friends, Allen pops in periodically with thoughts of his own.*

ON THE EARLY DAYS

*C*arl Reiner remembered Steve Allen's earliest television appearances "because he had been on radio. I thought he almost didn't need a straight line to make a joke. One word was enough for him to make a comment. So when he made the move to television, we were all very interested. As soon as we saw him, we knew it worked. The main thing about him was he used good humor. He found himself funny, and he broke himself up an awful lot of times and in doing so broke up America at the same time."

Sid Caesar: "I saw him when he first started. I watched him every night. Steve was funny. He had his own rhythm. Comedy is rhythm. Comedy is timing. A lot of times, the editors louse up the timing. They take out the essence."

Caesar recalled his appearance on *Tonight* with Allen in November 1955: "I was doing my show, and he said, 'Would you like to come on?' And I said, 'Sure.' And we did 'The Table Hopper.' Guy comes down and sits at your table and says [*warmly*], 'Hi, how are ya? I'll be with ya, just a minute.' And he goes to another table

311

and says, 'How ya doin'?' And he's sitting there, having dinner with you, but he's at five different tables. Table-hopping is just to get your name around. Not to see anybody or talk to anybody. He sat down at the table but never talked to you. It was done practically ad lib."

Allen fondly remembered Caesar's appearance: "The sketch ran about sixteen minutes. It consisted of a series of vignettes showing the different types of pests one meets in restaurants. The premise for each section of the sketch was, of course, determined in advance, but not one word of dialogue was written. Sid and I ad-libbed one set of lines during rehearsal and when we went on the air ad-libbed a completely new script, so to speak. It was Sid who, in rehearsal and on the air, ad-libbed about half-an-hour of the most hilarious material, lines, and pieces of business that I have ever seen."

The sketch worked because both of them could ad-lib, explained Caesar: "He knew when I was through, and I knew when he was through. We tried to complement each other. Not everybody can ad-lib. Comedy dell'arte is making it up as you go along."

Caesar enjoyed one of Allen's routines so much that he satirized it on his own show. Caesar: "He did a thing where you put a camera on the street with a big light. And the people used to walk by because they were attracted by the light like moths. I thought that was good, so I did it. I played the guy who walked by the camera [*pantomimes surprise and hams it up*]—do a little tap dance. People think that because they were in front of a camera, they had to do something. You walk past it first, then you come back and take a look, and then you go back and start to perform."

Allen booked Jonathan Winters on *Tonight* after Allen had seen him perform stand-up on an unlikely forum for his talents, *Omnibus*. A forerunner of serious high-culture programs like PBS's *Great Performances*, *Omnibus* was hosted by Alistaire Cooke and featured live musical and dramatic performances by a variety of distinguished artists, including Orson Welles, Joanne Woodward, Helen Hayes, Yul Brynner, Ethel Barrymore, and Leonard Bernstein. Winters was the first comedian ever to appear on the show. Winters: "I did Custer's Last Stand and the making of a basketball player—a kind of Frankenstein thing—a seven-foot player."

Winters landed the *Omnibus* spot after Ed Sullivan's people turned him down:

> You're standing there in an empty room with just a man sitting behind a table, fourteen pieces of paper in front of him and a pen, and you have to audition and especially be funny. So I did about five minutes. He said, "What is your name again?"
>
> I said, "Jonathan Winters."
>
> "I don't think Mr. Sullivan would understand your comedy."
>
> I said, "I don't think *you* understood it."

Fortunately, Allen did. In addition to appearing regularly on *Tonight* when it aired from the Hudson Theatre (which he did about twenty-five times), Winters was always first to be booked whenever the show went on the road. According to Allen,

> His most notable contribution on such occasions was one that the public never saw. When a regular television program originates in another city, the members of the company are like a traveling circus group or, I suppose, like any other encampment pulling up stakes. You all meet at some designated location to board a bus to the airport, you all get on the same plane, pile into another bus at your destination, are all taken to the same hotel and transported to the same auditorium or studio. From the moment we met him early in the morning at our first rendezvous point, Jonathan would be "on" and would never, even for a moment, stop his wild monologues until, a few days later, we were back in New York, exhausted not only from our professional chores but also from laughing at him.

Because Winters specialized in doing characters, Allen eschewed standard introductions like, "And now here's the very funny Jonathan Winters" in favor of introducing him as an airplane pilot, a member of the city council of the host town, a hotel manager, a sea captain, or any number of other characters: "It really didn't matter what sort of hat or costume we put on him." On a road show in Winters's hometown of Dayton, Ohio, he played all the characters—complete with sound effects—in a sketch about an island landing by a group of Marines, as well as a sketch about a pet shop incident in which the customer lost a finger to a carnivorous fish.

Reiner is forever indebted to Allen for pushing him and Mel Brooks to do something that continues to bring them great renown:

> He did one very unique thing that nobody else can claim. Being a fan of comedy, he was instrumental in getting Mel and I to do an album based on "The Two-Thousand-Year-Old Man." We performed it from 1950 to 1960 at many parties. We only did it for friends because it had a Middle-European Jewish accent. At one big party, George Burns came over to us and he says, "If you don't put this on record, I'm gonna steal it."
>
> Edward G. Robinson says, "I want to do that guy on Broadway."
>
> Steve came over and said, with great excitement: "Fellas, you *have* to do an album."
>
> We said, "No, this is only for friends. It's really very special. Inside stuff for Jews."
>
> He said, "Well, I'm a Christian. You guys own it. I want the world to hear how funny this is. *I'll* rent the studio. *I'll* pay for the session. You just do the record. If you don't like it, you can burn it." So we recorded it at World Pacific Jazz.
>
> And we said to him, "You want to be our partner?" He said, "No, no. I just want this to get out to the world."
>
> You can't not like somebody who in 1960 said something that you didn't have faith in would work. But he had faith. That

was a bond we had from 1960 on. If it wasn't for him, "The Two-Thousand-Year-Old Man" would only be heard at parties."

Reiner and Brooks's 1960 album, *2000 Years with Carl Reiner and Mel Brooks*, became an instant classic and earned a Grammy nomination.

ON WORKING WITH OTHER COMEDIANS

Allen's peers agreed—he loved comedy and comedians. Reiner:

> When you have a television program that lasts for an hour and a half, one of the easiest ways to entertain people is to get comedians on. It's one hand washing the other. He needed the comedians as much as the comedians needed him. And it's ever thus. The Seinfelds of the world will tell you how excited they were to get on the Carson show for the first time. The stamp of a host of a major talk show at night is the stamp of approval that you needed to send your career forward.
>
> Steve was the perfect guy to host a show. Not only did he need comedians, he loved comedians. He was able to select the good ones to bring on. And when he had his "Man on the Street," there were Bill Dana, Louis Nye, Tom Poston, and Don Knotts. Those guys were as funny as they get.
>
> He was an easy laugher. He appreciated other comedians, and he also appreciated himself when he said something funny. Or when he made a goof, he laughed at himself rather than get worried about the fact that people might censor him.

Caesar: "[Steve's *Tonight* show] paid the minimum to any guest, which was then a couple hundred, or a hundred, hundred-twenty dollars. But you didn't go and do it for the money. You did it because it gives you exposure, and you're talking with a very intelligent man."

Moreover, Allen resisted the temptation to outwit comedians guesting on his shows, adeptly presenting them to their best advantage. Reiner: "It was nice to have people like Steve who always knew the right questions to ask, as all the good ones do—from Paar on—because they give the guest leave to be informative or funny. And if they don't do that, then they're not good hosts, and all these guys are great hosts. And Steve sort of set the pattern of what a good host should be."

Winters: "I miss Carson a lot, and Steve. These guys always enjoyed talent, they knew how to use talent. And talent, in turn, knew how to produce for them. There was a kind of controlled insanity with Steve and all of us. You looked at Louis Nye doing Steverino, a very hip guy, and Knotts playing the funny weatherman. Good characters like radio days. They had departments—Fibber McGee and Molly and Fred Allen all had these departments of character people. You'd look forward to seeing Steve and the people he surrounded himself with."

About latter-day hosts, Winters opined: "Sometimes they feel that they're in competition with their guests. Maybe I'm wrong. Johnny or Steve wanted you to look good because you had just so many shots. I don't find the same rapport that I did with those guys. Johnny or Steve, they could feed you, they could play straight for you. And I don't think these guys want to do that necessarily, or maybe they don't know how to play with you."

According to Gelbart, "He was that thing that all really, really good entertainers are: a good audience. He didn't have to be on, and he was not stingy with his laughter when other people were being funny. He did that socially, too. It sounds like a simple thing, but it's not a simple thing. When a comedian lays back, he doesn't compete; he's really going against his nature in a way because that's what he does. But Steve was a gentleman, as opposed to a lot of other people who are terrific but not especially gentlemen or ladies. Steve was well mannered, which didn't make him any less wild in his comedy, or any less creative or imaginative. He wasn't polite—he did extremely physical, knockabout stuff. But with that all, there was the base of a very real sensibility."

ON ALLEN'S INFLUENCE

Caesar believed that Allen's *Tonight* show revolutionized television comedy and the prevailing entertainment model at the time, the vaudeville-style revue:

> The talk show was the death of the revue. The revue format is what we were doing. The *Tonight* show did away with all that. What Steve did by himself in his own format was to do a little revue with an interview. You had people come to talk to you about what they were doing. They wanna plug their book. So they come on, do a little performance, plug the book, and do a little performance. If they were a singer or a comedian, they did a little performance. So why do they need to spend all of the money for costumes and orchestras, when he could do it? It replaced the revue format. Not that it's just cheaper. But it's a faster form. You got almost the same values.

Once Allen established the *Tonight* show, it became, said Reiner,

> the template for all we're doing today. Steve Allen set the tone for a lot of madness that Letterman and a lot of other people do. Going out into the street for the first time and making fun out in the street. Letterman's still doing that. He's got the guy next door who has the little diner—made him a star. That was Steve doing all of that. Taking average folks and just asking them questions and eliciting funny answers, or just straight answers, and he knew what to do with them. He started that. He did set the template for all people who came after him.
>
> Things haven't changed that much from what Steve did. Every-

thing that exists today existed then. The only difference was that he was a musician. He loved to sit down at the piano, which for him was very entertaining—not as much for the audience. I think they would rather have another comedian. But that was catering to his needs as a performer, and he loved performing.

He did outlandish things. To this day, they'll do things that are the grandchildren of that: Will this float? Letterman does that—a big tank of water: "Will this ham float?"—and two pretty girls drop it in the tank. That's all based on what Steve did. The kind of silliness that late-night viewers appreciated because they're sleepy and they want to laugh. Everything that is done today, he did then, whether the people know it or not. Where it came from doesn't really matter to the people today.

And that, believed Caesar, is the problem—that contemporary audiences don't know that Allen's creation of *Tonight* "led up to the shows that you have now. That's the genesis." He bemoaned the apparent lack of interest in that fact among younger audiences. "They don't care—see, that's the terrible part. They have no tradition. Kids today look it up on 'dot-com.' So they don't have to have a memory. They know that two and two is four, but they don't know why. They don't respect anybody because they don't know anybody. To me, my heroes were Charlie Chaplin, W. C. Fields, Buster Keaton, Laurel and Hardy. They were the giants. Today, you got a few people who are very, very talented: Billy Crystal, Robin Williams. And they're not just joke tellers. They can act. They can perform. They can do several different things."

Kids today, said Caesar, are "not all dummies. There are some really smart kids out there. But they all look at what came before as old-time stuff. They don't realize that what they're doing is coming from what we were doing. If we didn't go through what we went through, they would never have anything. They would still be telling jokes. That's it."

On Changes in the Industry

Allen's friends noted some of the changes that permeated late-night shows over the decades. Reiner observed that Allen "had authors on very often. Today that has disappeared. That's something that I'd like them to reconstitute. He did have islands of literary intelligence coming on. Authors now are not as interesting, unless they're a celebrity author. He was more eclectic in his taste."

Winters lamented the loss of freewheeling merriment from current late-night shows:

> I think it's changed drastically. I look at Letterman and Leno. I think their major [focus] is "overnights." They're thinking about the ratings more than anything else. Steve was a giant, a guy who sat down and played the piano, he did movies, he did theater, he did colleges, he did it all.
>
> I don't see the fun in Letterman or Leno. And, very honestly, to me one of the funniest shows that went way out was *In Living Color* with the Wayans Brothers. And Jim Carrey. These guys were funny people. [Winters also singled out *The Bonnie Hunt Show* as an example of a contemporary program that followed the standards Allen established.]
>
> What we've lost, at least I've lost—how many people look forward to going to work every morning? How many people really thoroughly enjoy what they're doing? Rather than saying, "How long is my vacation? How much am I getting for this?" All these little things. For me, a lot of the fun has gone out. I can settle for the money. It's a question of fun: "Am I going to have a good time?"

On Vulgarity in Contemporary Entertainment

In his later years, Allen, who was known throughout his life for keeping his comedy clean, became vocally critical of the vulgarity that permeated contemporary entertainment. "Even people who fall far short of a state of personal sanctity—myself, for example—are revolted," he wrote. The mass media constantly bombard society with messages of encouragement to act in ways that have traditionally been, as Allen put it, "the province of the libertine, thuggish, coarse and depraved." At one time, aberrant messages could be ignored because they treaded quietly in the margins of society. But now aberrations are in the mainstream, especially on TV, "the most pervasive medium in the culture," wrote Allen in a November 1998 article in the *Wall Street Journal*.

In a 1998 interview, Larry King asked Allen, "Jerry Springer says he's in entertainment. Is he to you?"

"He's in it," replied Allen. "He ought to be thrown out if he continues to do what he's doing. I'm glad to have about eight seconds here to express my complete disgust at the degree to which filth and sleaze and vulgarity and every kind of offensive language is now dominant in our language. There's a place for the dirty joke or the 'goddammit' when I hit my thumb with a hammer. It's human nature. That's not what they're doing. They're resorting to sleaze in the most vile way for commercial purposes."

In the late 1990s, Allen became a spokesman for the Parents Television Council, an organization advocating family-friendly programming and awakening public consciousness on the subject. His criticisms of vulgarity in contemporary media became the theme of his fifty-fourth and last book, *Vulgarians at the Gate*, which he was working on at the time he died in October 2000. The book was published posthumously the following year and rose to number seven on the *Los Angeles Times* best-seller list.

Allen's friends had a lot to say on the subject.

Gelbart: "Steve came from a tradition in which [vulgarity] was unknown. His mother was a vaudevillian. Vaudeville was like radio, in a sense. It was family entertainment. And you didn't do any four-letter words. You didn't say 'hell' and a helluva lot stronger words. So he came from that. It just wasn't part of him to suddenly cut loose and do a Lenny Bruce. Steve didn't break away from tradition; I think he thought it was lazy, immoral perhaps, a very easy way to get a laugh to shock the audience, and he would rather really tickle their fancy rather than titillate them."

Caesar: "The trend toward vulgarity was brought by stand-up comedians—Lenny Bruce—which was good for the nightclubs. But I find that in mixed company, with men and women, sometimes children, you can't do that. Because if you say that in front of kids, they're gonna use it. It's just for the sake of a laugh. Because once you get hooked on saying that dirty word, it becomes a crutch. That they have to say that word; otherwise, they don't get the laugh."

Reiner: "The amount of continuity acceptance, of what could be said on television, was quite different. The other day, Johnny Carson and I were talking about a roast that was on the air with language that we couldn't believe—it offended us, and we used all that language in private. But hearing it coming over the air, we could not believe what we were hearing. We were pristine pure in those days about language. It always occurred to us [to use objectionable language], but we censored ourselves."

Today, continued Reiner, "The situation comedies have pushed the limits—the walls are rubber. I don't know how many times the word *ass* is said."

Caesar agreed. "Times have changed. They accept that. It's not only what you do, it's the time you do it in. And all of a sudden, it's time for this. You can say, 'asshole'—'he's an asshole.' Well, you say that, you might as well say the rest of it. And it lowers the caliber. Maybe it's good, maybe it's bad, but I don't like it.

"If vulgarity has permeated regular conversation, then what do people say when they get mad? [*nonchalantly*] 'Well, the cock f---er came over and talked to me, you know?' This is a regular conversation. When they say it out there, it's like, 'Yeah, okay.' They don't hear it anymore. It used to be, 'Oooh, I said. . . .' Now it's, 'Uh-huh,' it's like regular conversation. If you say it enough times, you got to accept it, it has no meaning anymore. Except that you're talkin' dirty, and you haven't got a good education because you have to use dirty words to express yourself."

Winters: "I agreed with Steve wholeheartedly [about vulgarity]. I know you can be funny without being dirty. There's being blue, risque, naughty, and then we have just out-and-out vulgar. I don't know. When you look back at some of the greats—Chaplin, Fields, Laurel and Hardy, the Marx Brothers—these guys had their moments when they were somewhat naughty, but nothing that you could classify as vulgarity.

"I don't know how we can hope to educate our children—which seems to be the big thing with the politicians—they want to educate everybody, and yet what we're facing constantly is vulgarity. Much of television is T&A—in commercials and in the body of the program itself. I know myself because I've proved through the years that I can be funny without being dirty. I think this is a copout for a lot of people—that [this is] what the audience wants—I guess these guys and gals are giving it to them."

Caesar: "I never use [vulgarity]. In a way, it was very good because it forced us to think. You can't just go for the dirty word. It's like dropping your pants. Aahh, big deal! It's like coming out in a very funny costume, and you get a huge laugh. Now, you've gotta be funny. The suit got the laugh. *You* have to be funny. And the suit becomes a hindrance. Because they're always looking at the suit."

Winters: "If this is the only way you can express yourself, then why spend time in college? Why hope to get any kind of an education? I can't imagine a real person in a major business, if you come in and just roll out all these four-letter words, that he would put you in a key position, unless he thought that this was the way to go himself. I'm for Steve 100 percent. And I'm constantly having to defend myself because people say, 'Oh, he must be some kind of reborn super-Christian.' I think it's also the way you were brought up. Not that my mother and dad didn't have a few words now and then, but nothing like what you hear on the screen today."

TV directors did not urge Winters to spice up his act, "but night club directors did years ago," said Winters. "'Talk about your pencil, and maybe make a comment about the chicks down there who are heavily endowed.' I just worked around it.

"My response: 'If you don't buy what I'm doing, then I don't know why I'm booked here. I'm not trying to change people's lives. This is the way I work. If you can't handle this, then I'm outta here.'

"People are saying, 'I'm so tired of dirt.' I remember when I worked the road, people would say, 'Do you get dirty? Do you get filthy?'

"'Naw, you can bring anybody—child, mother, sister, nun or a priest.'

"And they would say, 'That's great, because the last guy we saw here was just filthy.'

"Something to be said about that."

Said Reiner, "Steve and I didn't quite agree about [Allen's campaign against vulgarity]. I didn't mind language that was used in context to elicit a society or time. In the old *Show of Shows*, you couldn't say the word *hell*. And we're doing a war scene, and Sid had to say, 'War is hell,' with bombs bursting. And the censors said, 'You can't say *hell*.' So he said, 'War is *heck*,' and it got a laugh because everybody knew that he was saying *heck* instead of *hell*.

"I remember having the same discussion with Tennessee Williams where he said he didn't like foul language in the theater, where if you're trying to elicit the times, and you're talking about gangsters or hoods, people lived in the 'hood and they're using certain language, and it's appropriate to where they lived and who they were; [foul] language is almost necessary. If you cleaned it up, then it's not them. So we argued about that.

"I was a little more liberal about what could be said, not curse words, per se—look at Richard Pryor when he came on the scene and used all that language. He was allowed and should have been allowed to use that language because that was his milieu. He was born in a whorehouse. Someone was a madam in his house. That's what he heard. So when he's talking about his neighborhood and he doesn't say that, it's not true. And all of a sudden, when you hear the word, and it's said honestly and it's not said to shock, but it's said to shock in that—'Look what I lived through'—you have a perfect right to use it. I object when it's used by comedians who just use it to lift the audience out of their seats for a second."

Caesar felt that the trend toward vulgarity "has reached its peak. People no longer get shocked when somebody says a dirty word anymore, so it doesn't do it." He hoped to see a decrease in vulgarity, "but I don't expect it very soon because they depend upon that now."

Caesar also felt that today's ratings-driven TV industry has degenerated the quality of comedy. "All of a sudden, they get an idea, 'We wanna get that audience from seventeen to two. They're the ones who buy. They spend money.' They don't realize that the people who spend money are the guys in their forties who give it to their kids to go to the theater. They have a ninety-five-million-dollar weekend. Where'd the money come from? These kids don't go out and work."

ON STEVE ALLEN, THEIR FRIEND

Gelbart: "My first impression of Steve—and my last: a guy who really, really, really enjoyed himself, enjoyed people, enjoyed a silly side."

According to Caesar, "He understood what you were doing. You didn't have to explain it to him. He was an intelligent man. Intelligence. He was a renaissance man. I had very, very deep conversations with him about almost everything. You could talk to him about science. You could talk to him about physics. He knew.

"And he was a pleasant man to be around. A very pleasant man to sit down and just have dinner with. He worked hard, and when he wanted something done, he'd get it done. He was a good friend. If you were friends with him, he would come right to you and help you. And he also was a very kind man. Very kind. An understanding man. If you were sick or something, he would forgive you and say, 'Take it easy. If you can't do it, do it when you can.' And he was very tolerant, not only of other people's religions, but of other people's feelings. He knew. He never tried to belittle anybody."

Said Reiner, "I was the host of his memorial service, and I had a wonderful time introducing all these wonderful people. And there was a white piano on stage, and they found a digital recording of his, and there he was playing—'The Gravy Waltz' or 'This Could Be the Start of Something Big'—whatever it was, there wasn't a dry eye in the house. Talk about the aura hanging over the auditorium!

"I think he left a little too early. He could have stayed on television a little longer. He was good on a loosey-goosey basis, and when he went into the more formal Sunday night show, I don't think it served him as well as staying loose and being able to ad-lib. Nobody could ad-lib better than him. He was second only to Groucho, maybe on par with Groucho. He needed very short straight lines to make a joke. Usually, you need a bit of a setup. You say three words to him, he found a way to twist or turn it. He was semantically facile.

"He had one Achilles' heel. He came over one day and he was laughing so hard. He came up with this thing that he thought was hysterical. And he told it to me, and I thought he was kidding me. And he was really laughing. He thought [using] the names of Italian food for people was hilarious—[like] 'Chicken Cacciatore' and 'Clams Marinara'—and he'd laugh, and I'd look at him. And I said, 'Thank goodness, he's not perfect.' I told him, 'Except for that, you're the most brilliant man!'"

Winters: "Steve was a great audience. He appreciated talent, good talent. Exceptionally kind to fellow performers, went overboard to see they got the exposure they warranted, needed. Had a great laugh. When he'd break up, he'd just go. He took chances. We all did. Of course, it was a different time. It was live television. And you had to come out, there wasn't any canned laughter in those days. Canned laughter is embarrassing. They're telling us when to laugh. Bad."

Gelbart: "He was a model of industry. Everybody starts out wanting to do and wanting to be. Steve just seemed right from day one to do it. To sing it, to write it, to perform it, to compose it. He had an enormous amount of office space in his head for all of these different facilities of his. It may sound simplistic. He applied himself so thoroughly to it. It's a model for everybody. To use every minute of the day doing what he loved and needing to. There's a difference between wanting to and needing to."

Reiner: "The thing I miss most about him is he's not here. You always went some place and you were happy to see Steve pop into a room. And he doesn't pop in anymore. He only pops in because you've brought him in today."

* * * * * * *

While it is evident that Allen's friends sincerely miss him, perhaps Gelbart summed up most eloquently and poetically the feelings of many of Steve's peers in a tribute he wrote for *Emmy* magazine shortly after Steve's death.

Whenever he left us, it would have been too soon.

Given another ten, twenty, twenty-five years, his work would still never have been done.

Not in a hundred more.

A hundred more years, or a hundred more lives.

There would never be enough memo pads on the nightstand, staff paper on the piano, or cassettes packed into his tape recorder.

The choice was never really his. Steve Allen was forever taking dictation from a mind that ordered—compelled—him, by any means, any media possible, to get out the word, have the song sung, make the cause known.

It was not a matter of the kind of mind he had. It was more a matter of the kind of mind that had him.

His was not a mind that could be put on hold.

It was the head office for an imagination that seemed to stay open twenty-four hours a day.

Year in and year out. Steve Central.

A haven for inspired ideas.

The kind you never plan on having.

A place where a never-ending stream of thoughts and melodies intersected, overlapped, crossed over and under and traced back to one another; a creative complex of such crowded intricacy, what it most resembled was a cat's cradle (I know, Steve: that's why it was always so littered).

It was a trampoline of a mind, where the most common, the most often used words would bounce, fly and twist themselves into new and hitherto unused combinations, before tumbling out of his mouth that served as their delivery system—even as the next word, sentence, or whole paragraph was going through the same comic reconfiguration just one flight up.

If he often laughed at something he had said, it had nothing to do with vanity; Steve was simply sharing the same sense of surprise and delight that had just hit his audience; very often what he said was the very first time *he* had heard it, often without vaguest warning that it was what he was going to say.

So harmonious were the many parts within a man so fugal, there was no sibling rivalry between Steve Allen's comedy and his music.

His ability to extemporize on the piano was of a piece with the jazz quality of his humor.

Speaking or playing, he always worked without a net, offering others the opportunity of witnessing the thought process of a mind that was a work forever in progress.

Rare is the artist who will allow an audience to be present at the birth.

However diverse his gifts, they were grounded in his unfailing sense of decency, the touchstone of his graciousness and generosity.

He was, at his best, a quality he always demanded of himself, one of that rare, vanishing breed of American—a gentleman.

Coming to the medium of television when the clay was still wet, Steve helped to shape and define it. TV was his laboratory. It was his playground.

When he chose, he could be as gaga as Berle, as Dada as Kovacs. He was as conversant with literate comedy as that other masterful Allen, Fred.

With Allen, Steve, it was not a case of anything for a laugh.

It was *everything* for a laugh. Whether it took a funny hat or a prop or a pun.

By shtick or by Steinway. Highbrow, lowbrow or nobrow. Wilde, or Larry or Curly, with one mot after another.

The measure of how much he was entertaining us was always how much he was entertaining himself.

The man knew an expert comedian when he saw one.

If there was ever any doubt, he had only to look at a mirror.

Or, better still—listen in, as he talked to himself.

He knew that laughter says to the world, Do your worst—I'll find the ridiculous in it, and that will make it sublime.

Over the years, when called upon to compose an essay or a speech, or, far too often of late, to deliver a eulogy, I would always send Steve a copy of what I had written, shamelessly trolling for his praise.

In the larger sadness, I know it means little, but I'd give anything to be able to send a copy of this to Steve; then wait for his endearingly silly approval of what I'd written, leaving no term unstoned, endorsing it with his experienced, that is to say, well-trained seal.*

---

*"Steve Allen: In Memoriam," *Emmy* (December 2000). Reprinted by permission.

NOTABLE GUEST APPEARANCES ON THE STEVE ALLEN–ERA *TONIGHT* SHOW

(1954–1957)

ACTORS

Luther Adler	Kitty Carlisle
Stella Adler	Art Carney
Eddie Albert	Leslie Caron
Ben Alexander	John Carradine
June Allyson	Jack Carson
Dana Andrews	Dane Clark
Cliff Arquette	Lee J. Cobb
Lew Ayres	Charles Coburn
Jim Backus	Jackie Coogan
Orson Bean	Gary Cooper
Noah Beery Jr.	Jackie Cooper
William Bendix	Wendell Corey
Polly Bergen	Wally Cox
Janet Blair	Buster Crabbe
Ray Bolger	Jeanne Crain
Ernest Borgnine	Joan Crawford
Rory Calhoun	Arlene Dahl
Corinne Calvet	Dorothy Dalton

Linda Darnell

Doris Day

Laraine Day

Yvonne De Carlo

Don De Fore

William Demarest

Andy Devine

Brandon De Wilde

Kirk Douglas

Paul Douglas

Alfred Drake

James Dunn

Richard Egan

Anita Ekberg

Florence Eldridge

Faye Emerson

Dale Evans

Tommy Farrell

Parker Fennelly

Jose Ferrer

Rhonda Fleming

Ann Flood

Joan Fontaine

Anne Francis

Arlene Francis

Hal Frederick

Betty Furness

Clark Gable

Eva Gabor

Zsa Zsa Gabor

Eva Le Gallienne

Peggy Ann Garner

Billy Gaxton

Alice Ghostley

Billy Gilbert

Joel Grey

Andy Griffith

Jack Grimes

Uta Hagen

Margaret Hamilton

Carol Haney

Sir Cedric Hardwicke

Signe Hasso

June Haver

Helen Hayes

Florence Henderson

Paul Henreid

Charlton Heston

Howard Hill

Hal Holbrook

Judy Holiday

Anne Jeffreys

Van Johnson

Louis Jourdan

Katy Jurado

Danny Kaye

Jane Kean

Grace Kelly

Richard Kollmar

Jack Kosslyn

Veronica Lake

Fernando Lamas

Dorothy Lamour

Elsa Lanchester

Hope Lange
Charles Laughton
Peter Lawford
Sheldon Leonard
Joan Leslie
Viveca Lindfors
Gina Lollabrigida
Marjorie Lord
Anita Louise
Phyllis Love
Claire Luce
Ida Lupino
Betty Luster
Shirley MacLaine
Aline MacMahon
Fred MacMurray
Gordon MacRae
Karl Malden
Luba Malina
Nancy Malone
Jayne Mansfield
Frederic March
Rose Marie
Enid Markey
Melinda Markey
Al Markim
Frank Marlowe
Mary Martin
Ilona Massey
Virginia Mayo
Marie McDonald
Roddy McDowall

Siobhan McKenna
Audrey Meadows
Jayne Meadows
Susie Miller
Sal Mineo
Eli Mintz
Cameron Mitchell
Montie Montana
Victor Moore
Agnes Moorehead
Rita Moreno
Dennis Morgan
Chester Morris
Zero Mostel
Don Murray
Lorie Nelson
Julie Newmar
Mariko Niki
David Niven
Kim Novak
Maila "Vampira" Nurmi
Merle Oberon
Hugh O'Brian
Margaret O'Brien
Maureen O'Hara
Michael O'Shea
Bibi Osterwald
Jack Palance
Franklin Pangborn
Gregory Peck
Walter Pidgeon
Maggie Pierce

Dick Powell
Tyrone Power
Vincent Price
Rosemary Prinz
Charlotte Rae
George Raft
Ella Raines
Tony Randall
Basil Rathbone
Gregory Ratoff
Aldo Ray
Gene Raymond
Alan Reed
Don Reed
Donna Reed
Michael Rennie
Debbie Reynolds
Madlyn Rhue
Cyril Ritchard
Edward G. Robinson
Roy Rogers
Cesar Romero
Jane Russell
William Russell
Robert Ryan
Eva Marie Saint
Gordon Scott
Zachary Scott
Paul Shyre
Walter Slezak

Kim Stanley
Maureen Stapleton
Rod Steiger
Jan Sterling
Elaine Stritch
William Sylvester
Don Taylor
Elizabeth Taylor
Frankie Thomas
Arthur Treacher
Sophie Tucker
Judy Tyler
Jo Ann Val
Benay Venuta
Connie Vera
Gilbert Vernon
Robert Wagner
Jean Wallace
Eli Wallach
Jack Washburn
Willard Waterman
David Wayne
Johnny Weismuller
Cornel Wilde
Chill Wills
Shelley Winters
Natalie Wood
Gretchen Wyler
Keenan Wynn
Shirley Yamaguchi

COMEDIANS

Abbott and Costello
Don Adams
Joey Adams
Fred Allen
Gene Allen
Morey Amsterdam
Kaye Ballard
Gene Baylos
Jack Benny
Roy Benson
Milton Berle
Shelley Berman
Joey Bishop
Bob and Ray
Victor Borge
Eddie Bracken
Joe E. Brown
Lord Buckley
Red Buttons
Jimmy Caesar
Sid Caesar
Cantinflas
Joey Carter
Imogene Coca
Irwin Corey
Dagmar
Danny Dayton
Gabe Dell
Kenny Delmar
George De Witt
Jimmy Edmondson

Frank Fontaine
Phil Foster
Stan Freberg
Joe Frisco
Reginald Gardner
Dick Gautier
Jack Gilford
Hermione Gingold
George Gobel
Pedro Gonzales
Sid Gould
Ronnie Graham
Paul Gray
Dorothy Greener
Buddy Hackett
Tim Herbert
Bob Hope
George Jessel
Will Jordan
Milt Kamen
Beatrice Kay
Betty Kean
Buster Keaton
Al Kelly
Lenny Kent
George Kirby
Don Knotts
Jimmy Komack
Ernie Kovacs
Pinky Lee
Phil Leeds

Jack E. Leonard

Jerry Lewis

Beatrice Lillie

Paul Lynde

Charles Manna

Peter Marshall

Groucho Marx

Bob McFadden

Henry Morgan

Gary Morton

Ken Murray

Johnny Myhers

Cliff Norton

Jack Norton

Louis Nye

Lew Parker

Jack Pearl

Gordon Polk

Roger Price

B. S. Pulley

Roger Ray

Martha Raye

Jorie Remus

Slapsy "Maxie" Rosenbloom

Mort Sahl

Dick Shawn

Herb Shriner

Herkie Styles

Don Tannen

Theodore

Danny Thomas

Billy Vine

Oliver Wakefield

Betty Walker

Nancy Walker

Arthur Walsh

Doodles Weaver

Gene Wesson

Bernie West

Marie Wilson

Jonathan Winters

Ben Wrigley

Alan Young

Henny Youngman

COMPOSERS/LYRICISTS

Harold Arlen

Elmer Bernstein

Leonard Bernstein

Ralph Blane

Nacio Herb Brown

Irving Caesar

Hoagy Carmichael

Betty Comden

Aaron Copland

Don Costa

Howard Dietz

Vernon Duke

Sammy Fain

Mack Gordon

Adolph Green

Oscar Hammerstein

Otto Harbach

Gordon Jenkins

Grace Leboy Kahn

Nick Kenny

Ira Kosloff

Burton Lane

Gerald Marks

Hugh Martin

Jimmy McHugh

Johnny Mercer

Bob Merrill

John Redmond

Richard Rodgers

Harold Rome

Harry Ruby

Arthur Schwartz

Jack Shaindlin

Jules Styne

Jimmy Van Heusen

Harry Warren

Mabel Wayne

Victor Young

Schinichi Yuize

DANCERS

Diana Adams
Rod Alexander
Augie and Margo
The Blackburn Twins (Ramon
    and Royce)
Tony Charmoli
The Dunhills
Andre Eglevsky
Vera Ellen
Timmy Everett
Bob Fosse
Peter Gennaro
The Goldwyn Girls
The Habonim Group
Melissa Hayden
Ding Hayes
Geoffrey Holder
Iva Kitchell

Beatrice Kraft
Bambi Linn
Ray MacDonald
Ray Malone
Lucas Manu
Victor Moreno
Sono Osato
Al Priest
Pat Rooney Jr.
Rafael Ruiz
Peggy Ryan
The Schuhlplattlers
Mia Slavenska
Maria Tallchief
June Taylor
Tun Tun
Lou Wills Jr.

MUSICIANS

Toshiko Akiyoshi
Louis Armstrong
Jan August
Chet Baker Quartet
Charlie Barnett
Count Basie
Gus Bivona and Band
Art Blakey
Lawrence Brown
Les Brown
Dave Brubeck
Johnny Burnette Trio
Joe Bushkin
Billy Butterfield
The Cadillacs
Barbara Carroll Trio
Bob Casey
Carmen Cavallaro
Page Cavanaugh Trio
Buck Clayton
Van Cliburn
Cy Coleman Trio
The Commanders
Conti Condoli
Eddie Condon
Johnny Costa
Wild Bill Davis Trio
Wild Bill Davison Group
Miles Davis Quintet
Buddy De Franco
Paul Desmond

Dorothy Donegan
Bobby Dukoff
Marshall Eisen
Roy Eldridge Trio
Duke Ellington
Don Elliott
Don Elliott Quartet
Mario Escudero
Bob Evans
Tal Farlow
Maynard Ferguson Jazz Band
Ferrante and Teicher
Bill Finegan
Stan Fisher
Lawrence "Bud" Freeman
Stan Freeman
Slim Gaillord
Erroll Garner
Stan Getz
Stan Getz Quartet
Terry Gibbs
Terry Gibbs Quartet
Dizzy Gillespie
Carroll Glenn
Benny Goodman
Benny Goodman Quartet
Tony Gottuso
Raymond Graft
Jimmy Guiffre
Bobby Hackett
Sam Hamilton

Lionel Hampton
Louis "Moondog" Hardin
Art Harris
Coleman Hawkins
Richard Hayman
Neil Hefti Band
Woody Herman
Eddie Heywood
Richard Himber
Earl "Fatha" Hines
Jutta Hipp and Trio
Johnny Hodges
Hoosier Hot Shots
Peanuts Hucko
Byron Janis
Conrad Janis
J. J. Johnson
Jonah Jones Group
Jonah Jones Quartet
Philly Joe Jones
Max Kaminsky and His
    Dixieland Jazz Band
Stan Kenton
Lee Konitz
Gene Krupa
Gene Krupa Trio
Yank Lawson
Eric Leinsdorf
Les Jazz Modes
Oscar Levant
Henry "Hot Lips" Levine
Lou Levy
Liberace and brother George

Eugene List
Joe Loco and Band
Jack Lowe
Fred Lowery
Nellie Lutcher
Art Magyar
Richard Maltby
Shelly Manne
Jeffrey Marlowe
Ronald Marlowe
Freddy Martin and His
    Orchestra
Robert Maxwell
Lou McGarrity
Al McKibbon
Jimmy McPartland
Jimmy McPartland Jazz Trio
Marian McPartland Trio
The Mento Band
Charlie Mingus Group
Modern Jazz Quartet
Thelonius Monk and Trio
Joe Mooney
Pat Moran
Patricia Morrison
Rita Moss
Gerry Mulligan
Turk Murphy and Group
Phil Napoleon and Band
Paul Nero and Violin Group
Phineas Newborn Jr.
Phineas Newborn Piano
    Quartet

Red Norvo Trio
Norman Paris
Fletcher Peck
Leonard Pennario
Armando Peraza
Charlie Persip
Oscar Peterson
Oscar Peterson Trio
Oscar Pettiford
Terry Pollard
Bud Powell
Perez Prado and Mambo Band
Gerald Price
Sammy Price
Tito Puente
Boyd Raeburn
Ruggiero Ricci
Buddy Rich
Maurice Rocco
Shorty Rogers
Leonard Rose
Bobby Rosengarden
Rover Boys
Stan Rubin and His Tiger Town
    Five
Pete Rugulo
Salvation Army Band
Eddie Sauter
Gene Schroeder
Hazel Scott
Tony Scott
John Sebastian

Jerry Segal
Bud Shank Quartet
Charlie Shavers
George Shearing
Don Shirley
Bobby Short
Horace Silver
Roy Smeck
Johnny Smith
Willie "Lion" Smith
Harry Sosnik
Gunther Sprecher
Lou Stein Trio
Rex Stewart
Joseph Szigetti
Fal Tarlow
Art Tatum
Billy Taylor
Billy Taylor Trio
Sam "Bluzman" Taylor
Jack Teagarden
Dan Terry and The Band
Jean "Toots" Thielemans
Claude Thornhill and Orchestra
The Three Suns
Roman Totenberg
The Treniers
John Scott Trotter
Bobby Troup Trio
Fernando Valenti
George Van Epps
Charlie Ventura

Appendix

Joe Venutti
Leroy Vinegar
Cy Walker
T. Bone Walker
George Wettling
Arthur Whittemore
Bob Wilber
Mary Lou Williams

Teddy Wilson
Kai Winding
Kai Winding Group
Herman Wright
Sol Yaged
Lester Young
Florian Zabach

NOVELTY ACTS

The Amazing Randy (magician)
Bil Baird (puppeteer)
Cora Baird (puppeteer)
Harry Blackstone (magician)
Kuda Bux (magician)
Chan Canasta (mentalist)
Melbourne Christopher (magician)
Joseph Dunninger (mentalist)
Dr. Bruno Furst (memory expert)
Gene Gowing (square dance caller)
The Great Ballantine (magician)
Clifford Guest (ventriloquist)
Mr. Heckler's Flea Circus
Marshall Izen (puppeteer)
Kajar (magician)
Fred Keating (magician)
Rhoda Koren (magician)

Kukla, Fran and Ollie (puppet act)
Shari Lewis (ventriloquist for "Lamb Chop")
Ted Lloyd (ventriloquism teacher)
The Muppets (Jim Henson's puppets)
Bill Neff (magician)
Jimmy Nelson (ventriloquist)
Vic Perry (magician)
Dr. Franz Polgar (hypnotist)
Eddie and Lucille Roberts (mentalists)
John Scarne (magician)
Burr Tillstrom (puppeteer)
US Air Force Drill Team
Bobby Winters (juggler)
Sandra Wirth (baton twirler)

PUBLIC FIGURES

Gen. Omar Bradley (US Army)

Jacques Yves Cousteau (underwater explorer)

Gen. Colin C. Hamilton (World War II pilot)

Maj. James Jabarra (triple jet ace)

Carlene Johnson (Miss USA)

Lt. Gen. George C. Kenny (World War II pilot)

Henry Krajewski (presidential candidate)

Gen. Robert Landry (US Air Force)

Dr. Willie Ley (physicist)

Mayor J. N. Lummus (Miami Beach)

Sen. John L. McClellan (Arkansas)

Gov. Theodore Roosevelt McKeldin (Maryland)

Lee Meriwether (Miss America 1955)

Perle Mesta (socialite and diplomat)

Mayor Ernest Mirrington Jr. (Niagara Falls)

Zahra Norbo (Miss Sweden)

Mr. and Mrs. Ben Novak (Fontainebleau Hotel owners)

Dr. Irving Page (American Heart Association)

Ogden Reid (publisher, *New York Herald Tribune*)

Gen. Matthew B. Ridgway (Army Chief of Staff)

Lt. Gov. John W. Rollins (Delaware)

Hillevi Rombin (Miss Universe)

Eleanor Roosevelt (First Lady)

Lord Victor Rothschild (head of banking dynasty)

Mayor Harold Shapiro (Miami)

Gov. Robert "Allen" Shivers (Texas)

Secretary Robert Stevens (US Army)

Arthur E. Summerfield (Postmaster General)

Sarah Tal (Miss Israel)

Countess Alexandria Tolstoy (Leo Tolstoy's daughter)

Sen. Bernard Tompkins (Queens County, NY)

Margaret Truman (daughter of President Harry Truman)

SPORTS FIGURES

Tenley Albright (figure skating)

Sandy Amoros (baseball)

Max Baer (boxing)

Wrong Way Corrigan (aviation)

Bob Cousey (basketball)

Jack Dempsey (boxing)

Leo Durocher (baseball)

Whitey Ford (baseball)

Harry Gallatin (basketball)

Mrs. Lou Gehrig (baseball)

Jim "Junior" Gilliam (baseball)

Sandor Glancz (table tennis)

Marty Glickman (broadcasting)

Tom Gola (basketball)

Rocky Graziano (boxing)

Willy (William) Hartack
    (horseracing)

Sonja Henie (skating)

Jamaican Olympic Team

Lee Jouglard (bowling)

Marion Ladewig (bowling)

Joe Louis (boxing)

Sal Maglie (baseball)

Tony Martinelli (wrestling)

Bob Mathias (decathlon)

Willie Mays (baseball)

Ed McCauley (basketball)

Dick McGuire (basketball)

Willa McGuire (water skiing)

George Montgomery (boxing)

Willie Mosconi (billiards)

Carl "Bobo" Olson (boxing)

Bruce Parker (water skiing)

Johnny Podres (baseball)

Jack Redmond (golfing)

Dusty Rhodes (baseball)

Leo Robert (Mr. Universe)

Jackie Robinson (baseball)

Pauline Robinson (table tennis)

Antonio Rocca (wrestling)

Sandy Saddler (boxing)

George Santelli (fencing)

Al Schacht (baseball)

Kenny Sears (basketball)

Dolph Shayes (basketball)

Sam Snead (golfing)

Maurice Stokes (basketball)

Bill Sweikert (auto racing)

The Tritons (skin diving)

Jack Walsh (weight lifting)

Jack Wells (broadcasting)

Billy Welu (bowling)

Sylvia Wene (bowling)

VOCALISTS

Edie Adams
Anna Maria Alberghetti
The Ames Brothers
Charlie Applewhite
Eddy Arnold
Pearl Bailey
Mae Barnes
The Barry Sisters Trio
Carol Bennett
Solomon Burke
Cab Calloway
Thelma Carpenter
June Christy
Robert Clary
Avshalom Cohen
Al "Jazzbo" Collins
Dorothy Collins
Barbara Cook
Jill Corey
The Crew Chiefs
Alan Dale
Dorothy Dandridge
Sammy Davis Jr.
Davis Sisters
Gloria De Haven
The De Marco Sisters
Vivian Della Chiesa
Matt Dennis
Johnny Desmond
Elaine Dunn
Richard Dyer-Bennett

Bob Eberle
Skinny Ennis
Joan Fairfax
Frances Faye
Eddie Fisher
Ella Fitzgerald and Trio
The Fontaine Sisters
Tennessee Ernie Ford
Helen Forrest
The Four Freshman
Mort Freeman
Sunny Gale
Judy Garland
Genevieve
Anna Marie Genovese
Georgia Gibbs
Inez Giglio
Chuck Goldstein
Gogi Grant
Buddy Greco
Betty Ann Grove
Lalo Guerrero
Dolores Hawkins
Al Hibler
Jerome Hines
Billie Holiday
Lena Horne
Eddy Howard
Joe E. Howard
Lurlean Hunter
Burl Ives

Jackie and Roy
Herb Jeffries
Judy Johnson
Johnny Johnston
Alan Jones
Kitty Kallen
Helen Kane
Beverly Kelly
Bill Kenny
Morgana King
Peggy King
Teddi King
King's Point Glee Club
Ingeborg Kjeldsen
Gloria Lane
Joe Lautner
Peggy Lee
Ted Lewis
Abbey Lincoln
Roberta Linn
Julie London
Lonzo and Oscar
Dorothy Loudon
Tina Louise
Marilyn Lovell
Lulu Belle and Scotty
Betty Madigan
Elaine Malbin
Gloria Mann
Bob Manning
Micki Marlo
Dean Martin

Ellen Martin
The Martins
Barbara Mason
Jana Mason
Ray McKinley
Carmen McRae
The Mello Larks
James Melton
Mabel Mercer
Helen Merrill
Vaughn Monroe
Lou Monte
Ada Moore
Rosaria Morelles
Pat Morrisey
Doretta Morrow
Ella Mae Morse
Marc Murphy
Rose Murphy
Meg Myles
Ken Nelson
Portia Nelson
Anthony Newley
Erin O'Brien
Helen O'Connell
Anita O'Day
The Oranim Group
Tony Owens
Jackie Paris
Tony Pastor
Jan Peerce
Webb Pierce

Ezio Pinza
Ginny Powell
Leontyne Price
Ruth Price
Quartet D'Aida
Roberta Quinlan
Jimmy Randolf
The Ravens
Marge Redmond
Trudy Richards
Tito Rodriguez
Jimmy Rushing
Dorothy Sarnoff
Robert "Bob" Scheerer
Bobby Scott
Norman Scott
Dinah Shore
Frank Sinatra
"Smilin'" Jack Smith
Carl Smith
The Sons of the Pioneers
Jeri Southern
Joanne Spiller
The Sportsmen
Robert Sterling
Kirby Stone Quartet
Lee Sullivan
Maxine Sullivan
Yma Sumac
Sylvia Syms
Kay Thompson

Lawrence Tibbett
Martha Tilton
Mel Tormé
Bobby Troup
Bon Bon Tunnell
Jim Tushar
United Nations Choir
University of Pennsylvania Glee
    Club
US Air Force Glee Club
USS *Valley Forge* Choir
The Vagabonds
Jerry Vale
Rudy Vallee
June Valli
Carl Van Moon
Sara Vaughn
Ricky Vera
Dinah Washington
Ethel Waters
Wayfarers
Frances Wayne
Rick Wayne
Josh White
Kitty White
Barbara Whiting
Margaret Whiting
Lee Wiley
Lawrence Winters
Scotty Wiseman

WRITERS/AUTHORS/COLUMNISTS

George Adamski

Art Buchwald

Abe Burrows

Richard Carter

Bennett Cerf

John Crosby

Clifton Fadiman

Leonard Feather

Hy Gardner

Ben Gross

Richard Harkness

Moss Hart

Vincent W. Hartnett

Ben Hecht

August Heckscher

Randall Jarrell

M. K. Jessup

William Keating

Walter Kerr

Maj. Donald Keyhoe

Dorothy Kilgallen

Ann Landers

Max Lerner

Howard Lindsay

Walter Lord

Elsa Maxwell

James Michener

Ogden Nash

Arch Oboler

Drew Pearson

Pauline "Dear Abby" Phillips

Henry Pleasants

Henry C. Roberts

Carl Sandburg

Mel Shavelson

Everett Walker

Tennessee Williams

Earl Wilson

Thyra Samter Winslow

Pauline Woodruff Titus

Herman Wouk

OTHER CELEBRITIES AND GUESTS

Leona Anderson (World's Worst
  Singer

Hy Averback (announcer)

Ben Belefonte (inventor, audience regular)

Shannon Bolin (ear reader)

Al Capp (cartoonist)

Inga Christensen (oldest concert
  pianist)

Max Conrad (songwriting pilot)

Evelyn Curry (lion handler)

Salvador Dali (artist)

Valentine Davies
  (writer/director)

Mrs. Diehl (owner, laughing
  parrots)

Washington Dodge (*Titanic*
  survivor)

Mr. Drapo (instant dressmaker)

Frank Eschen (radio commentator)

Bill Esenwein (snake handler)

Jinx Falkenburg (host, *Tex and
  Jinx*)

Charles Feldman (movie
  producer)

George Feyer (cartoonist)

Rochelle Forrest (palm and foot
  reader)

Paul Frehm (cartoonist)

Allen Funt (host, *Candid
  Camera*)

Peter Furst (anthropologist)

Jolie Gabor (mother of Gabor
  sisters)

Magda Gabor (sister of Zsa Zsa
  and Eva)

H. S. Gatchell (dog trainer)

Dave Garroway (host, *Today Show*)

Irving Goldstein (radio
  announcer)

Bill Goodwin (radio
  announcer)

Peter Gowland (photographer)

Paul Gregory (movie producer)

Bill Haast (snake handler)

John Hammond (record
  producer)

Ejnar Hansen (artist)

Philip Harben (British TV chef)

Robert Harrison (magazine
  publisher)

Gaylord Hauser (nutritionist)

Jeffrey Hayden (director)

Don Herbert ("Mr. Wizard")

Harry Hershfield (cartoonist)

Eddie Hill (disc jockey)

Joe Interleggi, "The Human Termite" (strong man)

George Ito (fire eater)

Irving Kaufman (recording engineer)

Elia Kazan (director/producer)

Walt Kelly (cartoonist, *Pogo*)

Stanley Kramer (director/producer)

Lawrence Langner (founder of Theatre Guild)

Jessie Lasky (producer)

Octavio Leon (cigar roller)

Jack Lescoulie (host, *Today Show*)

Max Liebman (producer)

Lillian Lillian (audience regular)

Art Linkletter (host)

Alan Livingston (vice president, NBC)

Sid Luft (producer)

Det. Frank Malerba (NYPD)

Daniel Mann (director)

Marie Mann (Hat Check Queen)

Katherine Manning (*Titanic* survivor)

Dr. Conrado Massaguer (Cuban caricaturist)

Carmen Mastren (audience regular)

Dorothy Miller (audience regular)

Mitch Miller (head of A&R, Columbia Records)

Jim Moran (publicist)

Ripp Murray (exotic animal collector)

Jess Oppenheimer (producer, *I Love Lucy*)

Bill Pacarro (shoe sitter)

Suzy Parker (model)

Joe Phillips (animal handler)

Joe Pilates (physical fitness pioneer)

Otto Preminger (director/producer)

Bonnie Pruden (physical fitness pioneer)

Joan Rhodes (strong woman)

Madlyn Rhue (Miss California Grapes)

John Ringling North (circus owner)

Prince Robert (Prince of Hobos)

Dr. Rotondi (chiropractor and vegetarian)

Emanuel "Manie" Sacks (vice president, NBC)

Ivan Sanderson (animal authority and TV host)

Gen. David Sarnoff (RCA chairman)

John Schafer (audience regular)

Godfrey P. Schmidt (attorney vs. teamsters)

Blanche Scott (first licensed woman pilot)

Bill Silbert (NBC disc jockey)

Miriam Silverman (weight guesser)

Robert E. Simpson (president, B&O Railroad)

Mrs. Sparrow (palm reader)

Marian Stafford (Miss Hardshell Turtlewax)

Edward Steichen (photographer)

Mrs. Sterling (audience regular)

Vic Tanney (health club owner)

Mike Todd (Broadway producer)

Mr. Trowbridge (worm-farm owner)

William Tuttle (MGM makeup artist)

Professor Voss (health nut, audience regular)

Hudson D. Walker (art gallery owner)

Jack Warner (co-founder, Warner Bros.)

Sylvester (Pat) Weaver (president, NBC)

Perc Westmore (makeup artist)

Richard Willis (makeup artist)

Professor Wilner (animal hypnotist)

Don Woods (stunt driver)

Select Bibliography

Allen, Steve. *Hi-Ho, Steverino! My Adventures in the Wonderful Wacky World of TV*. Fort Lee, NJ: Barricade Books, 1992.

———. *Mark It and Strike It*. New York: Holt, Rinehart and Winston, 1960.

———. *Meeting of Minds*. Amherst, NY: Prometheus Books, 1989.

———. "Talent Is Color-Blind." *Ebony* (September/October 1955).

———. *The Question Man*. New York: Bellmeadows Press, 1959.

"Allen: A Third Titan?" *Newsweek* (October 11, 1954).

"Allen again Tops Sullivan." *New York Post* (January 29, 1957).

"Allen Cracks Top 10." *Variety* (July 4, 1956).

"Allen's Ratings Gain in Battle v. Sullivan." *Billboard* (November 1956).

"ARB Top 10." *Variety* (February 5, 1958).

"ARB: TV Report for June 1–7, 1957." *Broadcasting-Telecasting* (1957).

"ARB's Top 25 for Dec. again Shows NBC Segs Closing Gap v. CBS." *Variety* (January 3, 1958).

Barrett, Marvin. "Television's Biggest Battle." *Newsweek* (March 18, 1957).

Brooks, Tim, and Earle Marsh. *The Complete Directory to Prime Time Network and Cable TV Shows, 1946–Present*, 7th ed. New York: Ballantine Books, 1999.

Brownfield, Paul. "Late-Night TV Hosts Credit Allen with Giving Them Their Zany Format." *Los Angeles Times* (November 1, 2000).

Bruce, Lenny. *How to Talk Dirty and Influence People*. New York: Simon & Schuster, 1992.

Buckley, Gail Lumet. *The Hornes: An American Family*. New York: Alfred A. Knopf, 1986.

Bykofsky, Stuart. "For NBC's Tom Snyder, It's a Time of Recessions." *Philadelphia News* (June 6, 1980).

Carman, John. "Easy Duty: A Short History of 'The Tonight Show'—As Told by Steve Allen." *Chicago Tribune* (June 20, 1991).

Carter, Bill. *The Late Shift*. New York: Hyperion, 1994.

Clark, Norman. "Steve May Provide Ed with Stiff Competition." *Baltimore News-Post* (June 26, 1956).

Condon, George. "Ad Libbing Comic Steve Allen Reveals Serious Side." *Plain Dealer* (Cleveland, OH) (October 9, 1954).

Corkery, Paul. *Carson: The Unauthorized Biography*. Ketchum, ID: Randt, 1987.

Cox, Stephen. *Here's Johnny!* Nashville, TN: Cumberland House, 1992.

Deeb, Gary. "Did Carson Put Kibosh on Allen?" *Chicago Sun-Times* (June 18, 1980).

Delany, Kevin. "Sullivan Does TV Flip-Flop, Signs Presley for $50,000." *New York World-Telegram* (July 13, 1956).

Freeman, Donald. "Sullivan, Allen TV Battle Begins." *San Diego Union* (June 26, 1956).

Froug, William. "The Other Allen." *PIC* (January 1951).

Gelbart, Larry. "In Memoriam: Steve Allen." *Emmy* (December 2000).

Getlin, Josh. "The Perennial Steve Allen." *Los Angeles Times* (January 9, 1998).

Heimer, Mel. "Steve Allen: TV's Night Owl" (ca. 1954).

Hentoff, Nat. "Steve Allen Literate, Informal, Uses Jazz—And No One Gripes." *Downbeat* (March 24, 1954).

Holland, Jack. "Steve Allen: He's Loaded (with Talent)." *Tele Viewer* (January 15, 1955).

Humphrey, Hal. "Allen a Hit, Berle a Flop." *Mirror-News* (April 7, 1955).

Inman, David. "TV Q & A." *Boston Herald* (August 30, 1997).

Jones, Will. "Steve Allen: Late to Bed and Late to Rise Makes Him Wealthy and Wise." *New York Post* (March 10, 1955).

Kern, Janet. "Steve Allen Turns Author to Further Display Talents." *Chicago American* (April 4, 1955).

"KitchenAid on Steve Allen's Famous Network Show Tonight." *Housewares Review* (January 1955).

Kupcinet, Irv. "CBS 'Panic' Sparked by Allen?" *New York Telegraph* (May 1, 1957).

"Latest Ratings: ARB Top 10 Network Programs." *Broadcasting-Telecasting* (February 10, 1958).

Laurent, Lawrence. "Steve Allen: Ace Comic of the Casual School." *Post and Times Herald* (Washington, DC) (August 8, 1954).

Lester, John. "Steve Allen Takes 1st Round from Sullivan." *Newark Star-Ledger* (June 25, 1956).

Lewis, Darcy. "Goodbye-Ho, Steverino." *Wednesday Journal* (Oak Park, IL) (November 8, 2000).

Lin, Judy. "Friends Remember Steve Allen." *Los Angeles Times* (November 1, 2000).

"Lincoln out as Sullivan TV Sponsor." *New York Journal-American* (June 21, 1957).

"'Maverick,' Allen Clobber Sullivan." *Hollywood Daily Variety* (February 4, 1958).

McGuigan, Cathleen. "The Father of Late Night." *Newsweek* (November 13, 2000).

McMahon, Ed, with David Fisher. *For Laughing out Loud*. New York: Warner Books, 1998.

Miksch, W. F. "The Greatest Allen Since Fred." *1000 Jokes* (February–March 1955).

Millstein, Gilbert. "Portrait of an M.A.L: Master of Ad Lib." *New York Times Magazine* (January 9, 1955).

Moskowitz, Eric. "Catching up with 'Steverino,' TV's Pioneering Comedian." *Christian Science Monitor* (December 4, 1997).

Museum of Television and Radio. *Steve Allen: A Retrospective* (1994).

Nachman, Gerald. *Seriously Funny*. New York: Pantheon Books, 2003.

Natale, Richard. "Amiable, Quirky Allen Influenced Many." *Variety* (November 1, 2000).

"Nielsen Network TV: Two Weeks Ending Nov. 23, 1957." *Advertising Age* (January 6, 1958).

O'Brian, Jack. "DA Weighs Criminal Action over 'Pressure' on Allen." *New York Journal-American* (September 2, 1954).

———. "Script of Allen TV Show Changed by 'Pressure.'" *New York Journal-American* (September 1, 1954).

Paar, Jack. *P.S. Jack Paar.* Garden City, NY: Doubleday, 1983.

Pack, Richard. "The Maybe Golden Days of Live Local Television." *Emmy Online* (undated).

"Plymouth Division of Chrysler Corporation Signs as Full Sponsor of 'The Steve Allen Show' on the NBC Television Network during 1959–60 Season; Series to Be Colorcast Mondays from Burbank." *NBC Press Release* (April 20, 1959).

Pollock, David. "Steve Allen Remembered." *Television Quarterly* (2001).

Prall, Robert. "He's Costing a Lot of Sleep!" *New York World Telegram and Sun* (December 11, 1954).

Ramsay, Don. "Local College Students Admire Zany Steve Allen Radio Show." *Southern California Daily Trojan* (May 16, 1950).

Rector, Bob. "Steve Allen: Saddened by Medium's 'Filth,' One of TV's Original Superstars Fights Back." *Los Angeles Times* (April 25, 1999).

Reich, Howard. "TV Talk Show Bands Are a Peculiar Breed, But They Play a Crucial Role Few Viewers Ever See." *Chicago Tribune* (November 30, 1997).

Rothman, Clifford. "'Tonight' Creator Allen's Creativity Remains Undimmed." *USA Today* (December 11, 1997).

Samuels, Charles. "The Man Who Keeps America Awake." *Redbook* (November 1, 1954).

Saunders, Walter. "NBC Network Chiefs Elated By Steve Allen." *Rocky Mountain News* (Denver, CO) (May 28, 1957).

"Should Sponsored Entertainers Woo Controversy?" *Printers' Ink* (October 1, 1954).

Simon, George T. "Steve Allen: Presenting Jazz on Television." *Metronome* (July 1955).

"Steve Allen: Clock Stopper." *Newsweek* (November 29, 1954).

"Steve Allen Knocks Sullivan off Throne." *Columbus* (OH) *Citizen* (July 2, 1956).

"Steve Allen 30.9, Ed Sullivan 22.2." *Variety* (April 17, 1957).

"Steve Allen's Latest Show Receiving Critical Kudos." *Salem* (VA) *Times-Register* (July 13, 1956).

"Steve Allen's TV Show Gets Stink-Bombed." *New York World Telegram and Sun* (September 14, 1954).

Stevens, Dale. "Jonathan Winters, Ex-Daytonian, Clicks on Steve Allen Show Here." *Dayton Daily News* (February 12, 1955).

"Steverino 'Outrates' Sullivan, 'Maverick.'" *Philadelphia Inquirer* (April 2, 1958).

"Sullivan Unranked on Nielsen AA." *Variety* (May 22, 1957).

"Sunday Slugfest." *Rochester Times Union* (June 16, 1956).

"The Air Around Us." *Newsweek* (September 27, 1954).

"The Award" (cartoon). *Mad* (May 1958).

"The Big Switch." *Newsweek* (June 12, 1950).

"The Station Behind Those Many Miami TV Programs." *Broadcasting-Telecasting* (January 24, 1955).

"The Story of Caryl Chessman." *Court TV's Crime Library*. http://www.crime library.com/notorious_murders/classics/chessman. Accessed January 28, 2005.

"Tonight." *Variety* (September 29, 1954).

Traube, Leonard. "If Allen Wasn't 'Pressured' What a Buildup for 'Tonight!'" *Variety* (September 8, 1954).

Tucker, Ken. "Steve Allen, Comedy's Renaissance Man, Takes His Final Bow." *Entertainment Weekly* (November 10, 2000).

Untitled article. *Indianapolis Times* (December 27, 1957).

Watrous, Steve. "The Many Sides of Steve Allen." *Shepherds Express* (Milwaukee, WI) (May 11, 1995).

Williams, Robert. "Sullivan Snubs Allen at CBS Order." *New York Post* (July 16, 1956).

Wilson, Roy (cartoonist). Untitled. *Saturday Evening Post* (October 19, 1957).

Wolk, Josh. "In Memoriam 2000. Steve Allen." *Entertainment Weekly* (January 5, 2001).

Index

357